LOVE IN AFRICA

Love in Africa

EDITED BY JENNIFER COLE
AND LYNN M. THOMAS

The University of Chicago Press
Chicago and London

JENNIFER COLE is associate professor of comparative
human development and an associate member of the
Department of Anthropology at the University of Chicago.

LYNN M. THOMAS is associate professor of history
and adjunct associate professor of women's studies at the
University of Washington.

The University of Chicago Press, Chicago 60637
The University of Chicago Press, Ltd., London
© 2009 by The University of Chicago
All rights reserved. Published 2009
Printed in the United States of America

17 16 15 14 13 12 11 10 09   1 2 3 4 5

ISBN-13: 978-0-226-11352-4 (cloth)
ISBN-13: 978-0-226-11353-1 (paper)
ISBN-10: 0-226-11352-3 (cloth)
ISBN-10: 0-226-11353-1 (paper)

Library of Congress Cataloging-in-Publication Data
Love in Africa / edited by Jennifer Cole and Lynn M.
Thomas
        p. cm.
Includes bibliographical references and index.
ISBN-13: 978-0-226-11352-4 (cloth: alk. paper)
ISBN-13: 978-0-226-11353-1 (pbk.: alk. paper)
ISBN-10: 0-226-11352-3 (cloth: alk. paper)
ISBN-10: 0-226-11353-1 (pbk.: alk. paper)
1. Sex—Africa. 2. Sex—Social aspects—Africa. 3. Love—
Africa. 4. Love—Social aspects—Africa. I. Cole, Jennifer,
1966– II. Thomas, Lynn M.
    HQ18.A35L68 2009
    306.7096—dc22
                    2008043551

CONTENTS

ILLUSTRATIONS

ACKNOWLEDGMENTS

The shape of this volume reflects our belief that a combination of anthropological and historical approaches can contribute much to elucidating the complexities of social processes in Africa and elsewhere in the world. It also reflects the wisdom of our many, generous interlocutors. The volume first began as a double panel at the African Studies Association meetings in Washington, DC, in 2005. We thank the participants and the audience for their encouraging and thoughtful feedback. We gratefully acknowledge the constructive criticism of Jordanna Bailkin, Jessica Cattelino, Jean Comaroff, John Comaroff, Judy Farquhar, Mark Hunter, Julie Livingston, Danilyn Rutherford, and the participants in the African Studies Workshop at the University of Chicago on the introduction. In addition, John Comaroff graciously read and provided useful feedback on a penultimate version of the introduction. Our reviewers for the University of Chicago Press gave us thoughtful, detailed commentary on the introduction and each of the individual chapters for which we remain extremely grateful. T. David Brent and Laura Avey offered all the support two editors could want and expedited the publication of the volume in ways that made what could have been a difficult process a pleasure. And Maria Garrett, Elayne Oliphant, and Michal Ran helped with the details of getting the volume ready for publication. Thanks also to Laura Bevir for creating the index. Finally, we thank Julian Dibbell and Michael Sanderson, who have taught each of us, in their respective ways, much about love that we cherish.

Thinking through Love in Africa

Lynn M. Thomas and Jennifer Cole

A few years back, in a special issue of *Granta*, the Kenyan author Binyavanga Wainaina (2005) wrote a bitterly ironic essay entitled "How to Write about Africa." Wainaina explains that the author who writes about Africa and aspires to global circulation should always use words such as *darkness* or *safari* in the title, and that subtitles succeed if they include words like *Zanzibar*, *Masai*, *primordial*, or *tribal*. After further elaboration, he adds a list of what *not* to write about: "Taboo subjects: ordinary domestic scenes, love between Africans (unless a death is involved)" (92).

Wainaina is right to mock the absence of representations of love in writing about Africa for Western and global audiences. By contrast, within the continent, popular discussions of love abound. African novelists from Ngugi wa Thiongo to Ama Ata Aidoo have written poignant stories of African love, ones filled with heartbreak, suffering, and redemption. Love songs have been a staple of popular music across Francophone Africa for decades. English-language African newspapers and magazines have similarly long carried discussions of love, including advice columns. Today, in many African countries, it is hard not to notice the pervasive appeal of romantic movies or soap operas produced in Bombay or Hollywood, Brazil or Mexico. Moreover, from billboards sponsored by HIV/AIDS education and prevention campaigns to call-in radio talk shows, discussion of sexual intimacy, trust, and personal feelings seems to be everywhere. Yet despite

FIGURE 0.1 Tanzanian AIDS prevention billboard, 2006. Across Africa, numerous billboards warn people to protect themselves against HIV infection by using condoms, abstaining from sex, or remaining faithful to their partners. This Swahili-language billboard reads, "If you truly love him/her, you will protect him/her." *Photo courtesy of Aldin Mutembei, 2006.*

the sights and sounds of love in these varied African media, scholars have rarely addressed the topic. Like popular representations of Africa to which Wainaina so bitterly refers, historians and anthropologists have largely ignored love in Africa.

This volume examines how men and women have imagined and negotiated love—the sentiments of attachment and affiliation that bind people to one another—in sexual, predominantly heterosexual, relationships in colonial and postcolonial Africa. Such a project immediately raises thorny epistemological, methodological, and even political questions. To start with, why is there so little scholarship on love in Africa? This question is all the more curious given that there is a burgeoning body of work on love in other places (see below). Moreover, there is a significant Africanist literature on other emotions, namely, jealousy and anger (Douglas 1970; Harris 1978; Lambek and Solway 2001; Durham 2002). So why not love in Africa? Is it because scholars' epistemological and analytic concerns have blinded them to love's presence? Or is it because Africans have had powerful attachments that they did not formulate in terms of "love"? Or is it some combination of the two?

These questions remind us that to study love is to address head on the problem of universality and difference. Is love a universal emotion either intrinsic to the human soul or rooted in our bodies' psychological, physiological, and biochemical structures? Or is it produced through specific historical processes and cultural formations? Methodologically, how does one know if the word that informants use to signal passion or affect really maps on to the same conceptual and emotional field as "love"?[1] To use this word when

FIGURE 0.2 Sign for a marriage agency in Tamatave, Madagascar, 2006. In Madagascar, some young women seek marriages with foreign men. This sign advertises a marriage agency managed by a woman from Réunion Island that specializes in transnational arranged marriages. *Photo courtesy of Dominique Bois, 2006.*

one's informants use other idioms to describe intimate attachments runs the risk of creating an unwarranted impression of universality.[2]

Faced with these conundrums, we approach love as an analytic problem rather than a universal category. In so doing, we draw on anthropological and historical scholarship that explores how emotions are embedded in historically situated words, cultural practices, and material conditions that constitute certain kinds of subjects and enable particular kinds of relationships. Anthropologists working within a symbolic tradition have demonstrated how varying cultural symbols, practices, and lexicons enable different forms of feeling and emotional expression (Abu-Lughod 1986; Lutz 1988; Rosaldo 1980, 1984). Other anthropologists have elucidated the political economy of emotion—the way in which emotion is "a symbolic representation grounded in the basic material conditions" of people's lives (Scheper-Hughes 1992, 401; see also Rebhun 1999; Hirsch 2003; Gregg 2006). Historians, in turn, have drawn insight from these anthropological studies as well as cognitive psychology to chart significant changes in emotions over time (Reddy 2001; Stearns and Lewis 1998; Stearns and Stearns 1988; Stearns 1994; Lee 2007). Especially useful is Barbara Rosenwein's (2006, 2) study of "emotional communities" in medieval Europe. There she argues against grand narratives and for tracing the history of emotions through "relatively small increments of transformation and change."[3] Building on these studies, this volume makes two broad contributions to the scholarship on love and intimacy in Africa and beyond.

First, we challenge social scientific and historical scholarship that has reduced African intimacy to sex. Discussion of emotion has long been absent from Africanist scholarship on intimate relations. This absence, however, has become increasingly striking since the late 1980s with the explosion of analyses of the HIV/AIDS epidemic in Africa. Whereas countless studies have analyzed how sexual behavior fuels the epidemic, few have explored how that behavior is embedded in emotional frameworks. Although the reduction of intimate relations to sex is problematic anywhere, this is especially the case for Africa because of the long history of Westerners deploying arguments of hypersexuality to dehumanize Africans and justify degrading policies. Studies that dissect African sexualities while ignoring affect contribute to Westerners' persistent figuring of Africa as the "other" of European Enlightenment. This volume argues against that tendency by insisting that we cannot understand sex or intimacy without understanding ideologies of emotional attachment. We join a small but growing body of scholarship that seeks to better understand Africa's HIV/AIDS epidemic by examining the entanglement of sexual behavior and affective relations (Ahlberg 1994; Setel 1999; Parikh 2005; Mark Hunter 2002, 2005a; D. Smith 2001, 2006; Poulin 2007).

Second, we argue that anthropologists need to pay greater attention to how contemporary discourses, sentiments, and practices of love are the product of complex historical processes and intersections. Sociocultural anthropologists, largely working in locales outside of Africa, have produced a sizeable literature on love in recent years. Some have argued for recognizing passionate love—defined as a strong sexual and emotional attraction to another person that often results in a neglect of more ordinary obligations—as a universal phenomenon (Giddens 1992; Jankowiak 1995; Yan 2003; Hatfield, Rapson, and Martel 2007; Jankowiak 2008). Others, more aligned with the aims of this volume, have explored how shifting kinship practices, gender ideologies, and political economies shape intimate attachments (Collier 1997; Kendall 1996; Rebhun 1999; Gilette 2000; Ahearn 2001; Adrian 2003; Hirsch 2003).

Two new edited volumes locate the economic and cultural politics of such intimate transformations in the context of transnationalism and globalization. *Modern Loves* (Hirsch and Wardlow 2006) examines how companionate marriage has recently become a global ideal and, in the process, has been variously localized in ways that disrupt older social formations and facilitate claims to modernity. *Love and Globalization* (Padilla et al. 2007) explores how increased flows of people, media, and commodities are reshaping local economies of love, how new phenomena like Internet romance and sexual tourism are commercializing love, and how the performance of love facilitates international migration (see also Constable 2003, 2005; Brennan 2004; Faier 2007; *Etnofoor* 2006). These volumes effectively illuminate the way in which new transnational discourses and economic formations reshape love and intimacy around the world. By showing how claims to love are often claims to modernity, they also suggest some of the cultural politics that are a part of these transformative processes. But they tend to ignore the longer history of the imperial and cross-regional movement of affective ideals and practices, unwittingly confining such movement to the contemporary period of globalization.

Scholars working in colonial/postcolonial and queer studies, by contrast, have demonstrated how since the nineteenth century, at least, ideologies of affect have been an integral part of the disciplinary regimes through which imperial and liberal governments have sought to regulate their subjects and citizens. These regimes have worked in part by marking certain intimate relations—namely, those premised on the heterosexual monogamous couple—as more valuable and, hence, more worthy of political recognition than others (Warner 1999; Berlant and Warner 2000; Berlant 2000; Povinelli 2006; Stoler 2006; Matsuda 2005; Rafael 2000; Stoler 2002). Afsaneh Najmabadi (2005), for example, has explored how in late nineteenth- and early twentieth-century Iran, the promotion of a European conception of marriage rooted in romantic love depended on the normalization of heterosexual mores and affective ideals. This volume extends such attention to the history and politics of imperial and cross-regional ideologies of love into colonial and postcolonial Africa. It also enriches such scholarship by considering the politics of inclusion and exclusion manifest within *everyday* practices and discourses of love.

Together, our chapters demonstrate that Africans have long remade local affective ideals and practices by engaging those from elsewhere. Some of these engagements involved Christian missionaries and European colonial regimes; others reveal the mark of Islam or the mid-twentieth-century arrival of South Asian films. Contemporary discourses and practices of love in Africa emerge from the entanglement of such influences with endogenous ideologies and economies of affection. The apparently recent proliferation of discourse about, and practices of, love in Africa and other postcolonial contexts needs to be understood in relation to this longer history, a history that draws on multiple, even competing, conceptions of attachment and affiliation.

Readers should not turn to this volume to find an account of Africa's love "tradition." Rather, what you will find are analyses of the heterogeneous ways that people in Africa have deployed ideologies of love to elaborate generational and cultural distinctions and claim political inclusion;

how they have reconfigured affective relations amid the profound political, economic, and social changes of the past century; and how they have engaged ideals of romantic love to reimagine gender relations. Before turning to these specific arguments, we must consider more closely the question of why love has not, for the most part, appeared in earlier Africanist scholarship.[4]

The Problem of Love

Until recent decades, few scholars outside the fields of literature and psychology gave much thought to love in any context. In 1922, the German philosopher Georg Simmel (1984 [1921–22], 159) argued that although love was "one of the great formative categories of existence," it had yet to receive serious and nonreductive theoretical consideration from a range of intellectual disciplines. Similarly, Ann Swidler (2001, 2) has argued that love has generally seemed "too personal," "too mysterious," and "too sacred" a subject for sociologists to tackle. Anthropology, the social science discipline with the longest and most substantive engagement in twentieth-century Africa, devoted considerable attention to kinship, courtship, and marriage but shunned examination or explicit theorization of love.

Anthropologists' disinclination to consider love was due, in part, to the convergence of the epistemological foundations of their discipline with Euro-American folk theories of emotion. Western folk theories imply that emotions are psychobiological essences located within individuals (Lutz 1988). By contrast, anthropology has traditionally defined its subject matter as shared cultural practices and representations. This claim is particularly true for the British social anthropologists who dominated the formation of Anglophone African studies. These early anthropologists followed Emile Durkheim's, and later A. R. Radcliffe-Brown's, assessment that only collective representations that exist beyond the individual are the appropriate domain of sociological and anthropological study. For instance, the index to Isaac Schapera's *Married Life in an African Tribe* (1940), possibly the best-known volume on marriage and sex in Africa, does not include *love* as an entry. Insofar as anthropologists perceived emotions as a part of individual psychology and private experience, they considered love epiphenomenal to the proper subject of anthropological research.

Although this epistemological framing discouraged early anthropologists from examining love and other emotions, references to emotions and powerful attachments nonetheless crept into their accounts. Swiss missionary and scholar Henri Junod's (1912) brief discussion of love amid a cataloguing of folktales from southern Africa is typical. First, he tersely pronounced that "love, as we understand it, plays but little part in Thonga life." Then, after presenting two "love songs," one composed by a young woman prohibited from marrying the partner of her choice and the other by a jilted young man, he warned: "It would be erroneous to think Native lovers . . . are not capable of deep and lasting affection" (2:190–91). With these remarks, Junod acknowledged that passion and affection could animate Thonga courtship and marriage, and exhibited confusion—a confusion shared by subsequent scholars—about how to convey to a Western audience that affective ties among Africans are present but different.

Anthropologists also did not explore love because their informants distrusted its influence or disregarded its significance. Monica Hunter, for example, wrote that even though most Pondo marriages were "of choice" and elopement was a common and old practice, elders disapproved of young men marrying their "sweethearts" as they feared that they would "already [be] tired of the girl[s]" when they began living together (Hunter 1936, 188–90, 32, cited in Thomas, this volume). Similarly, in later fieldwork among the Nyakyusa-Ngonde of Tanzania, Wilson (formerly Hunter) reported that although passionate extramarital affairs often precipitated divorce, people repeatedly stated that "with us love is small" and insisted that marriages were premised on cattle exchange not affect (Wilson 1977, 166, cited in Shadle 2006, xli n30). Such accounts suggest that although emotional and physical attraction commonly animated courtship and affairs, it was not valued as a solid foundation for marriage. They also suggest how informants' cultural ideologies reinforced social anthropology's epistemological predilection to focus on kinship and exchange rather than emotion.

Yet even on those occasions when Africans did evoke love, anthropologists did not explore its meanings. Nowhere is this avoidance more striking than in accounts of love "medicines" or "magic." Such preparations entailed the combination and application of various animal, plant, and store-bought products to make a man or woman irresistibly attractive or guard a lover's affection from interlopers. Anthropologists described love medicines as among the most common treatments sought from healers (Hellmann 1935; Hunter 1936; Hellmann 1948; Krige 1936b; Kenyatta 1938; Schapera 1940). These scholars documented the prevalence of such medicines because of their broader concern with theories of magic, ritual, and witchcraft. Yet none considered what such widespread usage suggested about local conceptions of passion. In so doing, they missed an opportunity to explore love as an omnipresent health concern, an occult force, and an involuntary state of being.

Just as British social anthropologists' failure to engage these insights was an artifact of their discipline's epistemological foundations and their informants' values, it was also a product of the history of the West's relationship to Africa. Throughout the era of the Atlantic slave trade, European representations of African "barbarity" depicted African men and women as libidinous and licentious (Jordan 1968; Morgan 2004). Slave owners in the United States positioned blacks as moral inferiors by portraying them as hypersexual and devoid of emotional depth. Thomas Jefferson (2002 [1785], 176–77), for one, wrote: "Love seems with them to be more an eager desire, than a tender delicate mixture of sentiment and sensation. . . . In general, their existence appears to participate more of sensation than reflection."[5] Such racist accounts of black affect cast doubt on the fundamental humanity of Africans and their descendants. While evangelical abolitionists such as William Wilberforce rejected such ideas about the inherent inferiority of blacks, they argued that domestic life in Africa had been so corrupted by the slave trade that it could be righted only through the cultivation of Christian marriages and communities (Comaroff and Comaroff 1991). For most nineteenth-century missionaries, bridewealth exchange and polygyny demonstrated African women's "slave-like" status and the absence of deep sentiment within African courtship and marriage (Beecham 1841; Curtin 1964). By depicting lust as omnipresent and love as absent in Africa, thereby situating blacks as morally and spiritually inadequate, these European perspectives established a set of racialized polemics that would inform subsequent discussions and representations of black intimacy (Omolade 1983; Mama 1996; Hanchard 2000; Ratele 2004).

During the 1960s and 1970s, feminist scholars sought to write against racist representations that portrayed African women as oversexed and exceptionally fertile. As second-wave feminists, they also aimed to challenge sexist ideologies that occluded women's agency and situated women solely in the domestic realm by emphasizing the important economic and political roles that women performed in African societies (Paulme 1963 [1960]; Boserup 1970; Wipper 1972; Hafkin and Bay 1976). For these reasons, they avoided examining the affective dimensions of social life. But feminists' focus on women's strategies for securing livelihoods soon brought them face-to-face with women's exchange of sex and other domestic services for material resources (Schuster 1979; Obbo 1980; Robertson and Berger 1986; White 1990). While such scholars documented the dense persistent intersection of sex and material resources, they did not explore how sentiment also inhabited such exchanges.

love = modern

Other intertwined epistemological and political issues discouraged historians of Africa from following the lead of Europeanist colleagues who during the 1960s and 1970s made love into the subject of historical inquiry. As part of a broader effort by social historians to expand the discipline's thematic concerns to the family and everyday life, some Europeanists started to chart a history of emotion. Philip Ariès (1962), Edward Shorter (1975), and Lawrence Stone (1979) argued that the "increasing sentimentalization" of family life originated in northern Europe during the eighteenth century as the result of rising prosperity and life expectancy. This historiography linked love to modernization, a concept that Africanist scholars found increasingly suspect by the mid-1970s, as we detail below. The Eurocentrism of this early historical scholarship on love likely discouraged Africanist historians from embracing the topic. No doubt, intimate attachments also seemed irrelevant to the concerns that motivated most historians of Africa: reconstructing useable pasts for newly independent nations and analyzing the causes of economic underdevelopment (Cohen 1985).

Since the early 1990s, the influence of sexuality and queer studies has combined with the urgencies of the HIV/AIDS epidemic to focus much Africanist scholarly attention on sex. Historians of women and gender have engaged some of Michel Foucault's (1978, 1985) insights to demonstrate how the regulation of reproduction and sexuality were integral to colonial and postcolonial rule in Africa (Summers 1991; Vaughan 1991; Jeater 1993; Hunt 1999; L. Thomas 2003; Klausen 2004; Shadle 2006). Other scholars have documented the diversity of sexual identities and their politics in contemporary Africa (Achmat 1993; Epprecht 2004; Hoad, Martin, and Reid 2005; Moodie 1988; Morgan and Wieringa 2005; Murray and Roscoe 1998). At the same time, a plethora of studies have sought to understand the social underpinnings of AIDS.

Most anthropological research on AIDS and sexuality has deliberately eschewed broad cultural generalizations, fearing that such analyses simultaneously blame the victims and dehistoricize the causes of the epidemic. Instead, scholars have demonstrated how pervasive poverty and other forms of structural violence shape sexual practices (Schoepf 1992, 1995; Parker 2001; Arnfred, ed. 2004; Haram 2004; Mark Hunter 2007). Some scholars have used the concept of "transactional sex" to emphasize the centrality of material exchanges to everyday sexual relations and to avoid conflating varied forms of African intimacy with "prostitution" and its stigmatizing connotations (Mark Hunter 2002; Cole 2004; Wojcicki 2002; Zalduondo 1991). Such materialist approaches rightly elucidate how poverty and insecurity

steve + sally

facilitate the spread of HIV/AIDS. However, by highlighting the economic dimensions of these exchanges, such accounts once again background the role of emotions in intimacy.

Modernization and Love

There is, however, one body of Africanist scholarship that did make love the object of analysis. During the 1950s to 1970s, both Anglophone and Francophone sociologists, political scientists, and even some psychologists joined anthropologists in assessing whether urbanization and rapid social change were causing African societies to become more like Western industrialized nations, as modernization theory predicted. These social scientists sought to determine whether economic development was moving African societies from a communal, kin-based ethos to an individualist one (Cooper and Packard 1997). Similarly, policymakers, interested in everything from stabilizing labor forces to lowering population growth rates (F. Cooper 1996; Lindsay 2003; Sharpless 1997; Watkins 2000), took the existence of the nuclear family, founded on a couple's mutual attraction rather than the demands of wider kin groups, as an important indicator that modernization was actually taking place. As a result of these concerns, several scholars sought to understand the nature of African intimate relations, including the possible presence of romantic love.

Of particular interest was whether passion and individual choice served as a basis for spouse selection and marriage. Writing about marriage among Kinshasa schoolteachers—professionals often deemed the vanguard of modernity in Africa—Guy Bernard (1968) observed many cases where love or love at first sight (*coup de foudre*) dictated who married whom. One Mongo informant reported the following story of how he met his wife. He had just finished his teaching diploma and was in a store to buy provisions for the celebratory party when he saw a young woman from his region who had come to buy thread: "I was so attracted to this girl that it was impossible for me to stay where I was. I went closer to her and at the moment our eyes met, I could read on her face a joy that couldn't be faked (a smile mixed with shame). At that moment, I revealed my desires to the girl, and she agreed. . . ." (cited in Bernard 1968, 47; our translation). The young man invited her to get a drink at a café, where he proposed marriage. Bernard (1968, 46) concluded that while "a certain sympathy, that allows for the potential growth of love" is necessary, even among schoolteachers love does not always precede marriage. Similarly, Kenneth Little (1973, 133) cited a 1965 study of school leavers in Elizabethville (Congo) in which men said

(margin annotations: "modernization theory", "indicator", "an important ?", "anthropology + economy")

savage → transitional
modern

that love was important in the choice of a spouse, but they imagined it as a kind of sympathy that eventually developed into reciprocal affection. These accounts suggest that love had finally become a topic of discussion for both Africans and their ethnographers.

As a result of these findings, many scholars concluded that African societies were transitional—somewhere between older patterns of African kinship and marriage and those expected to emerge with modernization. Instead of finding nuclear families, ethnographer after ethnographer studying urban areas ranging from the Copperbelt to Kampala to Kinshasa discovered that divorce was frequent and relationships between men and women took a variety of different forms. These ranged from short-term exchanges of sex for money, to temporary unions, to enduring marriages (Powdermaker 1962; Southall and Gutkind 1957; Longmore 1959; Mair 1969 [1953]; Little 1973). Given these patterns of social organization that diverged considerably from a stable nuclear family, several scholars queried whether love in African intimate relationships implied the same kind of emotional bond as it did among Europeans.

In an analysis of letters written to an advice column of a Ghanaian newspaper during 1955, the psychologist Gustav Jahoda noted that many letters posed questions about how to recognize love and know that it was real. As examples of the basic question "Does she really love me?" Jahoda (1959, 183) found the following:

> I wonder if she is really in love with me. Please, how can I know that she has fallen for me?
> Is she a true lover?
> How can I be sure she will love me more than ever?
> Is this love really from Heaven?

Other studies similarly suggested that many urban Africans felt both eagerness and uncertainty with regards to love—implying that it was a new emotion, particularly in relation to marriage. For example, in her study of leisure activities in Kinshasa, Suzanne Comhaire-Sylvain noted that while she was not surprised that young women preferred films that featured love stories (*les films d'amour*)—because "all the young girls of the world dream of love" (1968, 91)—she was struck that girls themselves explained this preference by stating their desire to "learn about love" (*pour savoir quelques points de l'amour*) or to "better adapt themselves to love" (*mieux s'adapter à l'amour*) or to "better understand how to realize love" (*pour contempler la realisation de l'amour*). And in his study of engagement practices among teachers in Kinshasa, Bernard (1968, 153) judged that although couples exchanged love letters and used French words of endearment, they did so more to "make others believe the existence of a modern form of passionate love, which permits them to hide from themselves the lack of any true form of communication" (our translation). Taken together, this literature argued—often paternalistically—that Africans had not fully assimilated the practices and sentiments associated with romantic love.

In an analysis of Onitsha market pamphlets, literary scholar Emmanuel Obiechina (1973) echoed much of this social scientific perspective on love in Africa. According to Obiechina, the Onitsha literature, which originated in Nigeria after World War II, promoted an ideal of romantic love derived from Christianity, the English literature taught at West African schools, and popular romance novels imported from Britain. The novelty of the Western ideal of romantic love, Obiechina argued, lay in its privileging of individual desire: "In pre-colonial Africa, romantic love, whether as an autonomous experience or as a stepping stone to marriage, was played down and subordinated to familial and community interests" (34). But rather than celebrating the pamphlets' emphasis on romantic love, he evoked prior cultural suspicions of love as a basis for marriage in order to criticize it. Obiechina derided pamphlet authors' obsession with romantic love as "somewhat ridiculous" and in need of "serious reconsideration," believing it was out of step with West African affective values that stressed group over individual relations and idealized "complementarity" rather than "fusion" within marriage (71). Like other scholars who engaged modernization categories but concluded that African societies had not transitioned from a communal to individualistic ethos, Obiechina argued that radically different perspectives on intimacy were at play in postcolonial Africa.

These studies suggest that by the 1950s love had become a commonplace subject of social commentary and scholarly analysis in Africa. They also suggest the perils of studying love. Love became a subject of analysis because modernization theory proposed that nuclear families based on strong bonds between couples rather than kin groups were foundational to the creation of industrial society. But when modernization theory's predictions of economic development failed to be fulfilled in much of Africa, increasing numbers of scholars questioned the theoretical framework itself. While some scholars criticized modernization theory for ignoring the way First World economic superiority relied on plundering Third World countries for resources and labor (Rodney 1972; Palmer and Parsons 1977; Bundy 1979), others highlighted the way modernization theory implicitly located the subjects of anthropological study in a prior period of time, much

not quite / no white

as evolutionary thinking had done during the nineteenth century (Fabian 1983). Still others argued that the unilinear teleology of modernization failed to account for the reality of African experience that entailed many small-scale strategic adaptations to fluctuating social-economic conditions (Ferguson 1999).

Such denunciations discouraged subsequent scholars from developing the insights offered by the likes of Bernard, Little, Jahoda, Comhaire-Sylvain, and Obiechina. To suggest that Africans were trying to adopt new practices of love, but never getting it quite right, seemed to smack of ethnocentrism and an old colonial fear that Africans were somehow "not quite / not white" (Bhabha 1994, 131). Alternatively, to suggest, as Obiechina did, that in Africa love was valued differently ran the risk of aligning oneself with racist suppositions, like those espoused by Thomas Jefferson, that portrayed Africans as incapable of deep attachment. Subsequent Africanist anthropologists and historians largely responded to these intellectual and political challenges by avoiding the problem of love altogether.

en ethnocentrism

The Past and Presence of Love in Africa

Yet talk of love in Africa did not disappear. If anything, amid the elaboration of HIV/AIDS education and prevention campaigns and the proliferation of call-in radio talk shows, TV soap operas, and romantic films, it has become ever more visible and audible since the 1970s. In the remainder of this introduction, we draw insight from this volume's chapters to make three specific arguments about love in Africa. First, love is a crucial idiom through which people in Africa have debated generational and cultural distinctions and made political claims to inclusion, often by engaging new forms of media. Second, Africans have long forged intimate attachments through exchange relationships. They have also long grappled with the ways in which monetization strains this practice, a strain that has become increasingly visible in recent years. And third, although women in Africa have often embraced romantic love as a strategy for establishing more egalitarian gender relations, it is a strategy that has met with uneven success.

LOVE AND MEDIA: DEMARCATING DIFFERENCE AND CLAIMING INCLUSION

In her eloquent memoir of growing up the daughter of a Scottish mother and Sierra Leonean father, Aminatta Forna (2002, 129) offers the following

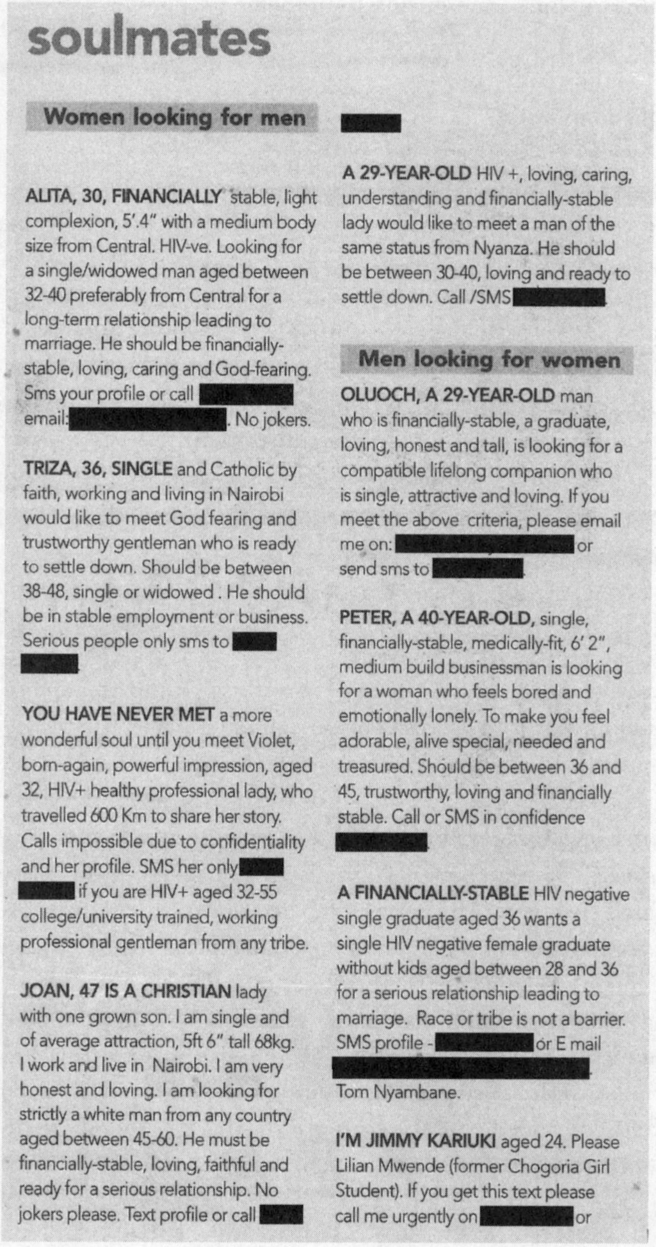

soulmates

Women looking for men

ALITA, 30, FINANCIALLY stable, light complexion, 5'.4" with a medium body size from Central. HIV-ve. Looking for a single/widowed man aged between 32-40 preferably from Central for a long-term relationship leading to marriage. He should be financially-stable, loving, caring and God-fearing. Sms your profile or call ███████ email: ████████████. No jokers.

TRIZA, 36, SINGLE and Catholic by faith, working and living in Nairobi would like to meet God fearing and trustworthy gentleman who is ready to settle down. Should be between 38-48, single or widowed . He should be in stable employment or business. Serious people only sms to ████ ██████

YOU HAVE NEVER MET a more wonderful soul until you meet Violet, born-again, powerful impression, aged 32, HIV+ healthy professional lady, who travelled 600 Km to share her story. Calls impossible due to confidentiality and her profile. SMS her only █████ ██████ if you are HIV+ aged 32-55 college/university trained, working professional gentleman from any tribe.

JOAN, 47 IS A CHRISTIAN lady with one grown son. I am single and of average attraction, 5ft 6" tall 68kg. I work and live in Nairobi. I am very honest and loving. I am looking for strictly a white man from any country aged between 45-60. He must be financially-stable, loving, faithful and ready for a serious relationship. No jokers please. Text profile or call ████

A 29-YEAR-OLD HIV +, loving, caring, understanding and financially-stable lady would like to meet a man of the same status from Nyanza. He should be between 30-40, loving and ready to settle down. Call /SMS ███████.

Men looking for women

OLUOCH, A 29-YEAR-OLD man who is financially-stable, a graduate, loving, honest and tall, is looking for a compatible lifelong companion who is single, attractive and loving. If you meet the above criteria, please email me on: ███████████████ or send sms to ████████.

PETER, A 40-YEAR-OLD, single, financially-stable, medically-fit, 6' 2", medium build businessman is looking for a woman who feels bored and emotionally lonely. To make you feel adorable, alive special, needed and treasured. Should be between 36 and 45, trustworthy, loving and financially stable. Call or SMS in confidence ███████.

A FINANCIALLY-STABLE HIV negative single graduate aged 36 wants a single HIV negative female graduate without kids aged between 28 and 36 for a serious relationship leading to marriage. Race or tribe is not a barrier. SMS profile - ███████ or E mail ██████████████████. Tom Nyambane.

I'M JIMMY KARIUKI aged 24. Please Lilian Mwende (former Chogoria Girl Student). If you get this text please call me urgently on ███████ or

FIGURE 0.3 Soulmates column from *Saturday Magazine,* May 2008. Personal ads are a regular feature in the *Saturday Magazine,* a popular Kenyan newspaper supplement that examines lifestyle issues (see chapter 7). The authors of such ads routinely disclose their HIV status and list qualities that they desire in their "soulmate," including a loving and caring personality, financial stability, trustworthiness, and faith in God. *Photo source:* Saturday Magazine.

the pressure Obama + michele

account of the affective sensibilities that shaped her parents' eight-year marriage:

> Our mother was the first person in her family to marry a foreigner. Our father was the first person in his to marry for love. When the passion leached out of their union and left a colourless husk, he offered her something else. An African marriage, my mother pronounced with scorn, where the men and women do their own thing. She could not accept such a compromise, for she was a European woman who deserved nothing less than to be loved and cherished.

By narrating her parents' marriage this way, Forna casts differences in love in particularly sharp terms. Forna's father distinguished himself from his parents and ancestors by marrying "for love." Her mother affirmed her European-ness by rejecting a marriage rooted in complementary spheres of action rather than passion and emotional fulfillment. While Forna continues on to explain that the collapse of her parents' marriage was likely less rooted in conflicting conceptions of love than in its inauspicious beginning—a premarital pregnancy—her mother insisted on representing the marriage as one precipitated by true love that also dissolved because of her commitment to this ideal. Like Forna's discussion, many of the essays in this volume illustrate how people have often constructed differences across generations, and between Africa and the West, through love.

Young people's claim that intimate passion differentiates them from their elders has a very long history in Africa, as elsewhere. Early colonial ethnographers such as Junod collected stories and songs of unrequited love or elopements. In contexts where people recognized the existence of passionate attraction—whether as part of youthful courtship or the product of love medicines—but regarded it as an unstable foundation for marriage, it was a perennial source of intergenerational tension. But people who embraced or defended the power of passion in their youth may have become more suspicious of it as they aged and gained influence within a social order that could potentially be destabilized by ungoverned feelings. Kearsley Stewart's comparison (2001) of the reproductive and sexual histories of grandmothers and their daughters in Uganda is a useful reminder that people's attitudes toward youthful intimacy often change as they age and that researchers should not take informants' narratives of drastic behavioral change across generations at face value. Stewart found that while "common sense" held that today's youth were beginning sexual relations at younger ages, demographic evidence revealed that the age of sexual debut had not changed much since the 1960s. Throughout this volume, we seek to approach claims that a specific generation was the first to marry for love or to introduce other affective forms as cultural commentaries to be explored rather than simple reflections of social reality. Such an approach does not deny that profound changes have occurred in affective discourses and practices over the past century. Rather, it demands a simultaneous attention to how conceptions of affective propriety can shift across an individual's or generation's life course and how claims to new forms of intimacy can also entail claims to power and prestige.

While passionate attraction and attachment had long been a source of intergenerational tension in many parts of Africa, the elaboration of European colonial rule—and specifically the spread of Christianity, Islam, and school education during the twentieth century—infused such tensions with new political dynamics and cultural meanings. Certain intimate and emotional relations were depicted as "civilized" "modern," and "Western" and contrasted with others deemed "primitive," "traditional," and "African." The elaboration of ideologies of love was part of this process. Turning attention to the specifics of this process enables us to move away from vague and often obfuscating references to tradition and modernity and, instead, to examine how people have variously deployed such categories to negotiate changing sensibilities and social processes, and to make political claims to inclusion (F. Cooper 2005; Ferguson 2006; L. Thomas 2006).

In *Modern Loves* (2006), coeditors Jennifer S. Hirsch and Holly Wardlow argue that companionate marriage—the ideal that situates emotional closeness as both the foundation and goal of marriage—has become a key trope through which many across the globe now claim a "modern identity" (14). Hirsch and Wardlow's argument diverges from that made by previous scholars who drew on modernization theory. Rather than understanding companionate marriage as a universal and inexorable by-product of economic and social development, they situate it as an ideal that has often taken root in places where people have not experienced increased material prosperity. They further depart from modernization theory by focusing on the *different* ways that people have interpreted companionate marriage and how its influence is part of "deliberate strategizing on the part of self-conscious actors" (11). This volume similarly seeks to challenge the logics of modernization theory by exploring how people in Africa have engaged various ideologies of love as part of broader efforts to claim "civilized" or "modern" status. But rather than situating such struggles as particular to our contemporary era of globalization, we seek to construct a deeper history of how people in Africa have deployed and reworked ideologies of love.

In her chapter, Lynn M. Thomas juxtaposes white South African anthropologists' discussions of sex during the 1930s to contemporaneous

Africa wanted to be civilized

debates about love that appeared in the black South African newspaper *Bantu World*. She demonstrates that while these anthropologists sought to document the transformation of African courtship and marriage by modern influences—including labor migrancy, the cash economy, urbanization, and mission Christianity—*Bantu World* writers sought to advise Christian readers on how to forge respectable heterosexual relations amid those transformations. The mission-educated African men and women who wrote in *Bantu World* elaborated a conception of "true love" that combined Victorian values with southern African mores to prioritize choice in courtship, emphasize a spiritual and singular connection between husband and wife, and idealize female self-sacrifice in marriage. For this aspiring black elite, discourses and practices of true love were part of broader efforts to claim "civilized" status and respectability amid the harsh racism of interwar South Africa.

In subsequent decades, discussions of how to recognize and manage true love, romantic love, and modern love proliferated in the advice columns of African newspapers and magazines and in pamphlet literature. As Jahoda (1959) and Obiechina (1972) examined in their studies of the West African press and Onitsha market literature, such discussions engaged conceptions of love promoted by mission Christianity and English fiction to contrast the affective ideals and courtship practices of school-educated young people with those of previous generations and less literate compatriots. In contrast to the love talk found in *Bantu World* during the 1930s, postcolonial and apartheid-era discussions were often characterized by less Christian moralizing. They were also far more explicit about sexual matters. Kenda Mutongi, in this volume, analyzes the popular English-language magazine *Drum* to reveal how during the 1960s and 1970s young people across much of Africa wrote to its "Dear Dolly" advice column to air grievances and gain counsel about heterosexual and homosexual intimacy. Former male readers of the column recounted to Mutongi how "Dear Dolly" letters often served as catalysts for conversations about how "modern men" should or should not behave. The column's didactic influences ranged from "Dolly's" self-assured responses—particularly strident when it came to same-sex relations—to readers borrowing the sentimental English words and phrases found in the column for their own love letters. For young readers across Africa, Mutongi demonstrates, "Dear Dolly" provided a sentimental education.

Recent scholarship has, in fact, identified readers' and audiences' didactic engagement of new cultural forms and media as a prominent feature of African popular culture. Stephanie Newell (2002) has argued that in much of Africa, popular fiction and especially romances serve as educational texts. She offers the example of Ghanaian readers who "take up the conjugal mod-

Dear Dolly

els" offered in romances and reference "familiar character types in order to prove their opinions about the opposite sex" (2000, 2–3). Similarly, Jane Bryce (1997, 122) argues that the popularity of romantic fiction in Africa should not be explained as mimicry or escapism but rather examined as a "testing ground for new ideas, new permutations and new constructions of gendered identity" (see also Nuttall 1994; Larkin 1997; Bastian 2002; Olaussen 2002; Odhiambo 2003).[6] African popular culture, according to Karin Barber (1997a, 2000), is largely defined by its capacity to rework imported genres for the purpose of moral instruction and, in the process, to muddle distinctions between the modern and the traditional.

Yet because public discussions of love in twentieth- and twenty-first-century Africa have often pivoted around technologies and media imported from elsewhere, difference has remained a prominent concern. New technologies and media have featured so centrally in debates about love because they graphically convey varying visions of intimacy and provide new venues in which those visions can be tested and enacted. For instance, the introduction of literacy in many parts of Africa through colonial mission schools exposed students to romantic themes in classical European literature and enabled them to access more popular genres. Moreover, it provided them with new ways to express desire and new forums in which to discuss its virtues and dangers (Barber 2006). Many young people readily embraced love letters as tools for establishing and sustaining romantic relations. Schoolteachers and parents, in turn, often deemed the furtive circulation and impassioned appeals of love letters as exerting a corrupting influence on youth (Breckenridge 2000, 2006; Parikh 2004; L. Thomas 2006).

Films too have offered varying visions of intimacy. In colonial Africa, government officials often censored romantic and sexually explicit films, fearing that they would incite licentious behavior and give black men the wrong impression of white women (Gutsche 1972; J. Burns 2002). While eschewing the racist logic of colonial censorship, African men and elders also voiced concerns about the influence of film. As early as the mid-1950s, debates raged on East African radio programs and in newspapers over whether romantic films were "harmful to women" and detrimental to the "sacred institution of marriage" (Strobel 1979, 120–21). Such debates frequently portrayed modern technologies and media from the West as endangering traditional African morality.

Yet, the most popular films have not always come from the West. In particular, Muslim viewers seem to find much in Hindi romance films that echo their own concerns about sexuality and intimacy; today, TV viewers across Africa watch Nigerian or "Nollywood" productions with similar interest. Laura Fair's chapter in this volume examines how people on the Zanzibari

Nolly wood

coast in the 1990s remembered the impact of the Bollywood blockbuster hit *Awara* on their visions of love and romance in late 1950s and 1960s. She persuasively argues that for these Zanzibaris, films that came from Bollywood resonated much more with local concerns about extended family interests versus individual desires than those from Hollywood (Larkin 1997; Fuglesang 1994; Fair 2004). Moreover, while the films provided vivid text and images through which to imagine the tensions between familial and individual preferences, wealth and poverty, the physical spaces of the cinema also proved important. Fair's informants described how movie attendance provided a sanctioned space for couples who could not otherwise spend time alone. In the darkened theater, couples could glance longingly at each other, sit close by, and, for the more daring, arrange trysts. Afterwards, film plots provided fodder for discussion (cf. Obiechina 1972). Whether imported from the East or West, foreign media have shaped how many Africans, especially young Africans, envision intimacy in their lives and how they distinguish themselves from their parents' generation.

Since the 1970s, media's role in providing sentimental educations and encouraging public discussion of love has persisted, if not intensified, with the rise and spread of audiocassettes, videos, the Internet, DVDs, cell phones, and satellite television. Two of the chapters in this volume engage the growing literature on the global circulation and local appropriation of these new media (Spitulnik 1993; Appadurai 1996; Ginsburg, Abu-Lughod, and Larkin 2002) to explore how young people in Niger and Kenya have reimagined intimate relationships and what it means to be modern. Drawing on fieldwork in a provincial town in Niger, Adeline Masquelier examines how young people use the Mexican telenovela *Rubí* to make sense of changing conceptions of intimacy and courtship. In recent years, youth in Niger—often reported as the poorest country in Africa—have been increasingly caught between their desires to consume foreign commodities, on the one hand, and their inability to obtain the income to purchase those commodities, on the other. Living amid heightened consumerism and overwhelming poverty, youth argue that *Rubí* offers fresh ways to interpret their daily dilemmas. Set in Mexico City and later New York, *Rubí* follows the escapades of the ruthless and ultimately lovelorn Rubí, a young woman who escapes poverty by marrying well but ultimately betrays all who surround her and ends up alone. Nigerien youth who watch the serial mine it for lessons about how to negotiate the growing tension between love and money. Masquelier concludes that far from providing these youth with an escape from reality, this Mexican telenovela, in fact, allows them to creatively transcend the limitations of the present by helping to imagine and enact alternative futures.

Although discussing a very different class of people—urban professionals—Rachel Spronk similarly argues that media provide young people in Nairobi with the tools to envision and forge new kinds of intimate relations. In Kenya during the 1990s, the liberalization of media as part of structural adjustment policies combined with the expansion of HIV/AIDS education and prevention campaigns to turn sex and love into prominent subjects of cultural representation and public discussion. Spronk explores how Western romantic films, locally produced magazines, and church counseling classes offer versions of love that range from "happily-ever-after" narratives to therapeutic discourses that emphasize emotional intimacy and mutual sexual pleasure and trust. In considering these various love scripts, young professionals portray the relations they desire as quite distinct from those of their parents' generation. Recognizing that other Kenyans often dismiss their practices—such as celebrating Valentine's Day—as "Western" and "un-African," some describe their own situation as an "identity crisis": "We are confronted daily in Nairobi with the fact that we are NOT the average Kenyan. . . . We fear that we are not part of it, but at the same time we hope that we are not part of it." This statement together with Spronk's analysis conveys young professionals' ambitions and ambivalences as they seek to forge intimate relations that are simultaneously cosmopolitan and African.

Read together, these chapters suggest how successive generations of African audiences have used diverse forms of media to imagine new ways of loving and to craft political claims to inclusion. Through the idiom of love, Africans have formulated and reformulated distinctions between the "traditional" and the "modern," "Africa" and the "West," and negotiated shifting economies of intimacy.

CONUNDRUMS OF LOVE AND MONEY

In her chapter, Jennifer Cole recounts the story narrated to her by a young Malagasy man, Dez, who, when asked about love, launched into an account about meeting his true love in a clothing stall at the marketplace. In an effort to earn the young woman's affection, Dez buys her the dress she admires. When she appears for a rendezvous wearing the dress he has bought her, he remarks, "My heart was beating like an earthquake when I saw her. I thought she looked like an angel." He went on to say that one day, if nothing prevented him, he would marry her. Dez's story suggests an interpretation of *fitiavina*—the Malagasy word often translated as "love"—in which affect and exchange are entangled rather than opposed. In arguing for material provision and emotional attachment as mutually constitutive, this volume joins recent Africanist efforts to complicate models of intimacy by emphasizing the power of material exchanges not just to reflect but to produce emotionally charged relationships (Cornwall 2002; Helle-Valle 2004). We also consider how increasing inequality and heightened monetization of social relations in much of Africa has strained the co-constitution of affect and exchange, introducing the more familiar opposition of love versus money and many of its attendant problems.

Although Western ideology and common sense often oppose emotional attachments and economic interests, much scholarship makes clear that they are entangled at the level of practice. Western folk theory implies that love is the emotion that makes us the most altruistic and the least selfish, while money is supposed to signal self-interest and impersonal ties. Yet, as Viviana Zelizer (2005, 32) has argued, far from being opposed, intimacy and exchange in the United States and elsewhere lead "connected lives": People continually assess how different intimate relations entail different monied duties and material expectations and rights. Eva Illouz (1997, 11) similarly breaks down the opposition between economy and emotion by arguing that in the United States, romantic love embodies late capitalism's core contradictions "between the sphere of consumption and the sphere of production, between a postmodern disorder and the still-powerful work discipline of the Protestant ethic, between the classless utopia of affluence and the dynamic of 'distinction.'"[7] Romantic love, according to Illouz, asserts the primacy of individual choice over and against the needs of the group, and yet, through the commodities that individuals use to express their sentiments, also reinstates class-based distinctions.

While Zelizer's and Illouz's insights about the entanglement of material provision and emotional intimacy center on U.S. cultures of intimacy, others have examined the political economy of love in less affluent locales. These studies show that what love means, how love is expressed, and what constitutes the purpose of marriage vary according to social class and particular economic circumstances. Jennifer Hirsch (2003, 82) documents how social and economic changes that have taken place in the context of transnational migration from Mexico to the United States encourage ideals of companionate marriage. She gives an example of how a young girl's ability to watch a television show that promotes new ideas of intimacy relies not only on the remittances sent home by migrants to pay for televisions and working electricity, but also on the availability of leisure time when girls are home alone rather than with their mothers grinding corn to make tortillas. While Hirsch points to the importance of the wider political economy, Linda Rebhun's ethnography of working-class communities in northeast Brazil (1999) focuses more squarely on the complex influences of money within intimate relationships. As she observes, "To survive in this confusing milieu, women must exploit their love to build necessary friendship networks and supplement their meager incomes" (86).

Historically, many Africans formed marriages through the exchange of bridewealth—a practice in which the groom's family typically gives cattle and other material objects to the bride's family. This practice shocked early missionaries to Africa (see Hunter, this volume). As one missionary to southern Africa observed, "They had no marriage, nor any proper domestic order, nor acknowledged any moral obligation to duties arising out of that relation. Females were exchanged for others, bartered for cattle, given away as presents. . . ." (Broadbent 1865, 204, cited in Comaroff and Comaroff 1992, 269). Subsequent Africanist anthropologists sought to rationalize these practices by demonstrating how they transferred productive and reproductive rights and responsibilities within and between kin groups (Comaroff 1980). Despite this anthropological emphasis on rights and responsibilities, our evidence suggests that bridewealth has also included affective dimensions. For instance, one elderly Malagasy woman proudly told Jennifer Cole how her former husband had "even paid a bull for her"—evidence in her mind not only of her productive and reproductive value but also of how much that man had loved her. Today, a language of romance increasingly pervades bridewealth exchanges, part of a more general shift from economies of production to those of consumption. To understand this shift and how it relates to the dilemmas raised in several of our chapters, it is important to consider what happens when money enters such exchange relations.

As part of their efforts to understand the emergence of modern societies, anthropologists have long argued about the social consequences of money entering exchange relations and replacing cattle or other items. Classical European social theorists such as Marx (1967 [1867]) and Simmel (1978 [1900]) argued that heightened monetization necessarily transforms the world either by alienating people from their labor or loosening social bonds. By contrast, much Africanist research argues against this perspective, suggesting that it is not money that transforms the world, but worlds that shape the meanings of money (Parry and Bloch 1989). Sharon Hutchinson (1996, 98), for example, has shown how among the Nuer in the Sudan during the 1980s and 1990s, "money's power of effacement was checked by an ideological elaboration of the unique bloodlinks uniting people and cattle . . . an elaboration that was developed so as to preclude the possibility of any direct equation between money and people." Similarly, David Lan (1989) has shown how in 1970s Zimbabwe, Shona distinguished between commodities acquired from forced relations of unequal trade and money that could be used to support shared social projects. Lan uses this example to argue that spirit mediums did not find money per se abhorrent; rather they rejected commodities that were iconic of exploitative social relations. These examples support the idea that cultural contexts shape the meaning of money, rather than money transforming social relations in a uniform direction.

By contrast, some of the chapters presented here challenge this perspective, suggesting that money *does* appear to have important and similar transformative effects on how people negotiate affective relations. They suggest that while older ideas of the mutual constitution of affect and exchange remain important, they have been challenged by heightened monetization, raising the questions of what constitutes true love and whether someone loves them for who they are or is using them for material gain. In some places such as urban South Africa, these tensions date back at least to the 1930s (see Thomas, this volume). However, this volume suggests that these kinds of dilemmas have become much more widespread amid rising consumerism and ever-sharper social inequalities. Of course, the balance between love and money can shift over the course of a relationship: What begins as love may end up as a ploy to obtain money and what begins as a relationship meant to gain money may turn into love. But what is clear is that many of our informants constantly wrestle with these ambiguities.

As already mentioned, Jennifer Cole's chapter examines the Malagasy concept of fitiavina. She shows how rural Malagasy conceptualize fitiavina as simultaneously material and moral, enacted in reciprocal exchanges of goods and labor distributed across social networks. Over the course of the twentieth century, however, missionaries sought to introduce new ideas of love as free from material self-interest, at the same time that colonization partially transformed the local economy. Today, in the context of growing social inequality fostered by neoliberal economic reforms, the opposition between fitiavina and money that first emerged through mission Christianity has both spread and intensified. Young urbanites feel themselves caught between their desire to attain Western commodities and the lack of jobs. Young women increasingly rely on men, ideally Europeans, to obtain material resources. Forced by their economic circumstances to use their relationships to obtain resources in ways that are anything but reciprocal, and hence have little to do with fitiavina, young Tamatavians have also started to reimagine fitiavina according to a more Western opposition of love and money. Young people now talk about "clean fitiavina" in which no material support is expected. Both young women and young men elaborate these distinctions as they increasingly foster some relationships because of emotional attachments and others because of the need for money.

Mark Hunter similarly draws on historical and ethnographic material from the South African province of KwaZulu-Natal to show how economic changes have shaped and reshaped the negotiation of affect and exchange. During the nineteenth century, Zulu speakers formed marriages through the transfer of *ilobolo* or bridewealth. As young men participated in wage labor under colonialism and after the formation of the Union of South Africa, they began to earn money to pay their own bridewealth, providing them greater control over choosing their wives. Amid increasing economic hardship, evidence of thrift and hard work and the ability to provide for a family became qualities that women found most stirring and attractive. Today in South Africa, Hunter argues, high unemployment and rising expenses have made it difficult for many men to forge marriages and to support families. Consequently, unmarried young women seek relationships with multiple men, in which the provision of material support is taken as evidence of emotional commitment.

That Malagasy and South African urbanites (see also the chapters by Smith and Masquelier) forge their emotional attachments through both physical intimacy and material exchange has implications for the spread of AIDS. This point is explicitly developed in these authors' earlier work on transactional sex (Cole 2004; Mark Hunter 2002). However, a long train of Western observers—ranging from nineteenth-century missionaries who denounced bridewealth as the buying and selling of women to contemporary AIDS activists and scholars who interpret transactional sex strictly in terms of economic survival—have missed this subtle and ubiquitous intertwining of emotions and materiality. By providing fuller analyses of conceptions of emotional attachment, this volume challenges scholars to historicize and relativize the long-standing Euro-American folk dichotomy between emotional and economic concerns. This dichotomy not only stigmatizes African intimacy, but also fails to recognize how all human intimacy rests on a complex blend of the material and the ideal, compunction and choice. Scholars studying the sexual transmission of HIV/AIDS need to recognize that emotional attachments as well as economic relations shape intimacy in Africa, as elsewhere in the world.

REPRODUCING AND CONTESTING GENDERED INEQUALITY THROUGH ROMANTIC LOVE

In his chapter on companionate marriage and infidelity in Nigeria, Daniel Smith cites a woman who compares her marriage to that of her parents: "My father had three wives and fourteen children. Often it was every woman for herself. My husband and I have a partnership. We decide things. There is love between us." This Nigerian woman is not alone in seeing her marriage rooted in the ideal of partnership as preferable to previous generations' marriages, especially polygynous ones. Contemporaries in many parts of the world have often described their embrace of romantic love and its cognate ideal of companionate marriage as part of broader efforts to achieve gender equality. But as scholars have also documented, they are frequently disappointed with the results (Wardlow and Hirsch 2006; Padilla et al. 2007).

In fact, some feminist theorists and scholars have long complained that romantic love assumes and perpetuates gender inequality. After World War II, Simone de Beauvoir blamed romantic love for cloaking and deepening women's oppression: "Love represents in its most touching form the curse that lies heavily upon woman confined in the feminine universe, woman mutilated, insufficient until herself" (1953 [1949], 669). De Beauvoir's insights were picked up by subsequent radical feminists who argued that love acted as an ideological smoke screen for gender inequality. Locating the roots of women's oppression in the division of household labor, some theorists understood love as a kind of false consciousness—a misguided conception of their interests—that encouraged women to work for free (MacKinnon 1989). Others, drawing on more psychoanalytic models, argued that romantic love enabled the abnegation of women and their achievements by encouraging women to sacrifice their own interests to those of men (Firestone 1970; Dworkin 1975). Social historians and cultural anthropologists have developed these insights by demonstrating how over the past century, as ideals and practices of romantic love that emphasize individual choice, self-sacrifice, and singular commitment have become increasingly widespread, they have often contributed as much to the reproduction of gender inequality as to its erasure (B. Bailey 1989; Collier 1997).

If romantic love is as detrimental to women's interests as these feminists claim, then why have so many women embraced its ideals and struggled to forge companionate marriages? Surely it is not because they suffer from false consciousness. Our chapters elucidate two reasons that some women in Africa have found romantic love and companionate marriage so appealing. First, these ideologies promise women greater independence from kin during both courtship and marriage. Individual choice in courtship has often signaled the advent of such independence. As Tina Kelobile, an unmarried black South African woman, implored in 1934: "Parents allow us, your daughters, a free hand in choosing our life partners, so that if things become dark, we may not blame you" (see Thomas, this volume). Once wed, such women have expected their marriages to be less encumbered by the meddling and potential financial burdens of natal kin and in-laws. Igbo women, Daniel Smith argues in his chapter, prefer "love marriages," in part, because they believe that they entail greater autonomy from their husband's extended family. Second, romantic love and companionate marriage have appealed to women because they promise more equitable and intimate relationships with husbands. For many, these ideals that valorize the singular bond between a husband and a wife entail the rejection of polygyny and the embrace of more egalitarian forms of decision making. As Laura Fair's informants explained, the romances in Bollywood films appealed to audiences in 1950s and 1960s Zanzibar because they involved greater intimacy and communication between spouses.

Yet the chapters assembled in this volume also suggest that women have often been disappointed by romantic love's and companionate marriage's promises of greater independence from kin and enhanced equity and intimacy with partners. Daniel Smith's chapter about Igbo women's strategies for dealing with their husband's infidelities in "love marriages" powerfully illustrates this point. Smith describes how older Igbo ideals of marriage, much like the marriage that Forna's Scottish mother bitterly characterized as "African," were premised on a conception of marriage as a joint project of social reproduction, in which men and women had separate but complementary roles. This ideal conflicts with that of love marriage, in which the quality of the marriage is judged according to ideals of emotional intimacy. While some men embrace ideals of companionate marriage, they nevertheless gain prestige from their peers when they engage in extramarital affairs because such affairs presume that the man has enough resources to support outside women and because they evidence sexual vitality. Smith argues that many women in such marriages choose to put up with these infidelities because divorce is highly stigmatized and because, in the context of a love marriage, cheating can imply that a woman has failed to satisfy her partner. "In such marriages," Smith notes, "a woman challenging her husband's extramarital behavior or asking for a condom may be undermining the very basis for the marriage and threatening whatever leverage she has with her husband by implying that the relationship itself has been broken." In Africa, where the productive and reproductive value of women has often cemented kin networks and been marked by elaborate forms of exchange, the potentially deleterious effects for women of an ideology that foregrounds couples rather than kin is particularly striking. Smith concludes that for Igbo women, "love is less than liberating."

Smith's argument resonates with other scholarship that highlights how the ethos of mutual trust that is supposed to characterize relationships premised on romantic love may increase women's vulnerability. Based on her research in northeast Brazil, Rebhun (1999) similarly argued that when notions of trust, monogamy, and singular commitment underpin a relationship, it is tricky for either partner to raise complaints, particularly about extramarital affairs, without throwing the entire relationship into question. Likewise, Abu-Lughod (1986) found that marriages rooted in romance have often made it more difficult for women to involve kin in their efforts to adjust or improve their intimate relations. Perhaps the starkest examples of how ideologies of romantic love can put women at risk come from studies on the HIV/AIDS epidemic in Jamaica, Mexico, Uganda, and Nigeria. This research shows how ideologies of male privilege and romance can easily combine to frame a girl's or woman's insistence on condom use as an affront to love (Sobo 1995; Hirsch 2003; Parikh 2004; D. Smith 2006; Hirsch et al. 2006).

Two chapters here suggest how, since at least the mid-twentieth century, some African women have recognized this ambivalent effect of romantic love. As Thomas discusses, the version of true love elaborated by *Bantu World* writers during the 1930s emphasized female self-sacrifice and subservience. Male writers, she explains, readily branded women who challenged this ideal—by either demanding more egalitarian forms of courtship and marriage or rejecting marriage altogether—as "modern girls" and corrupters of African tradition. Yet, female readers' angry responses and ethnographic accounts suggest that men generally did garner more power within both arranged marriages and love matches. Mutongi similarly argues that the version of romantic love promoted in *Drum*'s "Dear Dolly" advice column during the 1960s and 1970s fostered a double standard: It "stipulated that women assume submissive roles in heterosexual courtship, that men initiate all sexual encounters, and that women alone bear responsibility for the consequences of premarital pregnancies." Some young women voraciously read the "Dear Dolly" column and borrowed its language to craft love letters, Mutongi suggests, as ways to engage the pleasures of romantic love at a distance while avoiding venereal diseases, premarital pregnancies, and the label of "loose women."

Two other chapters focus on the gender dynamics that ensue in contexts where ideologies of love emphasize the importance of men providing for women at the same time that multiple partnerships are commonplace. In both Cole's and Hunter's chapters on Madagascar and South Africa, respectively, economic conditions have made it difficult for one relationship to fulfill all emotional and material needs. In response, both men and

liberating

women forge relationships with multiple partners. Women negotiate notions of romantic love based on singular relationships and harsh economic circumstances that require them to have more than one relationship. As Cole describes in her chapter, women's ability to gain money from their relationships with Europeans sometimes enables them to support other (Malagasy) men, thereby upending gender norms. But such arrangements also foster an idea that *real* fitiavina requires self-sacrifice, an interpretation that some men use to explain why women remain in abusive relationships. Meanwhile, in South Africa, as Hunter notes, marriage still has a high status among men and women. But many men's inability to secure *ilobolo* and women's resultant sense of betrayal makes this path an unlikely one for most young people. Here too, men's inabilities to fulfill the role of providers have become an important part of gender struggles between men and women.

In contrast to these analyses of how gender inequalities continue to structure contemporary romance, Rachel Spronk's discussion of intimacy among Nairobian young professionals offers a more optimistic perspective. She argues that this group's embrace of therapeutic discourses that seek to foster "healthy" partnerships stems, in large part, from their desire to achieve more equitable relations than those of their parents. Both Spronk and her informants view self-reflexivity, emotional openness, and deeper communication within courtship and marriage as an advance for Kenyan gender dynamics. This view is in keeping with Anthony Giddens's argument that intimacy became more democratic in the late twentieth century with the rise of therapeutic discourses and "a model of confluent love" that emphasizes autonomy and reciprocal sexual pleasure (1992, 61–64). Feminist scholars (Langford 1999; Evans 2003), however, have criticized Giddens for underestimating the persistent structural inequalities embedded in real-life heterosexual relations. Given the profound material poverty that informs so much gender inequity in Africa, it remains even more uncertain there than in the Euro-American contexts considered by Giddens and his critics whether therapeutic discourses and models of confluent love alone will lead to more equitable intimate relations.

Conclusion

If we began with a quote by Wainaina mocking the failure of Western popular representations of Africa to address love, our approach to the study of love in Africa both affirms and complicates what his remark implicitly assumes. Wainaina's reproach suggests that love is universal and that by providing representations of love between Africans (without death), Africa will look more familiar to global audiences. In keeping with the spirit of Wainaina's remark, we elucidate commonalities and connections between love in Africa and elsewhere. But rather than assuming love as a universal category, we examine how affective practices and discourses emerge out of the particular convergence of political, economic, and cultural processes. In so doing, we offer two broad contributions: one perhaps most relevant to researchers, policymakers, and others interested in HIV/AIDS in Africa, the other directed toward anthropologists examining love and its contemporary global framings.

African intimacy cannot be reduced to sex. This might seem like a commonsensical point, but in the context of the HIV/AIDS epidemic, scholars have largely examined sex to the exclusion of other facets of intimacy. Such a reduction denies the emotional, affective dimensions of all human relationships. When analysts focus only on the sexual or even the economic dimensions of HIV transmission, they may intend to explain the structural forces that produce the AIDS epidemic. Unwittingly, however, they also reinforce older, dehumanizing portrayals of Africa. To acknowledge the importance of affective attachments is to begin to paint a fuller picture of social life, its contradictions and consequences.

At the same time, any study of love must take into account the historical processes that shape and produce intimacy. In Africa—as in Europe, the United States, and elsewhere— contemporary ideologies and practices of love are the product of complex historical processes and intersections. What presently appears as an unprecedented explosion of public discourse about love prompted by globalization is, in fact, the result of a long history of the imperial and cross-regional movement of affective ideals and practices. From examining how Africans have deployed various ideologies of love to debate difference and claim political inclusion, to considering the intertwining of material support and emotional attachment, to exploring romantic love's promises and disappointments, we analyze how political, economic, and cultural formations specific, though not limited, to African contexts have profoundly shaped affective relations. We also insist that the only way to understand these processes is to trace the tangled, multilayered histories through which they emerged. Attention to these longer histories that include colonialism highlights how politics of exclusion and inclusion have so often animated affective discourses and practices. Moreover, it reminds us how social change, especially as regards intimate affairs, is far from linear but rather defined by uneven, circuitous, and submerged routes, as well as generational forgetting and the continual reformulation of cultural boundaries.

NOTES

1. The words *affect* and *emotion* are used fairly interchangeably in this introduction as in common parlance, though they also function as terms of art within particular disciplines. For example, in psychology and psychoanalysis, *affect* is usually used to indicate the physical manifestation of an emotion, while *emotion* is presumed to indicate an internal state specific to an individual. Within recent work in cultural studies, however, *affect* has been used to refer to a general state of bodily excitement that precedes the insertion of such excitement into a cultural narrative, where it then becomes a particular emotion (Massumi 2002; Berlant 1997).

2. The assumption of universality is especially problematic with respect to love, which does not even feature on psychologist Paul Ekman's (1980) well-known list of "basic" emotions that he derived from an analysis of everyday facial expressions.

3. We are indebted to Megan Vaughan, who alerted us to the usefulness of Rosenwein's work for approaching the history of emotions in Africa.

4. We cannot offer as complete a picture as we would like. We especially regret the absence of essays focused on queer love in Africa, a topic that certainly merits future investigation, particularly given the insights our own approach has gained from queer studies literature more broadly. We also hope that other scholars will push the study of love in Africa further back in time, before the late 19th century.

5. Thanks to Stephanie Camp to directing us to this quote from Jefferson.

6. In part, these arguments build on those made by scholars who have examined the popularity of romantic fiction in the United States and who have argued that while the ideals of romantic love—including self-sacrifice and singular commitment—promoted in such literature often reinforce "patriarchy," romance reading can be an "oppositional" act that allows "women to refuse momentarily their self-abnegating social role" (Radway 1991 [1984], 210).

7. These recent efforts to break down the opposition between love and money notwithstanding, one way to read the historiography on love in the West is that it recapitulates the ideology of a separation of love and money as history. According to this narrative, there has been a gradual transformation from marriages premised on the demands of property and the needs of the wider kin group to marriages premised on personal choice and emotional and sexual desires (Stone, 1979; Shorter 1975). Shorter sums up this argument when he says, "Romantic love unseated material considerations in bringing the couple together. Property and lineage would give way to personal happiness and individual development as criteria for choosing a marriage partner" (1975, 5). Though subsequent historians have contested and complicated this narrative, it has nevertheless proved tenacious, in part because the underlying narrative of increasing individuation and choice fits so well with narratives of modernization. More recently, Anthony Giddens has breathed new life into this teleological model and given it a libratory, political twist by suggesting that Western forms of intimacy are increasingly characterized by the democratization of personal ties enabling individuals to negotiate "pure relationships" that are free from material demands.

1

Love, Sex, and the Modern Girl in 1930s Southern Africa

Lynn M. Thomas

In 1938, the black South African newspaper *Bantu World* published a letter from Absolom Vilakazi, under the headline: "'To Be a Flapper': Is It Fashionable?" Vilakazi, at the time, was a student at a mission school in Natal. Remarkably, he later went on to earn his PhD in anthropology, to teach as a professor at American University in Washington, DC, and to become the president of the U.S.-based African Studies Association. When he was about sixteen years old, he wrote the following:

> I do not know what the standard definition of the word "Flapper" is . . . but I choose to use it here to designate a woman who, in the words of the Countess of Von Arnim, "is fluid"—a woman who is passing on perpetually; carrying on a petty love affair here, flirting with another man there, and playing at the same game of loving again elsewhere.
>
> It's astounding the way modern women act nowadays. They are so defiant and so rebellious. . . . They think nothing of planting a kiss on a man's lips in public and of caressing him and calling him some sweet names in the street and thus inviting publicity—things which our old-world maidens would have blushed to do.[1]

In this letter, Vilakazi drew on a definition of the *flapper* offered by the Australian-born novelist Elizabeth von Arnim to make sense of black South African women. During the 1920s and 1930s, people in many parts of the world ranging from Beijing to New York, Berlin to Bombay, used the terms *flapper* or *modern girl* to denote young women who appeared to disavow domestic duties and embrace an explicit eroticism (Modern Girl 2005, 245). Vilakazi evoked the flapper to condemn some black South African women's behavior as unseemly while linking it to foreign influences. In so doing, he ignored that previous generations of African young women had also enjoyed fleeting love affairs.[2]

As argued in this volume's introduction, scholarship on intimacy in Africa has focused a great deal more attention on sex than love. This chapter seeks to explain this disparity and help to correct it by analyzing two sets of writings on courtship, marriage, and the modern girl from 1930s southern Africa. These writings are among the very earliest and richest documentary sources on black southern African intimacy. The first set is the writings of white South African anthropologists who attended Bronislaw Malinowski's seminar at the London School of Economics and who pioneered Africanist studies of social change and sex. In recent years, scholars (Moodie, Ndatshe, and Sibuyi 1988; Burns 1995; Wood and Jewkes 2001; Delius and Glaser 2002; Mark Hunter 2005a, 2005b; Livingston 2005) inspired by feminist and Foucauldian theory, and a desire to address sexual violence, discrimination against gays and lesbians, and the AIDS epidemic have frequently turned to studies by Ellen Hellmann (1935, 1937, 1948[3]), Monica Hunter (1932, 1933, 1936), Eileen Krige (1936a, 1936b), and Isaac Schapera (1933a, 1937, 1940) to gain historical perspective on sexual relations. This chapter, however, approaches these interwar studies with a different purpose. Rather than mining them for evidence of past sexual practices, it examines the political and intellectual currents that encouraged these anthropologists to focus on sex while largely ignoring love.

By contrast, the second set of writings considered here—editorials, articles, and letters, like Vilakazi's, that appeared in the newspaper *Bantu World* during the 1930s—often did discuss love. As the first commercial black newspaper in southern and eastern Africa to offer women's pages, *Bantu World* was also the first to provide extensive discussion and advice regarding courtship and marriage. Rolfes Robert Reginald (R. R. R.) Dhlomo, the paper's "editress," wrote about such affairs and encouraged readers to respond. Present-day scholars researching the history of African intimacy, however, have overlooked these rich discussions. This chapter thus examines *Bantu World*'s unique women's pages to understand how school-educated Africans defined and debated love in the early to mid-twentieth century.

Juxtaposition of these two sets of sources reveals how in segregationist South Africa racial politics of representation combined with regional and international circuits of knowledge to shape who wrote what about black sex and love. These politics also encouraged some writers to deploy the modern girl. Through frameworks alternately rooted in liberal social science and a Christian-inflected African nationalism, anthropologists and *Bantu World* writers sought to make sense of changing practices of courtship and marriage in which young men and especially young women seemed to have more say than those of previous generations. Among the anthropologists, Schapera wrote most extensively about sex and was the only one to deploy the modern girl. As we shall see, Schapera evoked the modern girl to high-light social change, demonstrate the affinities between black and white in-timate life, and diminish the exoticizing effect of his detailed studies of sex. Like contemporaries elsewhere, many *Bantu World* writers also deployed the modern girl figure to consider the "possibilities and dangers of modern life" (Modern Girl 2005, 248). As Vilakazi's letter suggests, their deployment of the modern girl worked to blame "false" love on the foreign and the female. Exploration of these social scientific, Christian, and nationalist perspectives from the 1930s helps to illuminate why love has so long been a neglected topic within Africanist scholarship.

Social Anthropology and the Significance of Sex

For South African social anthropologists, changing practices of courtship and marriage were important research topics during the 1930s. Although from its nineteenth-century inception, anthropology had been concerned with issues of descent and kinship, sex received fresh attention in the 1920s as anthropologists drew on their fieldwork among "primitive" peoples to respond to universalist claims made by eugenicists, psychologists, and psy-choanalysts. Social reformers, like Ben Lindsey (and Evans 1925) situated sexuality as central to "the revolt of modern youth." In 1927 and 1929, Bronislaw Malinowski published *Sex and Repression in a Savage Society* and *The Sexual Life of Savages in North-Western Melanesia*. Partly inspired by the work of Havelock Ellis, Alexander Shand, and Sigmund Freud, these books explored how sex was "the most difficult" human instinct to control (Mal-inowski 1927, cited in Stocking 1995, 282). In 1928, Margaret Mead published *Coming of Age in Samoa,* her wildly popular study arguing that the emotional distress experienced by U.S. female adolescents was "a reaction to the re-straints put upon us by our civilization" (Boas foreword to Mead 1928, xv). Such anthropologists responded to reformers' efforts to tame modern youth and psychologists' theorizing of adolescence by insisting on the cultural determinants of sexuality.

South African anthropologists both drew on and departed from such works. Political preoccupations particular to the region also shaped their research agendas. During the interwar period, white eugenicists raised concerns about rapid growth of the black population and the "Poor White Problem," making interracial intimacy a decisive political issue. Passed in 1927, South Africa's Immorality Act prohibited sex between whites and Africans. The 1929 and 1938 election campaigns were dominated by parties' competing claims over who could better protect the white population from the "black peril" (Dubow 1995; Hyslop 1995; Klausen 2004). White conservatives, particularly Afrikaner nationalists, routinely sought to discredit anti-segregationist liberals by claiming that they advocated "miscegenation." In response, some prominent liberals spelled out their opposition to "race-mixture" (Hoernlé 1934; Macmillan 1989; see also Malinowski 1941). While black leaders and intellectuals denounced the racism that underpinned segregationist policies and black peril scares, their own engagement with eugenics, "racial uplift" ideology, and black nationalism meant that many of them also criticized interracial intimacy (Matthews 1938; Crowder 1988). Within this political context, anthropologists as well as *Bantu World* writers rarely discussed sex and love across racial lines. Likely, a related sense of respectable and objectionable relations also caused them largely to ignore same-sex intimacy.

Anthropologists at South Africa's English-language universities distinguished themselves from their metropolitan as well as Afrikaner colleagues by researching social change in urban and rural areas.[4] During the early 1930s, Monica Hunter (after marriage, Wilson) did fieldwork in the "reserves," towns, and white-owned farms of the Eastern Cape, where she had grown up as the daughter of white missionaries. Eileen Jensen Krige, raised in the rural Transvaal, did her early research there and in Pretoria. Jewish and born in Johannesburg, Ellen Hellmann studied that city's slums. Isaac Schapera, also Jewish, spent his early childhood in the rural northern Cape before attending school in Cape Town. During the late 1920s and 1930s, he researched the influence of "Western civilization" in the Bechuanaland Protectorate.

All four moved in South Africa's progressive political circles that drew together white liberals and leftists like themselves and blacks—mainly men—with advanced education (Elphick 1987; Hammond-Tooke 1997; Kuper 1999; Macmillan 1989; Kuper 2007). These white anthropologists also relied on school-educated African men as invaluable research assistants (Hunter 1936; Krige 1936b). Schapera's research assistants in the Bechuanaland Protectorate, for example, were teachers who had been temporarily suspended from their posts for impregnating students (Comaroff and Comaroff 1988, 559–60; Kuper 2002, 15). In addition to having firsthand knowledge of sexual matters, these men possessed the requisite English and Setswana language skills and the free time to help Schapera in his research. White anthropologists' findings were thus necessarily shaped by the views of learned and relatively well-off young men. As Lyn Schumaker (2001) has argued, school-educated blacks played a pivotal, if seldom recognized, role in the development of Africanist anthropology.

Schapera, Hunter, Krige, and Hellmann all participated in Malinowski's seminars at the London School of Economics (LSE) at some point during the 1920s and 1930s (Argyle and Preston-Whyte 1978). These South Africans were among the first participants to conduct fieldwork engaging the theory of "culture contact" that emerged from those seminars.[5] Malinowski acknowledged that he learned much from their work, particularly Hunter's *Reaction to Conquest* (1936), and his own 1934 visit to South Africa. Yet Malinowski (1938, viii, xvi) criticized some of them, especially Schapera, for abandoning a tripartite approach to culture contact that investigated "old Africa, imported Europe, and the New Composite Culture" as related yet discrete social realms in favor of an approach that examined the development of a unitary and "specifically South African culture" (Schapera 1938, 26).

A number of intellectual and political currents animated Schapera's desire to examine South Africa as a single social field. He was influenced by the more sociological perspective of A. R. Radcliffe-Brown, who taught at the University of Cape Town (1921–26), and the work of South African liberal historian W. M. Macmillan (Schapera 1934; Macmillan 1989; Gordon 1990; Schapera 1990; Kuper 1996, 2001, 2002). As already suggested, he was also shaped by his close interactions with school-educated Africans. Later in his life, Schapera recalled how he learned the importance of studying "people as they are, not as they were" when, early in his fieldwork, the influential Tswana Chief Tshekedi Khama reprimanded him for requesting a group of teachers to perform "traditional dances" when they had wanted "to show how they could do modern dance, ballroom dance" (Kuper 2002, 16). As a liberal Jew and the son of eastern European émigrés who faced dilemmas of "acculturation" in his own life (Kuper 2007, 19–20), Schapera sought to demonstrate how black Africans were "drawing more and more into the common cultural life of South Africa" (Schapera 1937, 387).

Among South African anthropological studies, Schapera's *Married Life in an African Tribe* (1940) is most comparable to Malinowski's and Mead's books in its monographic attention to sexual matters and in its ambition to reach popular audiences. While at LSE, Schapera served as Malinowski's

FIGURE 1.1 Tswana wedding, 1930s. This photo of a Tswana wedding party appeared in Issac Schapera's anthropological study, *Married Life in an African Tribe* (1940). In keeping with Schapera's commitment to documenting social change, this image illustrates the modern appearance of Tswana weddings. The three young women (on the left side) wear short skirts that Schapera described as typical attire for Tswana modern girls. *Photo courtesy of Royal Anthropological Institute Photographic Collection.*

research assistant on *Sex and Repression* and *The Sexual Life of Savages*, work that included surveying Freud's writings. In turn, Malinowski contributed an introduction to the U.S. edition (1941) of *Married Life*. Yet in his preface, Schapera (1940, 7) sought to distinguish his work from Malinowski's by describing it as a "social history" and stating that he did not intend "to add to the many theoretical discussions of either 'primitive' family [or] kinship problems." According to Schapera, a crucial impetus for his detailed research on sexual practices was a questionnaire sent to him in 1932 by Wulf Sachs, a Johannesburg-based Jewish psychiatrist who later wrote *Black Hamlet*, a study of the cross-cultural possibilities of psychoanalysis (Comaroff and Comaroff 1988; see also Sachs 1996 [1937]).

Married Life soon became infamous for its frank discussion of sex ranging from masturbation to physical intimacy between women to preferred heterosexual positions (Kuper 2007, 33–34). The publication of such explicit material was likely unimaginable to Hellmann, Hunter, and Krige. As young white women working in interwar South Africa where interracial sexuality was a politically explosive issue, they had to tread carefully when discussing black intimacy. As a Jewish man writing at a time of heightened anti-Semitism in South Africa (Furlong 1991; Shain 1994), Schapera, in fact, had a difficult time pulling off this feat.

Once *Married Life* appeared in South Africa, Douglas Buchanan, Chief Tshekedi's legal adviser in Cape Town, threatened to sue Schapera for publishing obscene material about the Tswana. Although Schapera had heeded Tshekedi's earlier reprimand to study Africans "as they are," he recalled ignoring this threat after deciding that Tshekedi's adviser had been offended by the familiarity of the sexual practices: "If they had been esoteric, it would have been all right" (Comaroff and Comaroff 1988, 561; Kuper 2002, 16).[6] Correspondence by E. Stanley Field, Schapera's legal adviser during the 1940 controversy, reveals that while Buchanan was indeed most offended by the accounts of "modernized" sexual relations, his complaints were not so easily dismissed.[7] Buchanan readily convinced a number of church leaders and University of Cape Town officials that the book should be suppressed within South Africa before "ill-disposed persons" use it to criticize "those interested in the welfare of the natives." After considering various responses, Field arranged for public libraries to place it on their reserve shelves, for Cape Town bookstores to take it off display, and for key newspapers and journals to refrain from reviewing it. With these actions, Buchanan's complaints subsided.[8]

In his correspondence with Field, Schapera expressed frustration that *Married Life* could be viewed as anything but "scientific" and noted that the complaints smacked of a "witch-hunt[]" as such concerns had never been raised about "Malinowski, Ben Lindsey, and the rest of them." Reminding Schapera of the particularities of South African racial politics, Field responded: "The difference is, of course, that the Malans and Erasmuses [conservative South African politicians] cannot make use of Malinowski or any of the others as the basis for any attack upon the Cape Town University, nor upon local liberals, nor upon South African Jewry."[9] While in later years Schapera downplayed the significance of his Jewishness to his anthropological career (Comaroff and Comaroff 1988), nonetheless it seems to have limited the dissemination of *Married Life* within South Africa. This incident also illustrates how scholarly accounts of African intimacy—especially ones that are sexually explicit—have long generated political controversy.

Schapera's commitment to documenting changes in African courtship and marriage was shared by Hunter, Hellmann, and Krige. All four anthropologists emphasized the transformations wrought by labor migrancy, the cash economy, urbanization, and Christianity. They argued that labor migrancy, by drawing men away from families in rural areas, fanned premarital and extramarital relations (Schapera 1933a, 1940). Hunter (1932) and Hellmann (1937, 1948) further documented how, by the interwar period, increased numbers of African women had begun to move to urban areas where they earned money by selling beer and providing domestic and sexual services. Hellmann (1935, 56) described how in the Johannesburg slum of Rooiyard "'back-door' husbands and sweethearts" were a common means by which even married women sought to make ends meet. These anthropologists also considered how Christian missionaries had reshaped courtship and marriage by banishing initiation, promoting monogamy, and condemning sexual practices that had previously been allowed such as premarital sexual play (including "thigh" sex, *ukuhlobonga* in isiZulu or *ukumetsha* in isiXhosa) and discrete extramarital affairs (Hunter 1936; Schapera 1940).

For these anthropologists, the increased prevalence of "illegitimate" births was among the most telling indicators of the social change. Anthropologists argued that rising rates of premarital pregnancies were evidence of African parents' inability to control their children and to hold young men responsible for their sexual actions (Hellmann 1935, 1937, 1948; Hunter 1932, 1936; Krige 1936a, 1936b; Schapera 1933a). Hunter (1936) described how many school-educated men in the Eastern Cape, in turn, blamed the problem on missionaries who, by denouncing *ukumetsha,* had left young people with little choice but to have intercourse. Rising ages of marriage also played a part by leaving young women sexually mature but unmarried for longer periods: African women living in urban areas tended to marry between twenty-two and twenty-five years of age while their rural counterparts usually married by eighteen (Hunter 1932, 1936; Krige 1936a). Hunter (1932) further argued that poverty, especially in towns, delayed families' and young people's efforts to raise the resources necessary for bridewealth and marriage celebrations.

Whereas many white South African commentators viewed colonialism as simply leading to the "break-up of the Bantu family" or "detribalization," these anthropologists offered more subtle accounts of social change that entailed the retention of "many features of the old [family system]" and the creation of "a new composite culture" (Hunter 1932, 686; Hellmann 1948, 115; see also Schapera 1933a; Krige 1936a; Schapera 1940). European "influences" including labor migrancy and schooling, they argued, gave young people a "greater sense of freedom" and fueled women's resistance to infant betrothals and to polygynous, levirate, and sororate marriages (Hunter 1936; Krige 1936a; Hellmann 1940; Schapera 1933b, 1940). They also fueled young peoples' greater say in the selection of marriage partners. Schapera (1940, 44, 58) described the following verse that scorned arranged marriages as the "song of the modern young Kgatla [a Tswana subgroup]": "The heart eats what it desires, but rejects what is sought for it."

Through discussion of marital choice, love surfaced in these anthropological accounts. Anthropologists agreed that passion had long been a part of courtship and that this emotion could lead to marriage or, if kin insisted on other partners, could persist in discreet extramarital affairs (Hunter 1936; Krige 1936b). Schapera (1940, 44, 58) provided examples of both "love matches" and "forced marriages" in interwar Bechuanaland, explaining that most young people accepted "any reasonably suitable mate chosen by their parents." According to Hunter, young peoples' preferences predominated in Pondoland. She wrote that even though elders disapproved of young men marrying their "sweethearts" as they feared that they would "already [be] tired of the girl[s]" when they began living together, most marriages were "of choice" and elopement was a common and old practice (Hunter 1936, 188–90, 32). While these anthropologists acknowledged that passionate love could animate courtship and prompt elopements and affairs, they did not examine how people described or understood this emotion. Instead, they heeded Radcliffe-Brown's call that social anthropology should be "independent of psychology" (Radcliffe-Brown 1923, 133, cited in Stocking 1995, 333) and left love unexplored.

On a couple of occasions, Schapera broke with this anthropological disregard for emotion by publishing a number of love letters translated from Setswana to English (Schapera 1933b, 1940). The most moving of these was written by a young migrant to his lover and appeared as follows in *Married Life*:

> I still think of how we loved each other; I think of how you behaved to me, my wife; *I did not lack anything that belonged to you. All things I did not buy, but I just got them, together with your body;* you were too good to me, and you were very, very sweet, more than any other sweet things that I have ever had. *We fitted each other beautifully. There was nothing wrong; you carried me well; I was not too heavy for you, nor too light, just as you were not too heavy for me nor too light; and our "bloods" liked each other so much in our bodies!* (46, my italics)

Seven years earlier, Schapera had published another version of this letter that omitted the passages italicized above, deeming them "too intimate to be published." The explicit aim of the earlier article that appeared in the liberal South African periodical *The Critic* was to convey "the Natives' genuine . . . concerns and interests" (Schapera 1933a, 20, 24). Schapera's decision to include the italicized passages in *Married Life* suggests that in writing for a mainly British and U.S. audience a few years later, he imagined that he could include more explicit talk about African intimacy. The complaints raised by Buchanan and his allies against *Married Life* confirm that such talk was not easily tolerated in South Africa. In an insightful rereading of these letters, Keith Breckenridge (2000, 341–44) has noted Schapera's failure to offer an "idiomatic analysis" of them. Yet for Schapera, the power of these letters lay in conveying how Africans shared the *same* sentiments as whites and Westerners; he had little interest in parsing cultural differences. Believing that such emotionally potent passages could speak for themselves, he deployed them to support his universalizing argument that South Africa was becoming a single society.

In a further foray into emotions, Schapera offered a rare psychological observation toward the end of *Married Life*. He argued that most Kgatla marriages lacked a strong emotional connection.

> It is evident, then, that the Kgatla conception of marriage does not make for loyal companionship and deep personal attachment between husband and wife. The unequal social status of men and women, the lack of daily intimacy in married life, the nature of the authority vested in the husband, the polygamous tradition and its modern manifestations in sexual promiscuity, and the growing spirit of revolt on the part of women, all render difficult the attainment of enduring harmony. (1940, 286)

Schapera noted that most women were unhappy in their marriages, even in ones that began as love matches. He blamed much of the problem on men's attitudes and disruptions caused by labor migration. Remarkably, Schapera, the lifelong bachelor, wrote: "Kgatla husbands have much to learn about the art of married love" (1940, 184). But he remained optimistic that the continued "'emancipation' of women and children . . . may yet possibly succeed in developing those conceptions of human personality that many thinkers believe to be the only suitable psychological foundations for stable personal relations under modern conditions" (1940, 356). By evoking psychological theory, Schapera worked to pull his particularizing criticism of Kgatla marriage back in line with his universalizing argument about a unitary South African society. In keeping with the views of contemporary liberal reformers in the United States and Britain (Seidman 1991; Collins 2006 [2003]), Schapera's conception of marital love was a companionate one in which husbands and wives enjoyed relative equality and shared physical and emotional intimacy.

Bantu World writers may well have rejected Schapera's assessment that most African marriages—or at least their Christian ones—lacked deep personal attachment. They may also have rightly asked whether all white women were so happy in their marriages. Yet, as we shall see, they shared his concern about how to achieve marital success under modern conditions.

Bantu World and the Importance of Love

As mentioned earlier, *Bantu World* was the first newspaper targeting black South Africans to offer women's pages and extensive discussions of love. The paper viewed women readers as crucial to increasing its early circulation figure of six thousand papers per week. Bertram Paver, a white advertising salesman, founded *Bantu World* in Johannesburg in 1932. In the midst of the Great Depression, Paver sought to expand the market for white companies by establishing the only black commercial newspaper with a nationwide circulation. About half of the paper appeared in English, with the rest appearing in the languages of isiZulu, isiXhosa, Sesotho, and Setswana, and, to a lesser extent, Tshivenda, Xitsonga, and Afrikaans. The women's pages—like the front page—appeared in English to ensure an audience that better cut across ethnolinguistic divides (Couzens 1978; Switzer 1988, 1997).

Liberal African nationalists edited and staffed *Bantu World* and held considerable sway in determining its content. R. V. Selope Thema, the editor from 1932 to 1952, was a leader of the South African Native National Congress (precursor to the African National Congress). He used his position at the paper to criticize discriminatory government policies and to highlight African achievements. According to historian Les Switzer, *Bantu World* quickly became "the arbiter of taste in urban African politics and culture and by far the most important medium of mass communication for the literate African community." Although this community (literate in any language) amounted to only about 12 percent of the total African population of 6.6 million in 1936, it was a vocal group. *Bantu World* embodied the concerns and aspirations of mission-educated Africans who worked mainly as clerks, teachers, clergy, domestic servants, and nurses, and who struggled, under increasingly difficult circumstances, to achieve elite status. In the face of white racism, the paper insisted on the importance of school-educated and Christian blacks to South Africa's future (Couzens 1978; Peterson 2000, 2006). Anthropologists also read and, on occasion, cited *Bantu World* (Hellmann 1940). For Hunter (1936, 554), black newspapers were an important source for understanding "what Bantu think of Europeans, and their influence upon Bantu society."

R. R. R. Dhlomo, the editress of the women's pages, was one of the period's most important black male writers in English and isiZulu (Switzer 1997). Although female columnists and letter writers appeared on these pages, Dhlomo and a handful of regular male contributors framed much of the discussion. Dhlomo's early life provides insight into the social background of the black men behind *Bantu World*. Born in Pietermaritzburg in 1901, he attended mission schools. In 1912, the Dhlomo family moved to Johannesburg where his father worked as a medical assistant for a mining company and his mother washed white customers' laundry out of their home (Couzens 1985). After further schooling, R. R. R. worked as a mine clerk and, in the late 1920s, turned his full attention to writing.

As *Bantu World*'s editress, Dhlomo sought to encourage black women's advancement. Under the masthead "Page of Interest to Women of the Race," the women's pages devoted considerable space to highlighting black women's educational and professional achievements and advising women on how to foster healthy families. Dhlomo argued that *Bantu World* itself could strengthen marriages by teaching women about the wider world and enabling them to hold "intelligent[]" conversations with their husbands.[10] Responding to the influx of black women into South African towns during the interwar period, Dhlomo and other male contributors to the pages sought to define and promote a respectable urban femininity that would distinguish their daughters and wives from the disreputable female figures of the prostitute and beer brewer that black leaders had long associated with town life (Webb and Wright 2001). Against the economic and sexual landscape of places like Rooiyard, the Johannesburg slum studied by Hellmann, *Bantu World*'s male writers sought to defend their womenfolk.

Other social patterns identified by the anthropologists also informed discussion in *Bantu World*. In 1932, a headline announced, "Bantu Girls Now Marry Later in Most Instances." The accompanying article explained how after completing training courses in teaching, nursing, or domestic service, many young women preferred to work for a period and help support their parents and younger siblings before marrying.[11] As in the anthropological accounts, the rising age of marriage was a piece of broader changes. *Bantu World* writers rarely defended or even mentioned polygynous, levirate, and sororate marriages, suggesting that such practices had become disreputable or even obsolete for mission-educated Africans. Moreover, like the anthropologists, newspaper writers situated "choice" of marital partners as a common, if sometimes contested, practice.

FIGURE 1.2 *Bantu World* women's page, April 1935. As the first commercial black newspaper in southern and eastern Africa to offer women's pages, *Bantu World* was also the first to provide extensive discussion and advice regarding courtship and marriage. In this edition, letter writers' definitions of love appear alongside complaints about modern schoolgirls, a photo of an all-female performance troop, and ads for household commodities. *Photo source:* Bantu World.

But unlike the anthropologists, *Bantu World* contributors offered few frank discussions of sex. When African men with advanced schooling worked as research assistants for anthropologists, they proved indispensable in gathering intimate material. Yet when such men wrote in *Bantu World*, they acknowledged sexual relations only implicitly, when lamenting increased immorality or offering marital advice. Christian and middle-class propriety helped to ensure that explicit descriptions of sex did not appear in the paper. Whereas anthropologists sought to document patterns of black intimacy, *Bantu World* writers, as an elite—if embattled—minority within the African population, sought to define and defend their own respectability. Like Tshkedi's legal adviser, *Bantu World* editors probably believed that such talk could harm African interests. Committed to a moderate African nationalism, they avoided material that might reinforce racist stereotypes of Africans as oversexed and immoral. Instead, they wrote about love and, at times, deployed it as a euphemism for sex.

Through regular columns, short stories, and letters, *Bantu World* writers debated what love could and should be. In 1936, a couple of male readers complained of too much love talk, writing that love had "absolutely nothing to do with . . . [a] leading newspaper."[12] Other readers—both male and female—responded by insisting that it was an important topic. "Love," as one woman wrote, "is not a little thing."[13] Editress Dhlomo defended discussion of love by citing women's most enthusiastic embrace of the topic compared to others raised in the paper. He dismissed as "sheer bosh" claims that the European press did not discuss love, explaining that it was a common topic in European newspapers, novels, and women's magazines. Until black South African women were able to "talk or read about" love in such varied media, Dhlomo argued, their newspapers had a duty to address the topic.[14]

A notable moment in *Bantu World*'s discussions of love came in April 1935 when Mildred Ntaba—possibly Dhlomo writing under a pseudonym—posed the question: "What is Love?" Ntaba noted that some people defined love as helping the needy while others defined it as loving the "opposite sex." She then asked readers for their views.[15] A number responded by describing the self-sacrificing and all-encompassing love of a mother for her children.[16] Others discussed Christian love, explaining that their God was the God of love.[17] As one writer put it, "It is through observing this law of love only, that we can demonstrate our love and obedience to Him."[18] For *Bantu World* writers, maternal devotion and Christian faith were poignant manifestations of love.

More than half of the approximately fifteen respondents discussed heterosexual love. For some, such love grew from Christian love. They quoted scripture to illustrate how love was a "natural" force that gave meaning and energy to all life. One writer described love between a man and woman as combining "spiritual sympathy" with a "strong physical attraction."[19] This unique combination, according to this author and others, laid the foundation for a strong marriage. W. S. Moeng wrote that "the desire for a mate, for affection, leads to marriage and home building. . . . There is always a definite need for an understanding comrade, for the warmth of real affection from love . . . for the sympathetic appreciation of a kindred spirit."[20]

A number of respondents distinguished "true" love from "false," associating the former with spiritual connection and sustained affection, and the latter with materialism and modern times. Over the past century, people living in a variety of colonial and postcolonial African contexts have deployed this distinction between true and false love (Jahoda 1959; Setel 1999; in this volume, Mutongi). Writing in *Bantu World*, Vivian Dube contrasted true love with the "morally weak way in which love is interpreted these days."[21] Other authors associated false love with youthful passion and film. Walter Nhlapo, arts columnist and musician, described how first loves cause "delights and deliriums," "heartbreaks," and "grief." Such passion and pain, according to Nhlapo, was indispensable for sustaining "bioscopes, talkies, theatres."[22] Dhlomo himself joked about young people who revel in the "stupid blindness" of "modern love" by following the "hot stuff" that they see in "bioscopes" where "two people with their mouths close together stand for an hour not knowing how to speak!"[23] Nhlapo and Dhlomo understood youthful romance, particularly as patterned after films, as shallow and unstable. Johanna Phahlane, a renowned musical performer and author of a women's page column, agreed. She wrote, "Passion and glamour are all very well during the engagement, but such qualities alone are [a] very unsuitable foundation for a happy home life." Young men and women should "get to know" each other, Phahlane advised, to determine if they will be able to "put up with one another's faults for the rest of . . . [their] lives."[24] For Nhlapo, Dhlomo, and Phahlane, successful marriages depended more on mature love than sexual passion. This perspective aligned true love with a long-standing southern African view (Junod 1912, vol. 2; Hunter 1936) that passion was an unstable foundation for marriage.

In debating what constituted true love, nearly all writers agreed that young people should be allowed to choose their partners. As one unmarried woman put it, love is "the thoughtful outgoing of one's whole nature to another.... It is ... [in] the realm of choice."[25] Others suggested how some rejected young women's right to chose. In a 1934 letter, Tina Kelobile wrote:

> ...There are some men, educated men, and teachers at that, who encourage parents to compel their daughters to marry them. They do this not because they love the girls, but because they are cousins of the girls, and because they are jealous of the courtship which exists between their cousins and some boys or young men.
>
> Imagine the shock a girl receives, when called to marry her cousin the very man, she has no love for. If she objects to this, she is called a disobedient child, whereupon she is thrashed until she consents. . . .
>
> How then can the couple live a happy life, bear each other's burdens, and sympathise with each other, when the husband knows that the wife loved and loves someone else?
>
> "Love swells like the Solway, but ebbs like its tide." Do the parents expect their daughters to be treated well, when they compel them to marry against their will! ...Therefore, parents allow us, your daughters, a free hand in choosing our life partners, so that if things become dark, we may not blame you.[26]

Kelobile's eloquent letter highlights a number of key features of love talk in *Bantu World*. First, she quotes European literature—the song "Lochnivar" from Walter Scott's *Marmion* (1808) in which a young woman defies her parents by eloping with her true love—to support her position. By citing Scott, Kelobile displays her erudition and reveals how texts taught at mission schools informed African conceptions of love. Second, she insists on each woman's right to choose her "life partner" even while acknowledging that she might not make the right choice. For marriages to be "happy," according to Kelobile, they needed to commence with free choice.

For many *Bantu World* writers, young women's choice in love was not incompatible with their obedience in courtship and marriage. Vivian Dube wrote that the girl who is true "keeps herself solely for the man she loves, because she hopes to be his pure wife one day. . . . She is even prepared to forego most of her former pleasures and pursuits, if her lover tells her to do so."[27] This ideal that placed men in charge, according to another writer, should be communicated from the outset: A woman should always wait with "reserve" and "shyness" for the man to "propose" love.[28] Absolom Vilakazi, whose 1938 letter opened this chapter, claimed that this power differential benefited women. As a very precocious fourteen-year-old, Vilakazi expressed concern that some African women would foolishly follow the "foreign tradition" of Leap Year and propose to men. He wrote: "In our old-fashioned world, women count it as a privilege to be denied the first advance in matters of the heart, they count it a man's delicacy to spare them the embarrassment of so forward a task."[29] A few weeks later, A. M. Xaba rejected Vilakazi's position, arguing that while "fifty years ago . . . [a girl] would have paid with her life" for proposing to a man, in these "modern days . . . marriage proposals should be on fifty-fifty bases," with women having the same rights as men to pop the question (on contemporary debates about "50/50," see Hunter this volume).[30] Although Xaba favored "forward" women, most others, particularly men, did not.

In many regards, the conception of heterosexual love advanced by *Bantu World* writers coincided with Victorian notions of true love that held sway among the middle classes in England and the United States from the mid- to late nineteenth century. Modeled after the Christian conception of self-knowledge through love of God, Victorian conjugal love entailed an intense spiritual bond between a man and a woman. This bond, chosen and forged through courtship, provided the foundation for a monogamous union in which the husband and wife maintained a unique and future-oriented connection to one another. While Victorians recognized sex as a healthy and necessary part of marriage, they prioritized the spiritual bond between husband and wife. This ideal also valued female acquiescence and self-sacrifice, granting men more power than women and relegating men and women to "separate spheres" (Seidman 1991; Giddens 1992; Illouz 1997; Collins 2006 [2003]).

Since the middle of the nineteenth century, mission-educated Africans would have encountered this Victorian conception of conjugal love through schooling and reading imported magazines, popular novels, and advice literature. By the 1930s, some *Bantu World* writers would have been raised in families where parents or even grandparents had espoused this ideal. As refracted through mission Christianity, the Victorian ideal of true love marked, in many ways, a sharp departure from courtship and marriage practices that had prevailed in black southern African communities. Whereas many communities allowed nonprocreative premarital sexual play and tolerated extramarital affairs—particularly husbands'—as long as they were discreet and not ill-timed, missionaries railed against such practices (Hellmann 1935, 1937; Hunter 1936; Schapera 1940; Mark Hunter 2005b). Moreover, missionaries opposed polygynous, levirate, sororate, and forced marriages for desecrating the voluntary and singular connection between husband and wife.

Yet it is crucial to recognize how Christian and Victorian conceptions of love also resonated with, and likely reinforced, existing southern African ideals. Anthropological accounts suggest that, like Victorians, non-Christian Africans did not regard passion alone as a stable foundation for marriage. The same sources indicate that young peoples' preferences often played a role in the selection of spouses; hence, choice was not entirely new (Mark Hunter 2005b). In addition, overlaps existed between Victorian values and southern African notions that young women should be demure in courtship and that marriage was a cooperative endeavor in which each spouse held clearly defined, though not equivalent, roles (Hunter 1936; Schapera 1940; Bryant 1949; Hunter, this volume). Given these strong resonances, the definition of true love elaborated in *Bantu World* is best considered a composite of Christian, Victorian, and long-standing southern African values.

At the same time that writers articulated this definition of true love, they lamented that it was under attack. In distinguishing true love from false, they described how the modern fixation on passion, glamour, and commodities was corrupting courtship and marriage. Their complaints were similar to those made elsewhere in the early twentieth century as contemporaries came to grips with new conceptions of "romantic" love that prioritized sexual pleasure and intertwined courtship with leisure and consumption (Seidman 1991; Illouz 1997). As Steven Seidman has written of Victorian conceptions of love in the United States, "true love was contrasted to a certain concept of romantic love which [was] said to rest upon more superficial and transient feelings" (1991, 50). During the 1920s and 1930s, South Africans, like people in other parts of the world, often contested these transformations through the figure of the modern girl. In particular, *Bantu World* writers and Schapera deployed the modern girl to discuss black intimacy amid South Africa's strained politics of race and difference.

The Modern Girl's Challenge to True Love

During the 1930s, *Bantu World*'s women's pages were filled with debates about young women, often with some schooling, who troubled social norms by wearing short dresses and pants, using makeup, attending raucous dances, smoking cigarettes, drinking alcohol, and fixating on romance. Writers usually referred to these young women as *modern girls*. *Girl* was first stretched beyond its reference to female children in 1880s England where it popularly denoted unmarried working-class and middle-class young women who seemingly occupied "a provisional free space" (Mitchell 1995, 3). It was this contingent independence from conventional female roles that people in Africa and elsewhere evoked during the 1920s and 1930s when they deployed *girl* or variants of it to reference young women. Whites' use of *girl* and *boy* to refer to African adults in segregationist South Africa, as in the Jim Crow United States, was a racial insult. But when black writers prefaced *girl* with *modern,* they signaled something humorous and unsettlingly progressive rather than decidedly pejorative (Modern Girl 2008).

One of the most common complaints about the modern girl was that she corrupted true love by having multiple sexual partners. Although in many international contexts, contemporaries often associated the modern girl with lesbianism, *Bantu World* writers always discussed her sexuality in heterosexual terms. A number of writers denounced girls who had more than one boyfriend at the same time or "change[d] their lovers as they do their dresses." By representing such behavior as a modern innovation, such writers ignored how premarital sexual play and discreet extramarital affairs had long been tolerated in many southern African communities. M. M. Mapumulo complained that "girls" deceived men by professing their love to many. If young women did not make themselves easily available through "irresponsible love affairs and wild night life," A. D. Petersen wrote, more men would marry. Like others who criticized the modern girl, Petersen deployed the word *love* as a euphemism for sex. Sexually forthright behavior by young women, writers argued, did not bode well for either the stability of future marriages or the African race.[31] Some, including female columnists and, on occasion, Dhlomo, blamed the corruption of true love on men who used love medicines, pawed women in public, and seduced and soon abandoned them.[32] More often, however, they held the modern girl responsible.

Criticism of the modern girl's corruption of true love coincided with concerns about her materialism. One *Bantu World* short story featured a foolish protagonist who dropped her "love" of two weeks for another man who was a "champion dancer" and managed a "big taxi."[33] In another fictional piece, Dhlomo insinuated that no self-respecting young woman would love a man just because he gave her "costly presents."[34] While Dhlomo portrayed the practice of earning affection through gifts as a modern innovation, this volume's introduction and chapters by Cole and Hunter argue that love has long been partially constituted through material exchanges including bridewealth.

Bantu World writers also criticized modern girls for their captivating appearances. In a 1936 letter published under the headline "All is Not Gold that Glitters," Walter Nhlapo wrote, "Modern girls look alike. They all wear the latest, in photo[s] they captivate you to lose you[r] head and heart. They have little or no personality in their faces, nor do they have good character, nor signs of ambition." Nhlapo described photos and clothes as if they were love medicines used by modern girls to trick men and conceal their own soullessness.[35]

Not all readers took these criticisms of the modern girl in stride. Miss Albertina Sikiti angrily dismissed Nhlapo as biased against "girls," "pedantic," and "absolutely repugnant." (And Dhlomo noted that he had edited out Sikiti's "very hot words."[36]) In the weeks that followed, Nhlapo and others responded. Nhlapo defended himself by insisting that he was attacking "girls of low morals [who] when powdered and painted look lovely . . . [and] ply . . . the unwholesome clandestine business which is not worth mentioning"—of course, he meant the business of prostitution.[37] A female relative of Sikiti, in turn, shielded her honor by explaining that Albertina was a nurse in training with "sincerity of purpose."[38] Sikiti's strong reaction to Nhlapo's letter and his rebuttal demonstrate how criticism of the modern girl could be intended as a veiled attack on prostitutes and read as an assault on school-educated young women. The modern girl was such a ubiquitous subject of social commentary because she could gloss a wide range of women who sought greater social and financial independence. This independence—whether embodied in the beer brewer with "back-door" husbands or the young woman with advanced schooling who delayed marriage—often challenged the authority of men and senior kin.

The modern girl was also ubiquitous because she provided *Bantu World* writers with a way to criticize aspects of black intimacy without attributing them to African "tradition." In a society structured by white racism and in a newspaper promoting a moderate African nationalism, writers interpreted the black modern girl's behavior in racial terms. Some criticized her obsession with love as a misguided aping of European ways. Locating the origins of such behavior in colonial corruption, they denied the reality that young women of previous generations also had multiple or fleeting love affairs.[39] Other writers emphasized how the black modern girl's love antics sullied their race's reputation in white eyes. Mary Zulu wrote that decent girls needed to combat Europeans' impression that "Native girls only think of dances, fancy clothes and love."[40] A European woman who occasionally wrote a column for *Bantu World* under the byline "M. P." confirmed this impression by urging African girls who spend "far too much time and thought . . . [on] love and sweethearts" to instead focus on work. Ignoring the immense racial barriers confronting black women, "M. P." suggested that black women follow "European girls" who had made great progress in recent years as typists, teachers, doctors, and business owners. In direct contrast to other *Bantu World* contributors who framed the obsession with love as a modern innovation, "M. P." traced it back to the "uncivilized races of long ago" who "in times of peace and plenty" had little else to think about besides love and sex.[41] Such rhetoric of racial superiority polarized the discussion, leaving little space for participants to consider how contemporary practices entailed the historical entanglement of old and new forms of intimacy.

Schapera also deployed the modern girl to navigate regional and international politics of race, love, and sex. In a 1933 article in the academic journal *Africa,* he noted the emergence of "what might almost be termed a class of flappers." Schapera located the rise of these flapper-like young women amid social transformations engendered by Christian schooling, labor migrancy, and the colonial cash economy. According to Schapera, what most clearly defined Tswana modern girls were their new dress, their active role in romance, and their unrestrained passion. He wrote:

> The modern Kxatla [Kgatla] girl, with her short European skirts and irresponsible behaviour, often herself takes the initiative in love-making. There has developed amongst them what might almost be termed a class of flappers. As one of the boys said to me: "we no longer want the girls chosen by our parents; we want girls like *bosejêwa ke pelo,* ('those eaten by the heart'), or *bomatsunya* ('those who are very pretty'), or *boengwe dipedi* ('those who trip along one-two,' referring to their walk as the shoe hits the ground), or *bo-'lexe e le teng xa ke utlwe sepê* (those who say, 'although it is there I don't feel anything,' i.e., they are so accustomed to sexual intercourse that their passion is not easily satisfied)." The old people look upon all this with dismay, and one of the old men remarked sadly to me, *batho ba ba bokôôa, ba kôafaditse ke basetsana xe e sale maxwane,* "these people are weak, they have been weakened by the girls while they were still *maxwane* [uninitiated]." (Schapera 1933b, 87)

By tentatively evoking flappers to describe these Tswana young women, Schapera sought to make their behavior familiar to the largely European and U.S. readers of *Africa* and to situate sexuality in black southern African communities amid the same social changes taking place elsewhere in the world. His hesitancy in using the term likely stemmed from a concern that some readers might criticize him for interpreting Tswana society through exogenous categories. But by providing a number of Setswana phrases used to describe the modern girl together with their literal translations, Schapera illustrated the endogenous resonance of the category. The old man's statement that uninitiated men had been "weakened" by girls posited female sexuality as a powerful and potentially debilitating force and insisted that its unleashing was a present-day innovation.[42] Like the *Bantu World* writers, Schapera deployed the flapper and modern girl to situate African sexuality and intimacy within international trends and to lessen the possibility that his writings could contribute to exoticizing interpretations of African life.

Nowhere in *Married Life* did Schapera use these terms. Perhaps by 1940, he felt that *flapper* and *modern girl*—whose usage in Britain and the United States had largely dissipated with the Great Depression of 1929—would appear dated to readers. He did, however, choose to commence *Married Life* with a modern girl story. The book begins with an excerpt from an English-language letter that Schapera had received from Sofania Poonyane, a research assistant who was then working as a messenger in Johannesburg.

> "I wish to tell you I have dropped my love with Miss R—K—of Mafeking. I did so because I discovered she was too considered [*sic*]. She thought too much of herself, and she was very expensive to marry, hark, where ever we went we should buy sweets or chocolates at 4/6 lb. What do you think of that? And we should always travel by taxi instead of by tram or bus at 5*d.* or 3*d.*, but taxi at 2/-, oh, no, I had to cut it off." (Schapera 1940, 15)

Schapera commented that the letter revealed the strength of European influences among Africans: The girlfriend's "extravagant tastes . . . are of a kind that could as easily dismay a young European citizen of Johannesburg as the Bantu tribesmen" (1940, 15-16). When discussing the state of Tswana marriages, Schapera's sympathies fell with women. In this case of courtship, however, he asked his readers to empathize with young men. By quoting Poonyane's letter, Schapera presented a humorous dilemma that black and white men in segregationist South Africa shared: the dilemma of how to handle modern girls.

More so than the other South African anthropologists, Schapera sought to demonstrate that African intimate relations were like those among whites and in the West. At the same time, Schapera offered the most explicit discussions of sex. These were two sides of the same coin. Through deploying the flapper and modern girl, Schapera sought to ensure that his detailed accounts of courtship and marriage supported rather than sabotaged his view that southern Africa was becoming a single society.

Conclusion

Analysis of anthropological studies and *Bantu World* writings from the 1930s reveals how international circuits of media and knowledge combined with contentious politics of race and difference to shape public discussions of intimacy in segregationist South Africa. Through *Bantu World*'s women's pages, Dhlomo sought to offer African women something enjoyed by other women in South Africa and elsewhere in the world: a place in print to read about and discuss love. *Bantu World* discussions of true love were a piece of the paper's broader efforts to counter white racism by demonstrating that school-educated and Christian blacks were respectable and important to South Africa's future. White anthropologists' interest in African intimacy, in turn, emerged from their participation in evolving international social scientific networks, particularly Malinowski's seminars at the LSE that encouraged research on sex and culture contact. South African racial politics shaped how Schapera, Hunter, Hellmann, and Krige engaged these disciplinary concerns and how their research was received. By deploying the concept of culture contact to demonstrate that southern Africa was becoming a single society, they challenged the logic of racial segregation. Yet in a context where intimacy was a deeply racialized and politicized issue, even liberal allies had difficulty tolerating their detailed studies of sex.

This chapter speaks to the contemporary concerns raised elsewhere in this volume by revealing the long history of debates over love in Africa. South African anthropologists documented that by the early 1930s, labor migrancy, urbanization, and mission Christianity had substantially transformed intimate relations. Most *Bantu World* writers espoused an ideal of true love that combined Victorian and southern African values to emphasize a voluntary, spiritual, and singular connection between husband and wife that entailed female self-sacrifice and unequal, if complementary, gender relations. In subsequent decades, discussions of intimacy in African popular newspapers and magazines shifted away from such explicit Christian moralizing. As Kenda Mutongi's and Rachel Spronk's chapters in this volume demonstrate, candid discussion of sex eventually became a sign of African media being modern and up-to-date. Yet like these more recent discussions, *Bantu World* debates focused attention on issues of companionship and fidelity. Read together with the anthropological studies, *Bantu World*'s editorials, articles, and letters suggest that the greatest challenge to true love was not the absence of love matches or young people's choice of partners. Both of these, by the 1930s at least, were widely accepted ideals among mission-educated Christians. Rather, true love's most stubborn sticking point was its insistence that heterosexual companionship should be found in a single relationship and that that relationship should last a lifetime (see Smith, this volume).[43]

Bantu World debates about love also raised issues of gender inequality. Writers often contested the gender politics of true love through the figure of the modern girl. Whereas female writers like Kelobile and Sikiti defended school-educated young women's prerogatives in love, male writers cast the modern girl as promiscuous and materialistic. Rather than interpreting some young women's forthright behavior as a rejection of the gender inequities embedded in true love, male writers cast their behavior as a betrayal of African tradition. In so doing, they interpreted contemporary gender politics through the lens of a middle-class African nationalism. To mission-educated black male leaders and intellectuals, the modern girl behavior of daughters, sisters, and cousins looked dangerously like that of the disreputable female figures—prostitutes and beer brewers—who they had long associated with urban landscapes. Yet the likes of Vilakazi and Nhlapo rarely named these lower-class figures. Instead, they traced the modern girl's indecent antics to foreign influences, ranging from films to the latest fashions from elsewhere. By adopting a nationalist perspective that blamed exogenous inspirations, they obscured how heterosexual relations in 1930s South Africa were the historical entanglement of (Thomas 2003) older and newer, regional and international ideals of love and sex.

Schapera's deployment of the modern girl partially resonated with that of *Bantu World*'s male writers. He used this figure along with translated letters to make his accounts of Tswana intimacy more familiar to his largely white readership. Moreover, he situated the African modern girl as the product of Christianity and colonialism. But by predicting that the continued "emancipation of women" would ultimately strengthen African marriages, Schapera's perspective was more in line with Kelobile's and Sikiti's than Vilakazi's and Nhlapo's. Like those women, he hoped that modern conditions would improve women's circumstances in courtship and marriage.

The three perspectives that dominated these interwar discussions of black South African intimacy—anthropology, Christianity, and African nationalism—are ones that have held considerable sway within African studies. This convergence helps explains why love has been a relatively neglected topic. The epistemological foundations of anthropology have encouraged the study of sex, not affect. While mission Christianity and schooling fostered discussion of true love, it did so in a moralizing and universalizing way that has made it difficult to consider how the entanglement of various ideals and conceptions have shaped love in colonial and postcolonial Africa. Similarly, African nationalism, influenced by mission Christianity and with a political commitment to combating colonialism and racism, has been ill equipped to consider gendered intimacy, particularly when it raises the specter of impropriety or difference. Perhaps these ideological overlaps make it a little less surprising that Absolom Vilakazi grew from being a precocious critic of the modern girl as a mission school student to become a professor of anthropology and president of the African Studies Association.

ACKNOWLEDGMENTS

An earlier version of this article was presented as a lecture at the Anthropology and Population Studies & Training Center, Brown University, in February 2006. I thank Dan Smith for hosting that event, the audience who attended, and colleagues who read other versions including Jordanna Bailkin, Jennifer Cole, Mark Hunter, Julie Livingston, Isak Niehaus, Uta G. Poiger, Priti Ramamurthy, and Sarah Abreveya Stein for providing insightful commentary. My conception of the modern girl has developed through my participation in the Modern Girl Around the World research group. For our joint publications, see the bibliography. The ACLS/ Charles A. Ryskamp Fellowship Program, National Endowment for the Humanities, and Graduate School and History Department at the University of Washington generously provided funding for research and writing. For collecting some of the sources for this paper, I thank the undergraduate and graduate research assistants with whom I have worked at the University of Washington.

NOTES

1. Abs. P. B. Vilakazi, "'To Be a Flapper' Is It Fashionable?," *Bantu World* [hereafter, *BW*], August 6, 1938, 12.
2. Within this paper, I use the term *black* as an umbrella term to refer to South Africans who thought of themselves or were viewed by others as nonwhite, coloured, African, Malay, or Indian.
3. Hellmann's 1948 book was the publication of an unrevised master's thesis completed in 1934.
4. The anthropological coursework and studies that developed at South Africa's English-language universities during the 1920s and 1930s differed substantially from that at the Afrikaans-language universities. Under the leadership of Werner Willi Max Eiselen of the University of Stellenbosch, the latter tradition drew more inspiration from German than British scholarship and emphasized "racial hygiene" (Hammond-Tooke 1997).
5. During this period, one black South African, Z. K. Matthews, also participated in Malinowski's seminar. I do not include Matthews in this analysis because his sole publication on marriage (Matthews 1940) focused on "traditional . . . customs" rather than social change.
6. Kuper (2007, 34) insightfully suggests that *Married Life* likely never became as popular as Malinowski's and Mead's studies of sex and marriage because of "the lack of exoticism" and because "the Tswana did not seem to be having more fun than anyone else." Schapera's gloomy representation of Tswana marriage is discussed later in this chapter.

7. London School of Economics Library, Archives and Rare Books [hereafter, LSE], SCHAPERA/2/2: E. S. Field to I. Schapera, July 25, 1940, and July 27, 1940.

8. LSE, SCHAPERA/2/2: E. S. Field to I. Schapera, July 25, 1940, July 27, 1940, September 19, 1940, September 24, 1940, and October 19, 1940.

9. LSE, SCHAPERA/2/2: E. S. Field to I. Schapera, September 19, 1940.

10. The Editress, "Men and Women," *BW,* March 7, 1936, 9.

11. "Bantu Girls Now Marry Later in Most Instances," *BW,* August 27, 1932, 2.

12. Quotation from "Night Scholar," "'Too Much' Love," *BW,* April 18, 1936, 12.

13. "Lost Sheep," "'Articles on Love Not Wanted,'" *BW,* May 16, 1936, 12.

14. The Editress, "Articles on Love," *BW,* August 1, 1936, 9.

15. Mildred Ntaba, "What Is Love?," *BW,* April 6, 1935, 11.

16. Maud J. Gacula, "What Love Is," *BW,* April 13, 1935, 11; Vivan Dube, "Love: What It Is," *BW,* April 13, 1935, 11; Jo. Nqoloba, "Love: What It Is," *BW,* April 27, 1935, 11; Selina Rampa, "The Love That Passeth All Understanding," *BW,* January 29, 1938, 12.

17. Mrs. A. E. P. Fisch, "What Is Love?," *BW,* May 4, 1935, 11; Israel B. C. Mbono, "What Love Is," *BW,* May 18, 1935, 12; Lady Porcupine, "This Is Love," *BW,* May 18, 1935, 12; Stranger, "What Is Love?," *BW,* May 18, 1935, 12.

18. Gacula, "What Love Is."

19. Nqoloba, "Love: What It Is."

20. W. S. Moeng, "A Vitalising Force," *BW,* June 8, 1935, 12.

21. Dube, "Love: What It Is."

22. Walter M. B. Nhlapo, "Love—You Funny Thing!," *BW,* May 11, 1935, 11.

23. "R. Roamer Talks About. . . . . . What Is Love?," *BW,* June 22, 1935, 5.

24. Lady Porcupine, "You Can't Live Without Love," *BW,* March 14, 1936, 12. Phahlane wrote under the pseudonym Lady Porcupine (Ballantine 1993).

25. Miss D. B. Mngadi, "'False and True Love,'" *BW,* March 28, 1936, 12.

26. Tina J. Kelobile, "Loveless Marriages," *BW,* December 8, 1934, 10. On the preference in some southern African communities for cross-cousin marriages, see Schapera 1940.

27. Dube, "Love: What It Is."

28. Nqoloba, "Love: What It Is."

29. Abs. P. B. Vilakazi, "Are Modern Women Too Forward?," *BW,* May 9, 1936, 12.

30. A. M. Xaba, "Should Girls Propose Love?," *BW,* June 6, 1936, 11.

31. Quotations from Enoch Follie, "Women Who Err," *BW,* March 14, 1936, 12; M. M. Mapumulo, "Girls Are Deceivers," April 25, 1936, 12; and A. D. Petersen, "How to Get 'Mr. Right,'" *BW,* December 3, 1938, 12.

32. Paroshe Mntande, "Stop This Love Making in the Streets Says Mntande," *BW,* November 10, 1934, 12; Editress's note to Abs. P. B. Vilakazi, "Are Modern Women Too Forward?," *BW,* May 9, 1936, 12; Windy, "Why Girls Change Lovers Like Their Dresses," *BW,* May 2, 1936, 12; "'Enemies of Women,'" *BW,* May 23, 1936, 12; Selina Rampa, "Men Not Women Play with Love: A Retort," *BW,* April 9, 1938, 11.

33. "Julia Tells Joshua That Her Love for Him Is Now Finished," *BW,* March 3, 1934, 10.

34. "Dora and Nora View Life Again: Bantu Girls Should Try to Make Men Trust Them," *BW,* January 21, 1933, 10.
35. Walter M. B. Nhlapo, "All Is Not Gold that Glitters," *BW,* July 4, 1936, 12.
36. Albertina Nt. I Sikiti, "All Is Not Gold that Glitters," *BW,* August 8, 1936, 12.
37. Walter Nhlapo, "Reply to Miss Albertina Sikiti," *BW,* August 29, 1936, 12.
38. Algernon H. Sikiti, "Miss Sikiti Supported," *BW,* September 26, 1936, 36.
39. Maxwell J. Khwela, "Growing Generation and Love," *BW,* December 7, 1935, 12; Follie, "Women Who Err."
40. Mary Zulu, "Decent Girls Should Also Be Mentioned and Helped Along," *BW,* January 28, 1933, 12.
41. M. P., "A Well-Balanced Mind," *BW,* April 4, 1936, 11.
42. Livingston (2005) has analyzed complaints about increased sexual immorality among women as a reoccurring trope in Tswana accounts of the past.
43. On the continued difficulties of meeting this ideal, see van der Vliet 1991 and in this volume, Smith and Spronk.

2

Making Love in the Indian Ocean

HINDI FILMS, ZANZIBARI AUDIENCES, AND THE CONSTRUCTION OF ROMANCE IN THE 1950S AND 1960S

Laura Fair

In 2002, while conducting research on the history of cinemas and movie-going, I asked Zanzibaris to identify what they considered to be the best films of all time. To my surprise, some two-thirds of those who attended films in the 1950s and 1960s—regardless of class, ethnicity, education, or gender—named the same film, *Awara,* as their favorite. Released in 1951, *Awara* hit the isles in 1954, where it played repeatedly to sold-out shows for more than a year. According to Zanzibaris, when people heard that it was returning after showing up-country, or elsewhere in East Africa, tickets would sell out before the film physically reached the isles.[1] *Awara* was so appealing that most people saw it more than once, with many people claiming to have watched it three, five, or more than ten times. *Awara* was one of those rare films that could be counted on to pack the house years after its initial release; a film that boatmen and traders would watch again and again as they traveled from Zanzibar to Pemba, Tanga and Mombasa, and other ports along the Swahili coast; a film whose themes and music inspired poets and musicians across the littoral; a film that tugged at the heartstrings and spoke directly to the romantic longings of a generation of East African youth.

What was it about *Awara* that so attracted East African fans? Why did Zanzibaris find this film, and other Bollywood productions like it, so appealing? How did the women and men living along the Swahili coast use films like *Awara* to initiate debates within themselves, and among their families and friends, about the meaning of love and romantic partnerships? What was the role of cinemas, as physical spaces, in the transformation of romantic practices over time? And lastly, how did the youth of the 1950s and 1960s use the discursive spaces opened up by the combined presence of Hindi melodramas and widespread discussions of nationalism and independence during this era to initiate fundamental transformations in dating and marriage practices over generations? These are the questions that drive this chapter.

Drawing on the insights of scholars of literary and performance cultures in Africa (Barber 2000; Newell 2000) this chapter emphasizes the didactic role of film, and popular culture more generally, within coastal East African society. Using art to talk about matters of the heart has a long history amongst coastal East Africans. From sexually suggestive dances done in the context of puberty initiation rituals, to lengthy poems composed as reminders of gendered duties and obligations within marriage, as well as popular *taarab* orchestral performances filled with nuanced use of double entendre and forlorn lamentations on the pains of a broken heart, coastal East Africans have a widespread appreciation for the power of art to express, rehearse, and instruct (Strobel 1979; Knappert 1983; Biersteker 1991; Fuglesang 1994; Fair 1996; Askew 2002). Film may have been a relatively new medium, but the didactic uses to which people put it were not. Again and again I was told by the people whom I interviewed that one reason, among many, for going to the movies was to learn. And one of the things they sought to learn about was how to make love within the context of the multigenerational patriarchal families in which most of them lived.

As other chapters in this volume also reveal, Africans have long engaged narratives from across the globe to define and construct their own notions of "true love." Many historians have linked fiction and print culture to the rise of romantic love in numerous times and places (B. Bailey 1989; Giddens 1992; Watt 1992; Shumway 1998; Breckenridge 2000; Lee 2001; Goodman 2006). In Zanzibar, and other places where literacy was the preserve of an elite few, visual and aural media, such as film and music, played a similar role. Of the total Zanzibari population of 265,000, in 1948, only 15,000 had attended schools where they might have become literate in Kiswahili written in Roman script, and fewer than 3,000 of these were women. As late as 1953, there were only 93 women enrolled in the Government Secondary School for Girls, where women were given instruction in English and literature, among other subjects.[2] Poetry, taarab music, and Hindi films, however, spoke eloquently about romance and longings for romantic love through idioms Zanzibaris could understand.

As Fuglesang argues in her pioneering study of the rise of video culture in Kenya during the 1980s, watching Hindi melodramas gave young women an opportunity to vicariously explore a range of emotions and "a 'language' for dealing with issues such as romance, sexuality and marriage" (1994, 157). Like the readers of romantic fiction in Ghana, examined by Stephanie Newell, film fans in Zanzibar stressed the educative potential of Hindi films, which "opened their eyes" to new ways of thinking about life's possibilities as well as new strategies for coping with life's heartbreaks and constraints (Newell 2000). Romantic longings had long been present in island society, yet up until the 1980s or 1990s, nearly all first marriages in coastal societies were arranged. Some couples in such marriages grew to appreciate each other deeply over time. Yet the Swahili have historically had one of the highest divorce rates in the world. Second and subsequent marriages, however, were often rooted in romances initiated by the couple themselves. The midcentury rise of the romantic couple as a key cinematic trope spoke to these romantic desires, and men, women, and couples who went to the show found their own yearnings validated. Many fictional romantic couples also embodied the nationalist rhetoric of class and communal harmony voiced in the years leading to the end of colonialism.

Setting the Proverbial Scene

«AWARA»

Many elements in *Awara* attracted audiences and kept them coming back for more. The film starred two of the most widely acclaimed actors in film history: Raj Kapoor and Nargis. Although this was not the first film in which they costarred, it was certainly the one that placed their romance center stage and lifted them to the status of the iconic romantic couple (Vasudevan 2000b). On screen and off, their romance was larger than life. Their open and very public affair filled the newspapers and film magazines, and despite the fact that Kapoor was married with children, and he a Hindu and she a Muslim, their romance was rarely portrayed as a transgression. Screen life and real life merged in the public eye. Drawing on their characters as Raj and Rita in the film, their love was commonly portrayed as "pure, blind, an all-consuming passion, and even divine" (R. Thomas 1989, 23). The combination of their superb skill on screen and their public lives and love made them household names not only in Zanzibar, but across the globe.

Unknown by most North Americans, *Awara* is perhaps "the most successful film in the history of cinema at large," having been seen in more countries, and by more people, more times, than any other film in history (Iordanova 2006, 114). *Awara* was dubbed into Turkish, Persian, Arabic, English, and Russian, where the popularity of Kapoor's character apparently inspired a generation of Soviets to name their sons Raj (Willemen and Rajadhyaksha 1999, 321–22; R. Thomas 1989, 23; Dissanayake and Sahai 1987, 42; Barnouw and Krishnaswamy 1963, 160; Thompson and Bordwell 2003, 409). Although no film was ever dubbed into Kiswahili, the main language spoken in Zanzibar, many people with whom I spoke claimed to have watched so many Hindi films that they could understand the dialogue completely. What is certain is that the characters of Raj and Rita spoke to deep human yearnings that transcended political, geographic, and linguistic divides. In the West, romantic fiction is largely considered a feminized genre (Giddens 1992; Radway 1991 [1984]), but in Indian films and island life, men too were encouraged to express their emotions and to yearn for the deepest of loves. As Haji Gora, a well-known Zanzibari poet, taarab composer, author, and avid Hindi filmgoer explained, "The love between Raj and Rita was of a totally fictional kind, but the kind that everyone, everywhere longs to have."[3]

Like all good Hindi films, *Awara* involves multiple, twisting-turning plotlines that take nearly three hours to develop and unfold. Love across class lines and marriage in defiance of family and community are two of the central themes explored. Raghunath, the emblem of patriarchy and power in the film, defies convention and the wishes of his family to marry a widow named Leela. During the early years of their devoted marriage, the indulgent couple escapes from the watchful eye of the extended family for a romantic weekend together on a remote island, where Leela is abducted by a villain. When Leela turns out to be pregnant, rumors begin to swirl that perhaps she was raped by the villain, casting Raghunath's paternity and masculinity, and the family's honor, in doubt. Raghunath's love is weakened by continuous pressure from his family and questions about the legitimacy of Leela's child, but when his associates from the upper echelons of society threaten his advancement from lawyer to judge, Raghunath finally caves to social pressure and throws Leela into the gutters, where she gives birth to their son Raj.

Told from the perspective of Raj, *Awara* (Vagabond) explores the issues of social legitimacy and class privilege from the vantage point of the poor. Modeled in part on characters played by Charlie Chaplin, Kapoor's character, Raj, addresses class head on. Leela struggles valiantly for years, trying to feed her son, send him to school, and raise him to be an upright man who can rise above the slums in which he was born. Effort, education, and moral strength, she tells her son, are the keys to success. Ultimately, however, ill health and poverty conspire against her, and Raj loses his place at school because she cannot keep up with the school fees. Quickly they descend down that slippery slope from the dignified poor to the criminal. Trying to save his mother, who is on the verge of death from malnutrition, Raj steals some bread and ends up in a reformatory. Schooled in the arts of petty crime, Raj graduates to become an important player in an underworld gang. One of the major themes developed throughout the film is the relative power of birth, social circumstance, and personal will to define one's fate. Individuals certainly have choices to make, but why, asks the film, are the poor sent to prison for stealing so they can eat, while the law studiously protects the thefts of capitalists and politicians who gorge themselves at the expense of others?

Yet a third major plotline in *Awara* revolves around the developing romance between poor, illegitimate, but totally lovable Raj and his wealthy and spoilt childhood sweetheart Rita, with whom he is reunited after twelve years when he tries to snatch her purse and steal her car. Despite the divergent paths their lives have taken since they were in school together as youth, the flame of love is rekindled between the two central characters in a heartbeat. Because of his desire for Rita, Raj attempts to renounce his life of crime and "go straight," but even the best efforts of this passionate couple cannot overcome the objections of Rita's guardian (who, as only an Indian film could have it, is also the father who abandoned Raj at birth). Raghunath reemerges as the patriarch protecting a woman's honor, and he refuses to hear of Rita's infatuation with a man well below her in class, status, and education. Despite his objections, Raj and Rita engage in a long and languid romance, and publicly pronounce their eternal love. Their love is socially affirmed after Rita, who has also been studying law, defends Raj in court against charges brought by her guardian, and in the process reveals that Raj is really the son of prominence, to whom fate has dealt a nasty hand.

This bare-bones sketch of the major plotlines—devoid of the emotive potential of stars, scenes, and songs—suggests that this film left audiences with a lot to discuss and debate. While Raj and Rita were the characters that audience members most identified with, people had a lot to say about the patriarch Raghunath as well. Some of those with whom I spoke in Zanzibar pointed to Raghunath's failures, and the costs born by his wife and son, as evidence that marrying for love against the wishes of family and community would result only in tragedy for all concerned. Love was, in the end, a very shaky foundation on which to build a family. Others, however, used Raghunath to illustrate that wealth and social power did not necessarily confer moral strength, and to say that any marriage could end in tragedy if the

FIGURE 2.1 Rita and Raj, the heroine and hero of *Awara*. Recounting the love between Rita and Raj, the Bollywood film *Awara* packed cinema houses along the Swahili coast throughout the 1950s. *Awara* was popular, in part, because its characters struggled with the tension between romantic love and family honor, a tension that resonated with Zanzibari audiences. The film also boasted a superb soundtrack. *Photo source:* Awara.

partners abandoned their commitments and obligations. Raghunath failed to stand by the woman he claimed to love. Still others used the plot of *Awara* to suggest that fundamental social change, such as moving from arranged marriage to love marriage, takes time. While Raghunath failed to stand up to his family and community, his children refused to relent to patriarchal pressure, and in the end their romance and love steals the show. Like academics, Zanzibaris examined texts for evidence, but drew on that evidence to support their own points of view. Films like *Awara* were widely popular because they provided men and women in the audience with characters with whom they could identify and relate, as well as others they could hate. Ultimately, what these films provided were ample opportunities for public sociability and endless fodder for moral debate.

CINEMA IN ZANZIBAR

Zanzibar, like the larger Swahili coast of which it is a part, is a polyglot place, home to a culturally rich and ethnically diverse population. From early in the first millennium, the Africans who lived along the East African coast welcomed traders and business partners from Arabia to India into their midst, and served as the brokers linking goods and markets from East and Central Africa with others across the oceans. While Swahili culture is African at its core, Swahilis have spent centuries selectively appropriating elements of the religious, artistic, and culinary cultures of others throughout the Indian Ocean. Beginning in the nineteenth century, Zanzibar and the Swahili coast witnessed the growing settlement of men, and eventually women too, from Arabia and South Asia who chose to make East Africa their permanent home. Attracted by the increasingly lucrative opportunities for trade with Africa, these newly arrived immigrants helped Zanzibar eclipse other Swahili port towns and emerge as the premier entrepôt and cultural center in the region.

Less than a decade after the Lumiere Brothers held their first public exhibition of moving pictures in Paris in 1895, this revolutionary new technology was on display in East Africa. By 1904, if not before, exhibitions of "moving pictures" became a feature of urban nightlife in Zanzibar town.[4] By 1926, an average of some 2,700 people were patronizing Zanzibar's cinemas each week, a surprisingly large number for a town with a population of well under 50,000.[5] The popularity of the cinema as a form of entertainment and leisure continued to grow over the decades, and throughout most of the period from the 1920s through the 1980s, the tiny town of Zanzibar continued to support three separate theaters, each of which had an official seating capacity of between 300 and 850.[6] Indian films regularly packed cinemas drawing capacity crowds of more than 3,500 people to the theaters in Zanzibar, two to three Sundays per month, from the 1950s thought the mid-1980s.[7] The same film would typically continue to play on Monday as well, in at least one of the town's theaters, and yet again at a special "ladies only/zanana show" on Tuesday or Wednesday. If a film was good, more than 5,000 people in Zanzibar might have seen it by the end of its first-week run.

In public and private spaces, wherever people came together, they discussed, critiqued, debated, imagined, and interacted with the issues that were presented on screen. Even people who did not go to the show themselves were drawn into the public lives the films assumed. To paraphrase one Zanzibari woman:

> Personally I wasn't a big fan, in fact I really didn't like films at all. But my sister and her friends were huge fans. They went to the cinema every Sunday, every single Sunday, and all week long they would talk about the

film. Whether I wanted to, or not, I knew all about the latest film. One of them might identify with this character, another with that, and they would argue back and forth about different scenes and the lessons they conveyed. I vividly recall how they argued and argued about characters and conclusions and how these debates would go on and on, at least until the next Sunday, when there would be a new film to discuss.

This group was not alone. Nearly everyone I interviewed said that discussions and debates about the latest film became a cornerstone of urban conversations. At home, at work, and among classmates at school, everyone talked about films, characters, and stars. "Heck," said one man, "even on busses and ferries people talked about films. You could always get a conversation going, even between complete strangers, if you turned the topic to latest films."[8]

BOLLYWOOD VERSUS HOLLYWOOD

Hollywood films were also commonly screened in East Africa, and in fact during the 1950s more than half of all films shown in Zanzibar were U.S. productions. These films also often centered on romance and love, yet Zanzibari audiences were not drawn to them to nearly the same degree. In U.S. films, as in U.S. children's literature, parents are often entirely absent, leaving youthful characters to sort out their dilemmas on their own. During the mid-twentieth century, however, many Africans viewed "modern" independent youth as dangerous characters (Thomas, this volume).

Bollywood films from the 1950s and 1960s echoed these concerns. Characters, male as well as female, who openly disregarded cultural norms or mimicked the West brought trouble to themselves and their families. Yet Indian films also placed generational struggles over changing ideals of love and marriage center screen (Vasudevan 1995; R. Thomas 1989). Patriarchal authority was called deeply into question in the films of the 1950s, and the desires of youth to marry for love was foregrounded. But at the same time, the affective family also served as the symbolic locus of resolution in Hindi films from this era. Youth were not obliged to rebel entirely or disassociate themselves from their families. In Indian movies, youth disobeyed, but within limits, and due to their pressure, patriarchs like Raghunath became kinder and gentler over time. In his study of Hausaland, in northern Nigeria, Brian Larkin found that there too Indian films were preferred because they raised issues and framed questions in ways that were more culturally resonant with the moral framework of the Muslim Hausa (Larkin 1997).

Bollywood, argues Larkin, provided a "parallel modernity" to the West, a cinematic script that addressed a complicated range of issues facing modern youth, but that did not necessitate "selling out" in order to be resolved. Indian films addressed global generational tensions, yet resolved them in ways that affirmed local moral codes. Bollywood was preferred over Hollywood, in part, because Hausas and Swahilis were attracted to fictional narratives that promised that individual happiness could be achieved without sacrificing family honor or the family as a multigenerational whole.

Bollywood films also developed themes and issues in ways that were far more relevant to East African life than those dreamed up by Hollywood. Social melodrama was the dominant mode of filmmaking in post-independence India, and many of the artists involved in the Bombay film industry were also leftists, including K. A. Abbas, who wrote the screenplay for *Awara* (Virdi 2003). Class and the social divisions separating the wealthy from the poor were given center screen in Bollywood, whereas self-censorship and the production code made class conflict resolved in favor of the poor a taboo subject in Hollywood films (Sklar 1975). Although poverty was never glamorized in films made by Kapoor or others of his generation, spectators were encouraged to empathize with the plight of the poor and to respect the honesty and integrity of underclass heroes and heroines (Vasudevan 1995; Nandy 1998; Mishra 2002; Virdi 2003). Such narratives found a receptive audience in colonial East Africa. As one woman said of her appreciation for the stories in films from this era, "Many stories were about the life of the poor, the trouble the poor had making ends meet. The films showed the real life conditions of the poor and how difficult it was. The stories were also about the wealthy and how they exploited the poor, how the poor were despised and looked down upon. That is what the stories were like in the old days. Many of the stories were like this, showing how the rich exploited the poor, or how the poor struggled and struggled, but never succeeded."[9] Characters commonly found in Indian films were also of the type that Zanzibari audiences could relate to. Villainous landlords, overbearing patriarchs, meddlesome in-laws, and corrupt police and politicians figured as prominently in Indian films from this era as they did in daily life in the isles.

Moral choices were as easy to see in Indian movies as the black and white film on which they were depicted, and this too resonated with patterns known from African folktales. While the evil and mean were always obvious, the dilemmas of the hero or heroine negotiating the path to success in the face of continuous temptations and obstacles revealed the murky road traveled by most of humanity. Indian films from the 1950s and 1960s directly addressed the "Third World" modernist dilemma: how to incorporate technological and scientific "advancement" into society without succumbing to a hollow mimicry of Western individualism, consumer capitalism, moral bankruptcy, and spiritual emptiness (Vasudevan 1995, 2000).

Moral and modernist dilemmas were often resolved through a reassertion of "traditional" values, where the hero or heroine is ultimately drawn back into the virtuous arms of the mother/family/nation (R. Thomas 1989; Vasudevan 2000). Morally upright, "traditional" characters were often juxtaposed with those who dressed, talked, and drank like those from Hollywood. These latter characters often manipulated state power or wealth to advance their own selfish ends, sending the message that those who carelessly mimicked the West might be wealthy, but they were morally bankrupt. In Hausaland and Zanzibar, people were deeply attracted to films that displayed modernity while simultaneously critiquing the West (Larkin 1997). Many people in Zanzibar stressed that one of the reasons they went to the movies was "to learn something,"[10] "to expand [their] mind to other possibilities,"[11] or "to compare [their lives] with those of people in other places."[12] The lessons people took were not necessarily that "the West is the best." As Mwalim Idd explained, "In those films you get to see [that the West] is more advanced in terms of technology, education or economy . . . but in terms of social life, social relations, and social values, we are ahead."[13]

The lessons on love that people took from Hindi films were also far more resonant with local social life. In most Indian films, the love of the young couple is complicated by love and commitment to one's extended family, and these complications mirrored realities in the isles. In partial explanation of her attraction to *Awara,* one woman who saw it at least four times remarked,

> The actors in this film were superb, truly superb! They could make you feel the pain that they felt right down to your core. You empathized with their struggles and hardships, and experienced their pain from their perspective. This problem of women being abandoned by their husbands, for whatever reason, was a common problem here in Zanzibar as well. I could identify with the struggles of Raj's mother because I had seen friends and even sisters struggle to raise their children without any help from the children's fathers. She portrayed that pain and those problems in a way that really hit home.[14]

Adam Shafi echoed her remarks when he said,

> *Awara,* I loved that film. I saw it more than ten times. Raj Kapoor and Nargis were outstanding! And the film shows real life, the inside of life,

and the ways in which family, traditions and culture can cause problems. The plot shows how a man [Raghunath] can abandon his wife [Leela], even though he loves her very much, because of family pressure.[15]

Couples did not always live happily ever after, and island audiences appreciated films that explored, rather than ignored, marital realities.

Marriage, Sex, and Romance: Between the Reel and Real Life

Casual visitors to Zanzibar are often struck by the visual presence of women covered in the black *buibui,* or *hijab,* and presume that this is an indication of sexual repression and gender oppression within the isles. Such facile conclusions belie a much more complicated reality (Fair 2001). In Zanzibar, and Swahili culture more generally, modesty in dress and appearance is upheld as a virtue, for men and women alike, but this does not mean that sexuality is considered a sin. On the contrary, sensuality is regarded as an art form, and young women have historically been given ritualized instruction on how to enhance their own and their partner's erotic pleasures. In the course of female initiation rituals, sometimes conducted privately or other times for small groups, older women teach young women through songs, dances, and play about the mysteries and wonders of sex, marriage, and procreation (Velten 1903; Farsy 1965; Strobel 1979; Le Guennec-Coppens 1980; Campbell 1983; Knappert 1983; Sheikh-Hashim 1989; Fuglesang 1994). Through ribald movements and lyrics performed in the context of *Chakacha, Msondo, Unyago,* and many other types of women's dance, young women are given the opportunity to recognize and validate their sexual desires. Here too young women are encouraged to "dance out" anticipated events, and in the process relieve some of the anxiety and fear associated with sex and marriage (Fuglesang 1994, 238). In ritual preparation for their weddings, an older woman physically prepares and beautifies the bride, massaging her entire body with sandlewood, perfuming her with aloewood, adorning her with henna, silk, and gold.[16] They also again perform the songs and dances the bride was taught during the course of initiation, trying to loosen her up, ally her fears, and encourage her to enjoy the consummation of her wedding night. These lessons and skills are refined throughout a woman's life. After a young woman is married, she is then recognized as an adult and is able to participate regularly in the full range of rituals that accompany other women's weddings. In the course of her own marriage, she will also continue to beautify herself with sandalwood, perfume her clothes and bedroom with aloewood (*udi*), and entice herself and her husband by wearing strings of

FIGURE 2.2 Bride ritually prepared by her *somo,* 1990s. In Zanzibar, older women referred to as *somo*s physically prepare and beautify the bride in preparation for her wedding, massaging her entire body with sandlewood, perfuming her every-where with aloewood, and adorning her with henna, silk, and gold. *Photo courtesy of Laura Fair.*

jasmine flowers (considered to be an aphrodisiac) in provocative places or sprinkling jasmine flowers on their bed.

The importance, or lack, of love within a relationship was also widely discussed and debated through the medium of poetry and song. Poets have a long and revered history amongst the Swahili. Great poets have used very complicated forms of rhyme and meter to praise the lord, condemn their political rivals, issue edicts on moral reform, instruct youth, give thanks, and address a host of other topics both worldly and divine (Jahadhmy 1977;

Abdulaziz 1979; Noor Sharif 1991; Knappert 1979; Biersteker 1991, 1996). The intense emotions associated with love, yearning, and heartbreak have also been expressed through classical poetic Swahili forms, but it was really only in the mid-twentieth century that romantic love and longing, rather than love of God or family, became common topics in classic metered verse. Nowhere near as bawdy or direct as the poems composed for performance within the homosocial environment of women's weddings and initiation rituals, these love poems—often shared in the public forum of taarab musical performance—focus on emotion and intense spiritual devotion to the object of one's desire (Askew 2002; Ntarangwi 2003). Romance, as expressed through taarab songs, explored the "deep mental and spiritual inclination toward a pleasurable love experience" (King'ei 1992, 131). In the 1950s, male taarab poets and performers in Zanzibar increasingly began to move away from religious, social, and political commentary, and to lay increasing emphasis on romantic love and longing in their work.

Again, local aesthetic cultures found resonance in Indian films, where music and song play important roles in enhancing emotion and conjuring deep sentiment (Skillman 1986; Pendakur 2003). Ethnomusicologists studying Swahili taarab, as well as Arab and Indian musics with which taarab shares certain affinities, have found that one of the key aesthetic criteria used to define "good" music is its emotionality, as well as its ability to evoke rapture, bliss, ecstasy, and the divine (Askew 2002; Larkin 2005; Eisenberg 2008). In Indian films, music and song are central mediums through which deep emotions, and particularly romantic longings, are expressed. If a couple says "I love you," they do it in a song. Songs are the "heart and soul" of Indian films (Pendakur 2003, 119). In the 1950s, taarab poets and musicians along the Swahili coast began to make the relationship between film music and their own poetic and musical traditions more explicit, by increasingly borrowing melodies from Hindi films onto which they grafted Kiswahili poems (Eisenberg 2008). Like all good Hindi films, *Awara* boasted a superb sound track that added to the emotional appeal of the characters and the film overall. Gramophone recordings of songs from the film were said to be among the best-selling Hindi releases of the 1950s (Willemen and Rajadhyaksha 1999 [1994], 300; Chatterjee 1992, 127–40; Iordanova 2006, 124). Larkin (2005) found similar, yet more complicated, intertextual references in Hausa *bandiri* music, where Sufi followers also borrow from the deep emotionality expressed in Hindi film tunes as they compose religious poetry in praise of the prophet Mohammed on top of Bollywood tunes. The emotionality of Hindi film music, often denigrated by viewers and critics in the West, was thus one of the principal appeals among affirming audiences in Africa.

The songbooks of Zanzibari bands from the 1950s and 1960s are filled with poems that idealize the loved one and liken her to the most beautiful flower, the brightest of stars, or the sweetest of fruits in the isles.[17] Poets and performers for the two most prominent male clubs, Michenzani and Ikhwan Safaa, also spoke openly of their frustrations in consummating their romantic desires. Swahilis may have considered sex to be far from sinful, but to be condoned, sex should be confined to the bedroom of a properly married couple. As young men bursting with desire, these poets and performers expressed their frustrations with local cultural patterns that kept genders largely segregated in public space and that gave elders, rather than youth, the power to arrange first marriages. By the 1950s women in Zanzibar were increasingly attending schools, and by the 1960s, a few were even finding waged employment outside of the home, where they met, and sometimes mingled, with members of the opposite sex. Brief public encounters sometimes led to "love at first sight," but men's songs from the period tell us that women might as well have been the stars and the moon, so far were they out of reach.

Cinemas and the Consummation of Love

In the 1950s and 1960s, cinemas were one of the few public places where men and women along the Swahili coast could gather and enjoy an evening of respectable leisure together. At a point in time when nearly all first marriages were still arranged by elders, newly married couples used the opportunities afforded by cinemas to dress up, go out, talk, and "date."[18] Going to the movies provided time and space for young couples, who often did not know each other at all before marriage, with an opportunity to be together and alone. Until fairly recently, it was rare for a young couple to have a home that was separate from the rest of a joint or extended family. In such cases, couples rarely had time or space, outside of their bedroom, to talk or be alone. As one African woman said of the dates she and her husband had at the cinema, "Going to the cinema helped us to get to know each other better. It gave us things to talk about, things to share, and most importantly it gave us time alone."[19] In his ethnographic study of filmgoing in India in the 1980s, Steve Derné (2000) also found many young men and women living in joint households who spoke of the cinema as giving them both the time and a place to be together and away from the rest of the family.

Many other men and women fondly recalled the time they went to the show as time that helped them develop a relationship as "a couple." Nostalgia for these earlier days, when their lives were focused on new love, allowed many to transcend the troubles of their current lives, such as two friends who were transported briefly by my questions from a hospital and the final stages of a lengthy fight with cancer, back to their early married days and their loving dates at the show. Issa, a Swahili cabdriver in Dar es Salaam, also recalled the important place of cinemas as physical and imaginary spaces in his early married life. "When we were first married my wife and I use to regularly go to the cinema. It was the only time we really got to be alone.... She preferred Indian films, those long, long love-story types. I liked action films better, but to make her happy I would take her to see these love-stories, and she too would accompany me to see action films." He fondly reminisced about how important going to see these films were to their young married life, giving them "something special to do alone."[20] Often they would make a day of it, casually making their way to the theater beginning in late afternoon, watching the film until nine o'clock at night, and then talking about the film the whole way home. "One of the things about these Indian movies," he said, "was that when you see them they force you to talk about love, about what real love means and how to love each other. This wasn't something we usually talked about after an action film."

In the context of the Sunday shows, when thousands of people would be milling in the streets or crowding the lobbies before and after shows, young people also had the opportunity to see members of the opposite sex in public and perhaps "fall in love at first sight." They may not have been able to speak, but at a time when cultural mores kept youth strictly segregated by sex, even being in the same room together provided an important thrill. On Sundays, as crowds gathered outside of the cinema halls waiting for the doors to open, small groups and individuals would mill about, greeting friends, neighbors and acquaintances, and quietly "checking out" members of the opposite sex. In the company of their families, young people who met at the show rarely engaged each other in direct conversation. "We might smile and look," said Nitesh Virji, "but rarely had the nerve to talk."[21] Nitesh said that if he or his male friends spied someone they wanted to meet, they would encourage a cousin or sibling to go and address a friend in the other group, allowing their eyes to follow and thus "meet" those of a new potential lover. Looks and glances were often far more communicative during these years than speech, and again, Hindi films provided visual models of evocative communication via eyes. Bolder groups of boys and girls would also go to talk to friends in other large groups of extended families, all the while slyly eyeing the potential mates in their friends' group. Intermissions, a deliberate twenty to thirty minute break in the film, also provided opportunities for milling and meeting while buying sodas and treats. One man, who did a lot of big-game hunting as an adult, likened these adventures from his youth to a photo safari, "You get an image rather than an actual trophy, but you get the excitement and adventure none-the-less." "Sometimes," he added, "a good picture is better than an actual mount anyway."[22] Like a spouse whom you see every day, he explained, the dead animal mounted on the wall is taken for granted, whereas "the one that got away" remains fresh and alive, evoking the thrill of further pursuit.

Another woman who used to go to the cinema regularly with her sisters and cousins confessed that she regularly met her boyfriend at the cinema. When asked how they arranged to sit together when they had these clandestine meetings, she said, "Sit next to each other? Heavens no! We were much too shy for this. Besides, if you ever did something like that you could be certain some auntie or cousin would see you and word would reach home before you did, and would you ever be in trouble then! It would be a long, long time before you were allowed to go to the cinema again."[23] You did not have to sit next to each other or touch to experience love, she explained. True love, like that in the Hindi melodramas, was an emotive, not a physical, love. Never in a Hindi film did you see a couple kissing, but the characters' love was of the most passionate kind. Another woman who partook in similar rendezvous explained:

> You would sit here, and your lover would sit in front of you 6–8 rows, on the side. We would glance at each other, and make love with our eyes before the show started and during intermission. It was all so romantic! Simply seeing each other gave you such a thrill! And the entire time you and your lover were watching the movie you were experiencing together the love you saw on screen. I still get goose-bumps remembering my first love from those days.

Comparing the love depicted in films of those years with that of today, another woman said, "These were serious stories, and the love, it was a deep, deep love. The actors and actresses knew how to love each other, really love each other. Love is still a theme in the movies today, but their love is superficial, it is about wiggling the body, not that deep love of the heart like in the old days."[24] Several men also contrasted the superficial love presented in today's Bollywood films, with the "true love" of the past, which they characterized as emotional, elusive, and divine.[25]

One self-proclaimed romantic described her marriage, to a man chosen by her parents, as simply a marriage—he provided her with safety at a time when young women of her community were being forcibly married to members of the Revolutionary Counsel in Zanzibar, and together they had children (Fair 2002; Glassman 2000). But the love of her life, her "true love-affair" was with a young man she had clandestine meetings with at the cinema. They too never sat next to each other and never even touched. Yet as she remembered this young man, she said:

> My heart still races when I recall our affair. We were so in love. It was like this movie playing now, *Veer Zara,* about a young couple who cannot marry because of the partition [of India and Pakistan]. He spends twenty years in solitary confinement, but he never forgets her, nor she him. Their love was true. It was divine. Politics separated us as well, but who knows, maybe someday we can be together again too.

Numerous men and women echoed her remarks, suggesting that in a society in which divorce held no stigma and subsequent marriages were common, Hindi films kept the dream of romantic love alive throughout their adult lives.

As texts, Hindi films may have inspired dreams of "true love," but as places, cinemas also allowed some the opportunity to advance a romance to the physical plane. Cinema seating was assigned, and occasionally a young couple would be so bold as to purchase their tickets ahead of time, thus assuring adjacent seats, even if each came in on his or her own. One trick was for a young man to make an advanced booking for himself, his girlfriend, and her friends. They could arrive separately, but when she approached the window to get the tickets for her group, the ticket agent, well aware of the plan, could let her know which seat she needed to take in order to sit next to her man. Sitting next to each other in the dark during a film was as intimate as most youngsters would ever get with a member of the opposite sex prior to marriage. For daring young couples, a large part of the thrill of such a romance was the adventure of sneaking out together in public and risking being, but certainly hoping never to be, caught.

Older, previously married lovers took more advantage of the time offered by the cinema than its space to advance their romance to a new level. Hindi movies are usually at least three hours in length, leaving ample opportunity for a romantic tryst. Lovers might feign they were going to the show and simply go someplace more intimate instead. Such romantic trysts were eulogized in a famous taarab song from the era known as "Ladies' Show" by the Mombasa stars Yaseen and Mimi.[26] Going to the Ladies' Show was a common and widely popular pastime for so-called respectable women observing purdah who did not attend the regular shows where men and women mixed. The song, or at least the stories surrounding it, suggests that purdah and propriety were not necessarily synonymous. One man told me that "Ladies' Show" became a common euphemism amongst members of his mother's generation for having an adulterous affair.

Another ruse, I was told by cinema employees, was for a man and a woman to each take their separate seats, and then at an agreed-on point in the film, such as the second song and dance number, leave the show. The cover of a *buibui* was a useful disguise for women attempting such feats. If a woman's brother or father was expected to come and escort her back home, the couple would return to the theater in time to see the end of the film, and she could emerge with the rest of the crowd as though she had been in the theater all along. Such plans had the potential to go awry, however, as in the case of one infamous married man in Malindi, who regularly used the cover of three-hour Indian movies to meet his lover. One day after such a tryst, he returned to catch the end of the film and found his wife sitting in his seat. Before the entire crowd in the theater, he was outed by his wife. In that particular case, it was his story rather than that of the film that circulated throughout town the remainder of the week. Twenty years later his tale continued to generate exuberant laughs.[27]

Just as important as the physical place of cinemas for inaugurating new loves, the imaginary space opened up by films also inspired men and women, and particularly youth, to fantasize about romance, love, and marriage in somewhat novel ways. As Larkin (1997) and chapters by Thomas, Mutongi, Masquelier, and Spronk in this volume argue, the transnational flow of mass media allows people to interact with narratives and imaginaries beyond their own lived reality. Loves like that of Rita and Raj depicted in *Awara* provided intellectual fuel for the smoldering fires of romantic love sparking up along the coast during this period. Youth of the 1950s were not the first generation to chaff under the yoke of arranged marriages, but they were among the first to be nourished on a regular diet of Hindi romantic melodramas. As both individuals and a generation, they drew on the characters and plots from these films to rewrite the narratives for their own emotive lives. Few real-life heroes or heroines had the hutzpah of Rita and Raj. Forging a relationship across the chasms of class and communal divides, committing to each other despite patriarchal opposition, defending each other in the face of immense social pressure, this was something that few mere mortals could manage. But as Radway and others have argued, fantasizing about what it would *feel like* to accomplish such feats is one of the main draws of romantic fiction (Radway 1991 [1984]). "Alternatives, hopes, wishes . . . the sense that things could be better, that something other than what is can be imagined and maybe realized," how it would feel to achieve such dreams, this is what films offer, argues Dyer, a vicarious sense of fulfillment, the momentary bliss of living in utopia (Dyer 1992, 22).

Numerous self-defined "romantics" said that the power of Hindi melodrama to ignite deep-felt emotion and to keep dreams of romantic passion alive was one of the factors that drew them to the show, and to films like *Awara*, again and again. As one woman said of the love between Raj and Rita, "they died inside of each other's hearts, and if you got a male friend, well you wanted it to be the same . . . without you he couldn't see, he couldn't hear, until you died you were together, inseparable in fact. This is what we saw in the films and this is how we wanted our loves to be."[28] This woman may have dreamed of a love equal to that of Rita and Raj, but instead she was married at the age of fourteen to a man at least three times her age. Like many young women in Zanzibar of her generation—be they Asian, Arab, or African—she had little to say when it came to making the arrangements for her first marriage.

Many of the women and men with whom I spoke lamented their early married life, but stated rather matter-of-factly that in those days (before the 1980s or 1990s) it was elders who chose your spouse, not you. You may have dreamed of romance and passion, but guardians typically chose a husband based on perceptions of his ability to provide for you financially, and older men were in this regard perceived as a safer bet. If he came from a wealthy and respected family, all the better, and missing teeth, warts, gray hair, and fat bellies were to be overlooked in favor of the improved status he would bring to you, your children, and, by extension, your entire family. Another woman spoke quite dramatically of her marital life history in this way: "I was married at the age of fifteen to a man who [was] not to my liking at all. He was arrogant, unattractive and patronizing, and treated me like I was nothing other than a slave."[29] But throughout their early adolescent lives both of these women had been avid Hindi film fans, and their dreams of romance and passion remained alive throughout their married lives. After some time, and the birth of a child, each made arrangements for a divorce. The first woman remarried a manager of cinema, a man who shared her passion for life and romantic love. The second woman remarried as well "to the man of her dreams," although she had to admit that the dreams quickly faded. "Now that I'm older," she explained, "I know that the passion you feel when you first meet, that deep, deep desire fueled by emotion, you know, like what you see in the films, is something that leaves after a spell. But I cannot help it, I am a romantic, and I live for that feeling."

Conclusion: Love and Revolution in the 1950s

The back cover of Adam Shafi's Kiswahili novel, *Vuta n'Kuvute*, describes the central themes driving the protagonists as "love and revolution." The novel, set in the 1950s, opens with a moving description of Yasmin, the desolate heroine, who has been married off by her parents, at the tender age of fifteen, to Raza, a fifty-two-year-old small-time shopkeeper in Zanzibar. Yasmin detests Raza. Not only is he old enough to be her grandfather, his teeth are stained and his breath reeks from the pipe he constantly has in his mouth. He is often so busy in his shop that he regularly goes four or five days without shaving, and many a night he falls down in bed next to her without even bothering to bathe. Yasmin, we are told on page two, "would rather die than give her body to this man" (Shafi 1999, 2). Going out to the cinema provides one of the few opportunities they share for mutual enjoyment. Yet even here, Yasmin's pleasure is somewhat tempered by the fact that she has to sit next to Raza in public.

Confined by purdah to the inside of their small home, Yasmin's days are filled with longing and loneliness. The only joy she experiences during the early period of their marriage is when she winds up Raza's gramophone and dances in the kitchen, pretending to be a Hindi film star. One day, while joyfully lost in her fantasy, dancing around the kitchen and making eyes at her imaginary lover, she is brought back to earth at the end of her performance by clapping and cries of "*Shabash!*" (Wonderful! Wonderful!) from the window across the narrow lane from her own. Thus, while dancing out her romantic fantasies to the tune from a Hindi film, Yasmin meets her future lover, the young and attractive Swahili man, Denge, who has studied in the Soviet Union and is now organizing for the overthrow of the British in Zanzibar.

Romantic love and political revolution are the central themes explored in *Vuta N'kuvute*. When I first read the novel, it resonated quite intensely with the oral histories I had gathered in Zanzibar. While doing research for my first book, *Pastimes and Politics*, I was made aware, in no uncertain terms, that the nationalist organizing of the 1950s and the "revolution" of 1964 were events that framed the lives of nearly everyone who lived in the isles. Arranged marriage, communal integrity, as well as cross-class and interracial sex were also issues that came up in this context, particularly as they had to do with the forced marriages that were part of state policy during the "revolutionary" years. These themes also emerged with surprising frequency during interviews on the history of cinema. When I asked about the place of cinemas in urban social life or about what were some of the best movies of all time and why, I was told by many elders of their own revolutionary struggles to marry for love, rather than marrying the partner their parents had arranged for them to marry. Shafi's novel seemed to capture these twin struggles that people had talked so much about. Yet when I asked Shafi, who was himself a young man involved in the revolutionary struggles of the era, if it was his intent to portray the struggle to choose one's own partner and the struggle for national independence as two sides of the same coin, he said:

> No. The novel is about nationalism and the struggles of young men, like Denge, to overthrow the British. I use Yasmin to locate the novel in Zanzibar, and describe her life because I wanted to describe how life was in Zanzibar at this time. Young people were taught to respect the elders, and girls their husbands, and never to question. In the 1950s there were many cases of old men like Raza marrying young girls like Yasmin. The beginning of the novel is intended to describe how her life was like, how circumscribed it was, and as the novel unfolds she too opens up and is exposed to many things she never knew existed before. I just wanted to describe how life was, not necessarily to link it with a duel colonialism.[30]

I include this exchange to illustrate that in the course of reading or watching, the reader or viewer always invests the narrative with their own meanings. As a feminist, it could not be more obvious to me that this novel linked personal freedom and national independence. Clearly this was not Shafi's intent. The point is that people take the narratives they have available and rework them to give them meanings in the context of their own lives. As Sabrina, a young Zanzibari said, "Films are filled with lessons—it's like reading a novel. There is a story and different issues inside, but it is up to you to interpret them, to think about them and decide what the meaning of the story is for you. . . . Each person comes with their own interests and takes from it what is meaningful to them."[31]

In coastal East Africa, the growth of romance, the rise of nationalism, and the avid consumption of Hindi films went hand in hand. The 1950s were a watershed decade for both lovers and nationalists on the African continent. It was during this decade that the struggles of peasants and wage laborers, women and men, ex-soldiers and students, frustrated entrepreneurs and heady intellectuals, coalesced and gave rise to the nationalist movements that swept the continent toward independence. While no nationalist I know of ever proclaimed the end of patriarchal control of youth and marriage to be among their goals, the growth of nationalist movements fueled the development of romantic love in several important ways. Most important, both nationalism and romantic love are based on fantasies, often very elaborate fantasies, of what one wants but does not have. Similarly, they both project into the future and infuse their subjects with hope that their dreams of fulfillment will come to pass. The 1950s were a decade in which nearly everyone on the continent was inspired to dream of liberation. *Freedom, independence,* and *self-determination* were words voiced in a thousand different languages, as people across the continent struggled to define the meaning of these imprecise terms and imagine what they meant when applied to individual, communal, and national lives. The wide-ranging debates about politics and economics helped to make this period—like that of the French Revolution—an era of "emotional liberty" as well (Reddy 2001). While nationalists from the Cape to Cairo and Cameroon took to the stage to rally support for national independence and freedom from colonialism, youth applied these vocabularies to more immediate personal concerns.

With the passing of time, newlyweds and nationalists everywhere have been forced to come to grips with the reality that mundane management of daily affairs is far more complicated and conflictual than they ever dreamed. But in the 1950s, the elderly men and women with whom I spoke were still quite young, and their dreams were still alive. Many of them directly commented on their own nostalgia for the past, for a point in their personal and national lives when everything seemed possible, and when the future was guaranteed to be more fulfilling, and their lives less filled with compromise than that of their parents. Such is the folly of youth, I was told. But many also commented on the importance of the larger changes taking place all around them for inspiring them to dream of different emotive and romantic lives. If nationalists could talk of overthrowing political economies based on colonialism, then why not talk of overturning patriarchal control of marriage as well? If politicians found willing ears for proposals to end racial segregation and ethnic privilege, then why couldn't parents hear of daughters like Yasmin falling in love with men like Denge? Scholars studying fiction and nationalism have found a similar pattern in other parts of the globe, where narratives of love conquering all have blossomed during periods of nationalist awakening (Sommer 1991; Vasudevan 1995). From Argentina and Ecuador to India and Zanzibar, the romantic couple emerged as an emblem for imaginary nations struggling to overcome deep historic divisions of class, race, language, region, and religion.

The 1950s did not mark the first time in African history that youth and elders had fought over marriage. Generational conflict over these issues had long been endemic. But in Zanzibar, the 1950s marked a turning point

FIGURE 2.3 Romantic couple, 1990s. Historically in Zanzibar most couples' first marriages were to partners of their parents' choosing, though typically second marriages would be for love. By the 1980s and 1990s, however, love marriages—such as the one enjoyed by this couple on their wedding day—were increasingly common. *Photo by Laura Fair.*

in public, as opposed to merely private, debate. Cinema certainly was not the only factor that contributed to the growing prevalence of these public deliberations, but it was an important one. By providing a regular infusion of narrative material to fuel imaginations, films inspired debate. The fact that there was such widespread consumption of films also meant that the dilemmas presented on screen became real life as men and women, elders and youth, everywhere argued among themselves over plots and the relative morality and immorality of characters and scenes. In bedrooms, on the streets, and in shops, tearooms, and buses, thousands of people talked and debated these texts each week.

For the most part people were unable to make their real lives as dreamy or steamy as those depicted in film, but the films opened up possibilities of fulfillment and gave them something to dream about, dreams many carried well into their old age. I know several sweet, quite elderly couples where the husbands still get a thrill out of bringing a special treat home for their wives, the love of their lives. The women too, though now in their sixties and seventies, still perfume their rooms with aromatic incense and sprinkle jasmine flowers on the bed. Most of these elderly couples dated regularly at the show during their early married lives, and for them the romance lives on. Others lamented that although they dared to love across class or communal lines, they never managed to consummate their romance like Rita and Raj. Instead, they married the partners of their parents' choosing and, in many cases, learned to accept conjugal love as a useful anecdote for a broken romantic heart. Still others said that while they were not inspired to choose their own loves, the narratives from Hindi melodramas nonetheless did become the soundtracks for collective discussions during their generation about the rights of young people to choose their own partners. Most of those married in the 1950s and 1960s were not able to follow their hearts in choosing their first mates, but when their children came of age in subsequent decades they were far more willing to empathize and compromise than their own elders had been at midcentury.

ACKNOWLEDGMENTS

For my son, Nassir, who died while I was writing the first draft of this paper. With fond memories of group hugs in the Indian Ocean and eternal gratitude for your love. *Mungu akulaze pema.* And special thanks to Lynn Thomas and Jennifer Cole for forcing me to push through the most difficult thing I have ever tried to write.

NOTES

1. *Awara* continued to play in Zanzibar and Tanganyika for more than a decade. Tanzania National Archives, hereafter TNA: Iringa Broadcasting and Films, cinematograph and Censorship Board, TNA 435 B/2/2; Mwanza Cinema Censorship Board, TNA 246/c.5/10. Haji Gora Haji, interview, December 24, 2004; Haji Faki Mohammed, interview, June 3, 2002, interview; Adam Shafi, May 18, 2005 (all interviews are by the author).
2. E. Batson, *Social Survey of Zanzibar Protectorate* (Cape Town: School of Social Sciences and Social Administration at the University of Cape Town, 1960), 10; "Women in Zanzibar," *African Women* 1 (1955): 49–51.
3. Haji Gora Haji, interview.
4. *Zanzibar Official Gazette,* December 7, 1904.
5. Zanzibar National Archives (ZNA), AB 5/111: Films, Their Educational Uses and Censorship.
6. Abdulhussein Marashi, Zanzibar (cinema proprietor), interview, May 7, 2002; Ferus Hussein (cinema proprietor), interview, June 25, 2002; Asad Talati (cinema proprietor), interviews, August 15 and 16, 2004.
7. Abdulhusein Marashi, interviews, May 7 and May 15, 2002; Ferus Hussein, interview; Ameri Slyoum, interview, May 16, 2002; Asad Talati, interviews. Ticket Books from Majestic Cinema, Zanzibar, 1972–1992.
8. Juma Sultan, interview, 2005.

9. Anonymous, interview, June 26, 2002.

10. Ameri Slyoum, interview.

11. Nasra Mohammed, interview, May 21, 2002.

12. Idd Farhan, interview, May 25, 2002.

13. Farhan, interview.

14. Bi Maryam, interview, February 16, 2004.

15. Adam Shafi, interview.

16. Some of my knowledge of this tradition comes from the ceremony prior to my own wedding, which is pictured in Figure 2.2.

17. Song books of Ikhwan Safaa/Malindi, 1959–63, courtesy of Mwalim Idd Farhan.

18. Bibi Amour Aziz, interview, June 20, 2002; Maryam Yahya, interview, June 3, 2002; BiSaumu, interview, June 16, 2002; Khamis Kombo, interview, June 15, 2002; BiMkubwa Said, interview, June 21, 2002; Mwalim Idd Farhan, interview, May 25, 2002; Adam Shafi, interview.

19. Bi Maryam, interview.

20. Issa, interview, February 2004.

21. Nitesh Virji, interview, April 25, 2005.

22. Patel, interview, April 24, 2005.

23. Fatma Alloo, interview, May 14, 2002.

24. Anonymous, interview, June 26, 2002.

25. Mwalim Idd Farhan, interview; Haji Faki Mohammed, interview, June 23, 2002; Haji Gora Haji, interview; Adam Shafi, interview.

26. I am extremely grateful to Andrew Eisenberg for his generous willingness to share with me copies of this recording, as well as Yaseen's *Sina Nyumba,* based on the title song from *Awara.* See Eisenberg 2008 for a discussion of the larger place of Hindi film music in Swahili taarab.

27. A friend, Ali Skandor, told this story in June 2005. Some twenty or more years after it had happened, people in Malindi still laugh heartily recalling this poor man's folly and the repercussions he endured.

28. Anonymous, interview, June 26, 2002.

29. Anonymous, interview, March 24, 2005.

30. Adam Shafi, interview.

31. Sabrina, interview, May 5, 2004.

3

"Dear Dolly's" Advice

REPRESENTATIONS OF YOUTH, COURTSHIP, AND SEXUALITIES IN AFRICA, 1960–1980

Kenda Mutongi

My girlfriend won't let me touch her breasts and refuses to have sex with me. The moment I make for her breasts, she grows cold and pushes me aside. I am 16 and she is 17. I feel she is not being fair to me.

> *Cindy, Ibadan, Nigeria*

It is a pity that at 16 you are beginning to have dirty thoughts and desires. Your girlfriend is a good girl. Don't corrupt her. You can have fun and be perfectly happy with her without touching her breasts or taking her to bed.[1]

Such was a typical exchange in "Dear Dolly," an advice column that dealt mainly with questions about sex and courtship from young men and women in English-speaking Africa. *Drum,* one of the most popular magazines in Anglophone Africa in the 1960s and 1970s, was home to this column. Financed by Jim Bailey, a white South African, *Drum* was first published in Cape Town in March 1951. Although white-owned, most of its writers were black, and Bailey hoped that these writers would help the magazine capture the "real" feelings and experiences of blacks in South African townships (J. Bailey 1982, 24). *Drum* was famous for its catchall editorial policy: It typically printed entertainment, sports, letters to the editor, and political news concerning Africans and African Americans. It had advice columns on

Anglophone?

this was going on in Europe too!

illness by a so-called Dr. Drum and a pen pal section, as well as advertisements promoting correspondence colleges, radios, skin-lightening lotions, weight-gaining tablets, and medicines for pimples, malaria, and stomachaches. It was also famous for its vivacious and titillating cover girls. In addition, the magazine prominently featured pictures of ordinary Africans, an innovation that marked a great departure from colonial publications that rarely included Africans on their pages. This generous mix of the popular and the political became so well liked that, in the early 1960s, Bailey extended the magazine's readership outside South Africa, publishing separate and local monthly editions in Ghana, Nigeria, and Kenya. As in South Africa, *Drum* immediately became popular among Africans in western and eastern-central Africa, particularly because it vividly documented the independence movements that were occurring in these areas. Clearly, *Drum* had a little something to offer to young and older men and women, both in the cities and rural areas: As many as 300,000 copies sold every month in English-speaking Africa (Morris 1989, 52). In many ways, *Drum* not only helped revolutionize the nature of journalism in Africa, but it also popularized the social life of Africans—especially that of the new urbanites.

Like any new magazine that tries to meet the changing needs of its readers, *Drum* experimented with different subject matter and columns, and various layouts, designs, and bindings. Several columns, a book review section, a "women's corner," a comic section, and so on appeared abruptly, lasted for a short period of time, and then disappeared if they did not attract enough response. However, "Dear Dolly," the column that answered the courtship and sexuality questions of young men and women, was published every month until *Drum* closed its offices in East and West Africa in the mid-1980s.[2]

What was it that made "Dear Dolly" such a popular column in the 1960s and 1970s? Its discussions of sex and courtship certainly contributed to its popularity.[3] This article focuses on the East, Central, and West African editions of *Drum* and examines these editions' representations of homosexual and heterosexual sex and courtship.[4] The language employed in the "Dear Dolly" column of these editions suggests that the editors intended the column to entertain as well as to instruct, and these intentions shaped the way in which the courtship discourse was represented. Much of the entertainment tended to come from the letters by lustful young men eager to have sex with reluctant or bashful young women. These letters, and to some extent the editors' replies, were often written in jocular and titillating language that was occasionally facetious or ironic. That the letters and replies were sometimes less than straightforward is borne out when the reading habits of men are taken into consideration. Oral evidence suggests that men read

FIGURE 3.1 *Drum* (East African edition), "Dear Dolly" column, January 1965. "Dolly" advised young people about love and sex in *Drum,* a South African-based publication that grew to be one of the most popular magazines in Anglophone Africa during the 1960s and 1970s. In this column, Dolly offers frank and moralizing advice about lesbian love, unfaithful partners, polygyny, and marital prohibitions. *Photo source:* Drum, *East African edition, January 1965.*

the column loudly to their male friends, commenting on and imaginatively rewriting the events in the letters in order to reveal their opinions on sexuality and courtship matters. Thus the men generally conceived the reading of, and writing to, the column as a social and fun event.

Hilarity was not always the editors' intention. Their desire to instruct was apparent in their responses to letters from men in homosexual relationships and young women in both heterosexual and homosexual unions. These men and women were given seriously didactic and moralistic replies. While the women in heterosexual relationships wrote to the column inquiring about how they might go about requesting their boyfriends not to pressure them into premarital sex—largely because they were in school and were afraid of getting pregnant—the men and women in homosexual unions were mainly concerned with the legality of their relations or with finding ways to end them. Hence, the editors catalogued the vices of out-of-wedlock pregnancies and of homosexuality and extolled the virtues of abstinence for women in heterosexual relations and the value of heterosexuality for those in same-sex relations. While I lack evidence to describe the reading habits of men and women in homosexual relationships,[5] oral evidence suggests that most young women in heterosexual relations often read the column surreptitiously, extracting romantic vocabulary they needed to write letters to their boyfriends. Since societal norms postulated that women generally practice restraint in matters of sexuality, letter writing became a safer form of correspondence for the women because it allowed them to communicate furtively with their lovers; these women dared not employ too racy a vocabulary in spoken language, but letters allowed them to express themselves yet keep a safe distance. In any case, gender and sexuality were crucial in determining the courtship discourse in the column.

Who wrote the letters printed in the column? Who replied to them? Who was Dolly? How might we read these letters? Each of the three *Drum* offices in Accra, Lagos, and Nairobi received at least twenty letters every month, out of which the staff selected about ten to fifteen letters to print (with Kenya, Uganda, Nigeria, and Ghana having significantly more letters than the other English-speaking countries of Tanzania, Zambia, and Sierra Leone). The criterion used to select the letters was not clearly evident, but according to the publishers, most letters printed were chosen from several that concerned common dilemmas—interethnic marriages, unreciprocated love, premarital sex, homosexuality, and so on.[6] Initially, the magazine editors had difficulties finding the appropriate editor for the column. As Anthony Sampson, one of the early editors of the South African *Drum* indicated, "Dolly was a worried syndicate of men. . . . Being Dolly was a job that everyone tried to escape. We [Sampson and the mostly African male staff writers] ended by discussing the trickier problems around the office" (Sampson 1957, 122). Sampson noted how he "tried all kinds of people for the job—a missionary, but he was too severe; Henry [one of the African news editors], but he was too frivolous; myself, but I was too patronizing" (1957, 122). He eventually settled on the mostly male staff of *Drum*, who sat down together and edited the letters and then concocted replies that were prepared months in advance, often in the Lagos office, and then distributed to Accra and Nairobi for inclusion in the upcoming months.[7] Only one version of "Dear Dolly" was printed in all the three editions for Accra, Lagos, and Nairobi.

The answers provided by the editors, together with the visual and written advertisements that accompanied the column, indicate that the editors were trying to feminize the column. The passport photograph of Dolly Rathebe—a renowned South African music and film star—that graced the top of the column implied that the editors wanted the readers to view the column in sensational and intriguing terms.[8] On the other hand, written advertisements portrayed Dolly as an older female relative, as an aunt or a sister. But since the editors' intentions were notoriously idiosyncratic (both in the ways they edited letters and in their replies) and seemed geared more toward selling *Drum* than seriously addressing the problems posed by youth, it would be misleading for us to read the letters in the column as "true" experiences of courtship and sexuality among the youth. Instead, the letters are perhaps better read simply as representations of the changing sexual mores in 1960s and 1970s Anglophone Africa.[9]

While Africanists have begun to pay close attention to youth culture,[10] the topic of courtship has generally received little more than lip service from African historians—even though marriage, a likely product of courtship, has been the topic of several monographs.[11] The assumption behind most of these studies has been that many marriages were arranged by the families of the brides and grooms. Representations of courtship in "Dear Dolly" suggest a different picture, however (see also Thomas, this volume). They reveal that as literacy increased in the mid-twentieth century, and as the print media facilitated courtship discussions, courtship became less a family affair and more a preoccupation of youth.[12] These changes gave young men and women the opportunity to adapt the courtship language found in advice columns like "Dear Dolly" to express their sexual desires.

Even though research on heterosexual courtship is scarce, heterosexuality is at least a more commonly discussed topic in historical literature than same-sex courtship. The cultural taboos against homosexuality and the sensitive nature of these relations (and especially their illegality in many *arcane ?*

African countries) have made it hard for historians to find data to work with.[13] The few available studies have often associated homosexuality in Africa with arcane initiation rituals or have tended to overrationalize the reasons people enter homosexual relations (Evans-Pritchard 1971; Junod 1912; Moodie, Ndatshe, and Sibuyi 1988; Shepard 1987). In other words, scholars have often treated homosexuality as either an adolescent phase or the male migrant laborer's temporary means of coping with the unavailability of women, and hence of no serious consequence to the "proper" functioning of society. These interpretations are lacking in some important ways. As Mary Porter has recently argued, such conclusions overlook "people's erotic desires for others of the same sex," as these sentiments are "completely obscured by attention to rational and material choices" (Porter 1995, 134). In the column, however, there were several letters that not only testified to homoerotic desires, but also denounced same-sex relationships as abnormal and illegal.

Representations of Dolly through Advertisements

Recent studies of advertisements have argued that in order to broaden our understanding of mass consumption, we need to pay attention to the ways in which both the producers and consumers gender commodities (Burke 1996; de Grazia and Furlough 1996). Many of these studies have assumed each gender category to be monolithic and have examined only a single form of femininity or masculinity. In the case of the "Dear Dolly" column, however, the *Drum* editors tried to lure youth to the column by presenting the character of Dolly as exhibiting multiple femininities. Her character was both consolingly authoritative and intriguingly sexual. Since the editors intended to persuade the youth of the advice-giving value of the column, they created a Dolly who was an aunt-like figure, imbued with wisdom and authority, yet also friendly and full of kindness. At the same time, in order to keep the column titillating and sensational, the editors exploited the sexual and seductive attributes of Dolly Rathebe's photograph, as well as her stardom. Evidently, the editors believed that a combination of the sexual and the authoritative, the amiable and the caring, would help entice young men and women to read and write to the column.

Throughout the 1960s and 1970s, a passport photograph of a smiling and elegant Dolly Rathebe was placed at the top of the "Dear Dolly" column. She appeared beautiful, youthful, and sexy, and the editors aggressively promoted this image.[14] Throughout, they printed letters that young men had (supposedly) written proposing marriage to the Dolly in the photograph. For instance, in January 1963, Joe from Lagos, Nigeria, wrote:

> My love for you Dolly is so great that I can't sleep well without having first taken a glance at your photograph in *Drum* every night. I do not know how to get in touch with you. Where can we meet and what can I do to win you over? I am still a student but my father is very rich.

The editors replied:

> Poor boy! Why don't you forget about me and concentrate on your studies. You are still a young boy and there is still some way to go. The fact that your father is rich does not necessarily mean that the world will bow at your feet. Anyway, thank you for your compliment.[15]

In yet another equally bold proposal, Willie, an eighteen-year-old boy from Accra, wrote to the column, saying:

> Help me, Dolly, I'm really in love with you since I started buying *Drum* just recently when I got my job. And when I first saw you, I forgot myself. You are the only woman I rely on, and without you one can faint a long time. Dear Dolly what can I do to see you face to face?

Willie received the following answer:

> Down boy! Don't try to flirt with me, you silly boy with [all] the girls around you. I am sure there is someone else you could rely on to hold your hand.[16]

In a letter entitled "Darling Dolly," Joe from Tanga, Tanzania, wrote:

> When I last spoke to a girl about love she laughed at me and ran away. So, Dolly, although I am not worthy of you, I would be happy to call you my girlfriend. I respect and love you very much and will try to make your life as happy as it should be. What do you say?

Joe was answered:

> Down, boy! I am perfectly happy, thank you. You do not say how old you are, but from your letter I suspect I have too many years for you. My advice is to choose your prospective girlfriends more carefully. I know there are lots of girls who would like a boy as sensitive as you.[17]

This is a small sample of the flirtatious letters printed in the column. The fact that the editors printed these letters shows that they intended infatuated young men to view Dolly as sexually appealing. Their replies to the letters, however, require further investigation. Why, for instance, do they rebuff the men while at the same time encouraging them to flirt with Dolly? A possible answer is that the editors believed that a tantalizing correspondent like Dolly added spice and intrigue to the column. In other words, they were making Dolly play hard to get. In fact, we can safely argue that a more receptive response might have dulled the column and perhaps turned it into something verging on sleaziness. In some ways, then, the editors' snappy replies helped maintain the column's respectability and credibility as a source of advice, while at the same time encouraging young men to flirt with the sexualized character of Dolly. Indeed, a combination of the stern and tough, with the flirtations, contributed to the multiplicity of Dolly's character.

Another feature that might have added to the titillation of the column was the sensationalized titles that the editors used for the letters proposing to Dolly—titles like "I faint for you Dolly," "Dolly I love you," "Marry me Dolly," "Darling Dolly." In addition, lurid titles assigned to other general letters in the column—like "Give me the secret of a happy sex life," "Crucially in love," "My charming, but oh so naughty *Don Juan*," "Bosom pal grabs girl," "I am in jitters," "How can I learn to love"—heightened the sexual nature of the column even more. These titles vividly spectacularized the column, turning it into a place where the editors imagined young men could venture to flirt with the sexualized Dolly.

The aunt-like Dolly, on the other hand, was created in written advertisements for the column. In a rather amicable and sympathetic tone, the column editors tried to convince young men and women that this Dolly possessed the knowledge to guide them through Cupid's intractable maze. At the end of the column, especially in the early 1960s when the column was still relatively new, was a note saying, "Let Dolly mend your broken heart. Write to Dolly at . . ." Later on, other solicitous phrases at the top of the column repeatedly reminded readers of "Dear Dolly's" mission: "Do you have a problem that you can't discuss with anybody? Perhaps I can help. Write to Dolly at . . ." In other, even more persuasive advertisements, the editors urged young people to feel free to write to Dolly because in doing so they would be helping others with problems similar to theirs. They wrote: "If you have a personal problem, write to Dolly who will probably be able to help you. . . . You will find her most sympathetic. And remember there are probably many others with the same problems and by getting Dolly to help you, you will be helping others." The column editors wanted the youth to believe that this Dolly was capable of acting like their gentle confidant.[18]

The aunt-like Dolly was therefore presented as authoritative and self-assured. She could firmly disregard those whom youth sometimes viewed as their adversaries—usually parents and guardians. She often told her advisees to bypass their parents, for instance, and do what they felt was right for themselves. When Nsiah, a young woman of eighteen from Accra, wrote to the column saying that her father was forcing her to get married, she was answered:

> I do not agree with him imposing a husband on you since such marriages are always short-lived. If your father still wants you to be his daughter, then he must allow you to go to college. Tell him Dolly advises that you would be very useful to him if you are working as a fully certified teacher. Do it my dear, and best of luck to you.[19]

In a letter with similar concerns, Dapo Samaru from Zaria, Nigeria, wrote:

> I am 21 while the girl I love dearly is 23. Before I left Lagos for Zaria we used to take a stroll hand in hand down the streets of Lagos and discuss things of common interest. I thought we were of the same age until I saw her testimonial and found out that she was 21 in 1975, when I was 19. My problem now Dolly is that our parents object to our marriage because of her age. Please advise me.

The wise and authoritative Dolly replied:

> Age is no barrier where there is love. There are many cases like yours where the couples are today happily married. That she is older does not mean that she will not respect you as the head of the family. So if you love each other dearly, keep her and marry her when you are ready.[20]

Apart from conveying Aunt Dolly's authoritative voice, the above exchanges also reveal her friendliness and affability toward the youth. She often took their side. In replies to the letters that addressed this Dolly, the editors usually employed phrases like "my friend," "you have my sympathies," "my dear," "my son/daughter," and so on. Certainly they hoped that such genial phrases would touch the hearts of those who had written to the column asking for advice or—for that matter—other general readers of the column. And Dolly's affability also responded directly to the letters' imploring tones— "Help me Aunt Dolly for I am going to pieces," "Dolly what shall I do," "Please Aunt Dolly what must I do," "Please Sister Dolly help me as you have helped others," "Please, Dolly, you are my last hope." Clearly, the editors wanted to portray the aunt-like Dolly as a source for help. Their Dolly would not be a killjoy authoritarian but a well-meaning friend, not an intimidating parent but a kind and affable advocate. She would be in your corner fighting courtship battles with you. And, as the editors hoped, you would want the help of this imaginary advocate: She was knowing and steadfast.

friend + aunt

"Let Dolly Mend Your Broken Heart": Gender and Heterosexual Courtship

Premarital sex was one of the main problems the two Dollys discussed with youth in heterosexual relationships. At least half of the letters printed in the column dealt with this topic. Of these, half were written by young men plotting ways to get women to have sexual intercourse with them. Young women wrote the remaining half, asking Dolly how they might escape their boyfriends' premature sexual overtures. While these women wished to maintain their relationships with their boyfriends, they were afraid of getting pregnant before they completed their schooling or got married. In response to the men's questions, the editors often adopted a playful tone by humorously reprimanding the men's sinister schemes and telling them to lay off. On the other hand, the wise, aunt-like Dolly tended to answer the young women's queries, advising them to be cautious and savvy in their interactions with their boyfriends. Gender was therefore very crucial to the ways in which questions and answers about heterosexual courtship were generated, framed, and conveyed.

This gender bias is not surprising. Studies of public discourse in postcolonial Africa have shown the ways in which African men have used humor to avoid confronting important issues in the lives of ordinary people. Achille Mbembe, for instance, has eloquently examined the tendency among ordinary men in postcolonial Togo and Cameroon to employ grotesque and obscene language in political discussions so as to avoid confronting state oppression (Mbembe 1992). In my own work, I have argued that the use of excessive humor by male officials in public discussions of women's problems in postcolonial Kenya have rendered these discussions ineffective since the officials have spent more time trying to outwit their colleagues than in seriously engaging the concerns of women (Mutongi 2007). Similarly, the *Drum* editors' use of humor when responding to questions posed by young men seems to invalidate the serious issues generated by these questions.

A letter from Stephen in Dar es Salaam, Tanzania, demonstrates this point quite succinctly. The following letter was printed in the column in January 1967:

I am 19 and have been having a great admiration for a 16 year old girl. From the way she greets me and behaves in my presence I have come to the conclusion that she too likes me. Now I want to make her my girlfriend and have sex with her, but I do not know how to go about it. My fear is what would happen to me should she turn me down. I may drop dead. Please help.

Stephen received the following reply:

You are more likely to die wasting away if you don't speak than dropping dead if you do. Courage man, courage.[21]

A letter from Townson in Lagos, Nigeria, echoes Stephen's concerns:

I am 18 and my girl is 17. I want to have sex with her but I don't know how to tell her. Your advice is needed please.

The editors replied:

Hey man! If you do not know how to tell her then do not tell her.[22]

Another letter with similar concerns from T. T. in Nigeria noted:

I am 20 and in love with a girl of 22. We have interests in common but any time I introduce the topic of love-making she tries to brush the idea aside.

T. T. received the following answer:

Take it easy man. Easy, man! Aren't you lucky! The fact that she refuses to make love to you does not mean that she does not love you. I would advise you to keep cool, and let things take their natural course.[23]

It seems that the editors preferred clever and dismissive phrases like "Courage man, courage," "Hey man," and "Easy, man," rather than trying to tackle the important problems of premarital sex generated by the young men's letters. Of course these problems affected women the most since they involved pregnancy, illegal and expensive abortions, loss of honor, and the possibility of single mothers remaining unmarried for the rest of their lives. A letter by Cecelia Ikate of Kaduna, Nigeria, is very suggestive of these concerns:

I am 24, I attended a modern school with the hope of obtaining a certificate but, unfortunately, I fell in love with a boy, by whom I also had a baby. My problem now, Dolly, is that I want to marry but cannot get a suitable suitor. As soon as they make love with me, they vanish. I cannot get someone trustworthy to marry, so please help me.

The editors advised her:

> It is a pity that you have made the first mistake of your life. But at 24 you can still make up for the mistake, so don't lose hope. I advise you not to allow every Tom, Dick, and Harry to make love to you if you want to settle down to a better life. When suitors come, play your cards carefully and never allow them to make love to you. Keep on trying your right man will come along.[24]

A letter with similar concerns from "worried girl" in Lamu, Kenya, noted:

> I am a 19-year-old student. I am in love with a 24-year-old man. We had sex and it resulted in pregnancy. When I told him he at first denied responsibility but later he asked me to abort it so I could complete my studies. He promised to refund the money which I borrowed from a married neighbor. To my surprise the man has not refunded it to me. I have however refunded it to the woman. I have heard that the man tells people he is going to sue me for killing his child. I do not know what to do. Please help me.

"Worried in Lamu" received the following reply:

> It is your fault that you are in this mess. The man has taken you for a ride and you have lost your honor, money, and the baby. You would be a fool to continue with him. Concentrate on your studies and strive to make a good grade in your final examination.

Surely it was not just women who needed to be warned about the consequences of premarital sex; young men needed to be made aware of them as well. Premarital sex often resulted in pregnancy and caused tremendous anguish for many young women (Molokomme 1991; Bledsoe and Cohen 1993; Mikell 1997). Apart from the economic burdens that many women endured raising the child on their own, premarital pregnancies also hurt the women's chances of ever getting married. According to youth opinion polls, frequently taken by *Drum* and other similar magazines, it was not so much that the men wanted to marry virgins, as had been the case in the previous decades, but rather the fact that the women had children.[25] In other words, for many people in the 1960s and 1970s generation, engaging in sexual intercourse was permitted as long as the non-virgin status of the woman was not made public through conception. Yet the unavailability of contraception for unmarried women and the illegality of abortion in many African countries meant that premarital sex resulted in many cases of unwanted pregnancies (Bledsoe and Cohen 1993). Of course, the presence of a child publicly proved that the woman was no longer a virgin, and this was seen as a stigma by suitors—especially single men. Since most African communities valued matrimony and the social and political aspects (like establishing a household) that accompanied it, prolonged single motherhood became increasingly disgraceful (Allman 1991, 1996). Clearly, these are some of the issues the editors needed to address in their correspondences with young men. Instead, they tended to blame the women for the pregnancies while they whimsically dismissed men's lustful desires with lighthearted, conspiratorial answers to their questions.

Another issue that determined the seriousness of the young men's questions was the salacious and scheming language in which their questions were framed. Note, for example, the tone of this letter by Chiko from Nsukka, Ghana:

> I am 18 and in love with a girl of the same age. We are both students, and love each other very dearly, and we cannot go [for long] without seeing each other. I would like to take her to bed but I do not know how to tell her. She will soon go away with her brother and I am anxious to sex her. Dolly let me hear from you or I will go mad.

The editors reprimanded Chiko:

> You should think more about love and less about sex! It is plain from the tone of your letter that you do not really love her, but are only interested in sexing her. I wonder what you think you stand to gain. Do you not think of anything other than sex?[26]

Chiko was not the only promiscuous young man. In April 1977, for instance, the following letter from O. O. in Nairobi was printed in the column:

> She is 15 and I am 17. I am in love with her and I have spent a lot of money on her. But whenever I ask her for sex she tells me she is ill. When we meet again she tells me that it will be all right on a certain day, but I have found out that I have got a bad relationship with her. Advise me on how I can get this girl to bed and then leave her.

The editors responded:

> Nothing doing, chum. Even if I did know the secret of luring young girls to bed for adolescents who mistake lust for love, I would not tell you. You should be ashamed of yourself. Save your money for the right girl—and I hope she has as much sense as this one.[27]

Even though they reproached these naughty men, the editors' use of jaunty and dashing phrases like "nothing doing, chum" and "sexing her" in their replies diminished the seriousness of their message to some degree. These humorously reproachful responses were in many ways like those given to the young men discussed above who wrote letters proposing to Dolly. These answers suggest that the editors intended to keep the column tantalizing without making it appear too serious or reproachful.

Such rhetorical liberties seemed to be available to men only. Women were seriously advised to be cautious in their dealings with their boyfriends. In their replies to women's letters, the editors consistently warned the unsuspecting women against philanderers. See, for instance, the following advice to Ronke of Ibadan, Nigeria, who wrote:

> Two months ago, I fell in love with a boy who has promised to marry me. But whenever I pay him a visit at home, he discusses nothing but sex with me. I will be taking my final papers soon and as I do not want any obstacle to stand in my way, I have asked him to wait. But my boyfriend still insists, saying that I do not love him and that there can be no true love without sex. Is this true, Dolly?

The editors answered:

> Don't listen to him but concentrate on your studies. If your boyfriend can't wait, then you will do right to give him a boot.[28]

In a similar instance, Margaret from Tema, Ghana, wrote:

> I am 18 and my boyfriend is 20. When I visited him the other day, he made an indecent advance which I rejected. But he told me that if I could not give in, I should allow him to take an additional girl with whom he can do that sort of thing. Dolly, I am not in favor of his suggestion and I do not want him to take another girl. I love him. How do I bring him down?

The editors agreed with her, saying:

> You are sensible in rejecting this boy's indecent approach. If he sincerely loves you, I do not see why he should not wait until the two of you are married. Tell him this. And if he insists that he can't live without sleeping with you, back out. He sounds morally weak.[29]

Another letter from Deborah in Nigeria stated:

> My boyfriend is 20 and has left school, while I am a 17 year old girl and still in school. My problem is that every time I visit him he asks for sex, and this I do not like. But to keep him happy I sometimes yield. I take

the pill but my boy is opposed to it. I am afraid that I will get pregnant if I stop taking the medicine and thereby be unable to finish my education. What do you say.

The editor replied:

Don't mind your boy. I would advise you to use contraception unless you are ready to stop your studies and take up the responsibilities of a mother. But then is your boy prepared to meet his responsibilities should you get pregnant?[30]

Philanderers, the editors admonished, were unlikely to offer any support after they had (as the familiar expression went) "put a woman in a family way." They thus advised women to "resist temptation," "to practice self-discipline in matters of the flesh," "to be strong and sensible girls," "to play their cards carefully," and to "look before they leap."

So concerned were the editors about the women's vulnerability that they warned young women interested in initiating relationships with men to tread carefully by writing letters to their boyfriends instead of verbally communicating their romantic feelings. Letter writing, they believed, would not only give women the opportunity to explain their feelings carefully, it would also allow them to act "properly"—that is, submissively and bashfully—especially since women who expressed their sentiments verbally were often construed as prostitutes. Consider, for example, their answer to Willie from Obo, who wrote:

A boy of my age—18—approached me one evening and told me that he was in love with me. Frankly, Dolly, although I have had an eye on this same boy for a long time, I couldn't just bring myself down to say I love him too. What I did was to run away. . . . Since that evening I have been trying to find a way of telling him that I am madly in love with him too. Please come to my rescue.

Willie received the following reply:

You were over-excited and naturally did what most girls your age in your position would have done. I would suggest that you write a nice sweet letter to him. And next time he accosts you, please don't run away—you won't get frozen. Good luck.[31]

A similar letter from "Lovesick" in Kisumu, Kenya, noted:

I am a girl of 21 at college in Kisumu and there is a boy with whom I am madly in love, but I fear to approach him and express my feelings. I am frightened that he will call me a "prostitute." What can I do in order to approach him without fear?

The editor replied:

> You could write him a letter, explaining your feelings, or ask a friend to approach him suggesting that you could meet him, perhaps at a dance. . . . But don't be disappointed if he doesn't live up to your starry-eyed dreams. Love is not all physical appearance.[32]

Letter writing, however, put women in a secondary or reactive role when it came to creating the courtship discourse in the column. Unlike verbal communication, letter writing provided no immediate response.[33] It is no wonder that men set the tone of the courtship discourse in the column since they could express their desires freely and verbally. To them, women and not men were to be blamed for all the consequences of premarital pregnancy. Respectable women did not sleep around and thus did not get pregnant. Yet just as the men insisted that women remain virtuous, they continued to pressure women to have sex with them. It was clearly a no-win situation for the women.

Homosexual Courtship

While the editors listened carefully to problems about heterosexual dating and were sometimes willing to offer wide-range advice, their responses to youth who practiced homosexuality was generally negative. About an eighth of the letters printed in the column addressed this topic, often inquiring whether homosexual relationships were socially or culturally accepted. The editors' replies to these letters indicate that "situational" homosexuality could be tolerated as long as the practitioners did not express their feelings for each other publicly or in explicit terms. Because situational homosexuality was temporary, the editors did not view it as "real" and did not therefore perceive it as dangerously threatening to the dominant heterosexuality. However, young people who referred to their homosexual relationships in erotic or intimate terms, showed a strong aversion to establishing relationships with members of the opposite sex, or made their relationships public were often admonished. Their homosexuality was too "real," too abnormal, to be tolerated.

The reply given to a letter by Susie, an eighteen-year-old woman from Ibadan, Nigeria, who related her intense sexual relationship with another woman, attests to the editors' strong opposition to explicit description of homosexual sex. In January 1965, the following letter by Susie was printed in the column under the headline "Girls Love Each Other":

> I am a girl of 18 and madly in love with another girl of 18. I am so fond of and used to this girl that I have no interest in boys. My day is never complete until I have seen and played with this girl. Dolly, I am becoming very worried about this. How can I divert my love from her to boys?

The editors replied without mincing words:

> Your use of the word 'love' in describing your relationship with this girl frightens me because it suggests that you are developing lesbian tendencies. Well, this is a most disastrous thing to happen. You need to see a psychiatrist—and that immediately. . . .[34]

In yet another confessional letter printed in the column, C. L. from Kitale, Kenya, wrote enthusiastically about her intense sexual encounters with young women:

> I am a 17-year-old girl and out of school after completing my O-levels last year. My problem is that although I have many girlfriends there is one I adore and there is nothing that thrills me more than my lover's kisses. I have heard of the word "homosexual" but I don't really know what it means. Please tell me what it means and its advantages and disadvantages. I do not like boys at all; all I care for is this girl.

C. L. received a categorically negative answer:

> A homosexual is someone who is sexually attracted to or engages in sexual activity with a person of the same sex. The main disadvantages are that a homosexual is considered abnormal and therefore a social outcast, and homosexuals cannot achieve the degree of fulfillment of a heterosexual couple—or, for that matter, have children. The advantages are nil.[35]

It appears that what bothered the editors more than anything else was the fact that both Susie and C. L. derived great pleasure from their sexual encounters. To the editors, the young women's use of terms like "lover's kisses" meant that these women were elevating their same-sex romances to the level of heterosexual romances. Yet the editors insisted that the pleasures they described could be achieved only in heterosexual relationships. What C. L. and Susie were experiencing was therefore abnormal, so abnormal that it warranted psychiatric intervention. In addition, the fact that lesbianism hampered reproduction rendered it inexcusable, especially so since many African societies valued children as a source of wealth.[36]

On the other hand, the editors tended to excuse occasional male homo-sexuality, perhaps because it did not hinder reproduction as one man could impregnate many women and thus produce many children (Sweet 1996). Note, for instance, their reaction to Hophni, a twenty-five-year-old married man from Jos, Nigeria, who confessed his homosexuality:

> I desperately need your help. I am 25, married, and have a child. I also have many girlfriends. But I am rarely attracted sexually to either my wife or my girlfriends. Instead I fall for handsome boys. They are my life. I go to any length and expense to befriend them and get them to "mate" with me. I know that this is a very bad habit, but I have been indulging in it in the last ten years. Please how can I give it up?

The editors wrote back stating emphatically:

> This is a serious disease. The practice itself is a criminal offense under the laws of our country. You need to see a psychiatrist but meanwhile try to develop a strong will to resist the temptation. It is in your interest to try and give it up as it could land you in real trouble. It would not be so bad if you had one male friend, but if you chase after different boys all the time, you are promiscuous and morally wrong as well as break-ing the law.[37]

What is startling about Hophni's case is that although the editors knew that male homosexuality was illegal, and were even capable of calling it a disease, they condemned promiscuity rather than the homosexuality itself. Their reply to Hophni implied that young men could engage in occasional homosexuality so long as they confined themselves to one partner and did so privately. Promiscuity could result in publicity, which could land the practi-tioners into great trouble with the law since homosexuality, often referred to as sodomy, was illegal in many African countries.[38] Secretly practiced situational homosexuality was thus what the editors seemed to advocate for youth who could not contain their attraction to part-ners of the same sex. Note, for instance, their mild response to the letter by M. L. from Tanzania, who wrote about her husband's homosexuality:

> Two years ago I married a divorced man who assured me that he loved me from the bottom of his heart. He had broken off with his wife some years before I met him. Now his former wife has married a friend of his and the amazing thing is that they frequent our place. One day when my husband's friend brought his wife to our house, my husband became very hostile. I have found out that my husband is a homosexual and is

very keen on his former wife's husband, who returns his sexual interests. What should I do?

The editors responded:

I think your imagination is running away with you. If your husband has twice been married it seems a bit unlikely that he is a homosexual. Have a good talk with him and suggest to him that as he doesn't get on with his ex-wife, it might be a good idea if he ended his friendship with her current husband.[39]

In a letter with similar concerns, Mary Okello from Kisumu, Kenya, wrote:

I have recently got engaged to a very handsome man. We get on very well and we share similar interests. He is working and so am I, and we plan to get married towards the end of the year. Recently some friends of mine told me that he is gay because they have seen him in the company of such a crowd. What should I do?

Okello received the following reply:

Ask him, as he is the only one who is likely to know the truth. Don't believe rumors as people thrive on talking about others. Your boyfriend might be hurt with the question so try and do it in a good manner.[40]

For another rather mild response to what appears to be a case of situational homosexuality, note the editors' reply to this letter by Julia from Nairobi:

I have always had a lot of girlfriends and got on well with them. While at college I have been out with guys and enjoyed myself. But of late I have noticed that I prefer women to men. I see an attractive woman and act as if it were a man. I feel frightened of these emotions and to begin with felt that there was something wrong with me. Can you please help me.

Julia received this reply:

What you feel is quite natural. Accept your new feelings and do not feel guilty. There are quite a lot of men and women who feel the same way as you do. They have husbands, wives, or lovers of the opposite sex but turn to people of the same sex for sexual relationships. Tread gently and do not force yourself on your friends. You should try to discuss this with a friend who can talk you out of it or help you come to terms with your feelings.[41]

The editors' support for secret situational homosexuality is remarkable given their negative attitude toward homosexuality in general. To them, as long as the young women or men had partners of the opposite sex, their occasional romantic involvement in same-sex relationships did not interfere with the proper functioning of society. Reproduction and heterosexual relations would continue unabated. Situational homosexuality has been a topic of immense discussion among Africanists (Moodie, Ndatshe, and Sibuyi 1988; Moodie 1994; Shepard 1987; P. Harris 1990). In his study of mine workers in South Africa, Dunbar Moodie, for example, has argued that temporary or situational homosexuality was accepted by members of the miners' communities. He has noted that younger boys or "mine wives" engaged in sexual relationships with older men because the latter paid them cash. But after the "wives" accumulated enough money to pay bridewealth and establish new households with women in the rural areas, they not only quit the mines but also abandoned their "mine husbands" (Moodie 1994). For Moodie, then, homosexuality was a practical financial arrangement, simply a stage in the process of achieving heterosexuality or in avoiding proletarianization. In other words, homosexuality facilitated heterosexuality; it had a beginning and an end—it was temporary, never to be repeated after heterosexuality was achieved. M. L.'s, Okello's, and Julia's cases, however, indicate that homosexuality in other parts of Africa was not as rigidly situational or circumstantial as Moodie's study suggests. That is, it did not begin and end during a specific time but could coexist with heterosexuality. In M. L.'s, Okello's, and Julia's cases, the sexual boundaries appear to have been much more fluid (Sedgewick 1990; Butler 1990).

Nonetheless, in spite of this occasional toleration of situational homosexuality, the column generally presented homosexuality as abnormal and illegal. To the editors, heterosexuality was the only normal and acceptable sexuality, and they were not afraid to say so: They castigated young women like C. L. who were enthusiastic about their homosexuality, but also confirmed the fears of others like Hophni and Susie who were trying to escape same-sex relations.

Reading "Dear Dolly"

My evidence on the reading of the column is largely from interviews with young men and women in heterosexual relations. The interviews suggest that reading the column was also a highly gendered process: For young women reading the column was often a secret venture, while for young men it was a public social event. As I have noted, men often read the column loudly to their male friends, commenting on and rewriting the events in the letters in order to reveal their opinions on sexuality and courtship matters.

Young women, on the other hand, afraid of being labeled promiscuous, tended to read the column secretly. Despite this secrecy, many women read the column in order to learn romantic vocabulary to use in writing letters to their lovers. Inevitably, then, reading the column allowed both men and women to remake themselves in different ways (Barber 1997a; Newell 1997; Larkin 1997). I will focus on the reading habits of women first.

Since explicit sexual talk was not generally condoned, especially in places like the missionary schools attended by many of the youth, the column became one of the few places where young girls could learn explicit sexual language. Some of these girls were not necessarily interested in the column's recipe for a successful courtship or in its warnings about the dangers of homosexuality for that matter, but they were merely curious. And the column served their curiosity well. In other words, the column was not always as wholesomely didactic as may have been intended. Part of its popularity depended on its appeal to the young women's guilty imaginations, as the women considered turning the language in the column to their own immediate uses. For instance, some of the women copied the romantic language in "Dear Dolly" and used it to write letters to their boyfriends or girlfriends. According to Amy Kisia,

> In those days, you could not tell your boyfriend to his face how much you loved him. But you could write your boyfriend a letter and in there you could express your love openly. But you could not tell him—in person— the same words you had used in the letter.[42]

Kisia noted how women crammed romantic words from "Dear Dolly," a habit some of them had learned when studying vocabulary for their exams in school. Alternatively, the women wrote down the words on pieces of paper so that they were handy when they needed them to write letters to their boyfriends; they avidly cribbed suggestive idioms for courtship—lest they forget the important phrases. But, as Kisia noted, "You made sure that no one saw the piece of paper with the words on it because people did not use those words in conversation. They were considered bad words." So for many young women the language of romance became a written one rather than a spoken one.

Finding a secret place to read the letters was therefore crucial. Many of my interviewees noted that they read "Dear Dolly" late at night with a flashlight—or while in the toilet. According to Mary Emali, "You read quickly because you did not want people to wonder what you were doing in the toilet."[43] Other teenagers, even more ingenious, cut out the column from the magazine, hid it in their schoolbooks, and read it while doing homework. As Ester Njoki noted, "If you were reading and heard someone come into the room, you hid the pieces of paper in your other books. Thus to read the column safely, you had to surround yourself with lots of books and papers for emergency."[44]

The fact that "Dear Dolly" was only two pages allowed for a quick, surreptitious reading for the women who were under intense scrutiny and surveillance at home or at school. According to Njoki, "You did not want your friends, even your girlfriends, to see you reading because those things [romantic pursuits and sex] were supposed to remain a secret."[45] Since the letters relied on the use of a basic syntax and romantic clichés—like *charming, sugar, sweetheart, Romeo and Juliet*—a large stock of descriptions and formulaic characterizations were readily created that could be understood immediately by even the most inexperienced of readers (and, as noted, often deployed by future letter writers).

It is also possible that some of the women read the column in order to identify vicariously with the writers' romantic experiences. Janice Radway, in discussing bored and homebound women in the United States' Midwest, has shown that these women often identified with the heroines in the romance novels they read (Radway 1991 [1984]). Similarly, in many parts of Africa, the fear of being labeled a loose woman, of contracting venereal disease, or of getting pregnant because of the absence of contraception may have led many young women to live vicariously through others' romantic experiences. Fear and repression can incite the imagination, and the language of the letters—graphic, imprudent, and lustful—described situations that were far more vivid than those normally encountered. Available nowhere else, the intense and vivid descriptions in some of the letters to the column conceivably transported the women into a romantic utopia, and made prospective romantic adventures seem possible and even likely—at least for a time. How many of "Dear Dolly's" women readers may have been caught reading with one hand it is impossible to tell, but it is probably fair to speculate that many young women could not resist the temptation to participate in the excited thoughts to which the letters lent themselves—especially as no serious consequences accompanied their excited daydreams. Indeed, judging from numerous replies given to letters written by young men and women asking about safe ways to relieve their sexual frustration, this bluntly practical behavior was certainly in the realm of the editors' advice.

> Whenever you have the urge, try as much as possible to divert your thoughts by reading good books or doing some other useful things. You can try masturbation if you feel you are really pressed.[46]

While some of the reading experiences of young men might have mirrored those of women, most of the men I interviewed read the letters in the company of their friends—largely in order to air their views on the various aspects of sexuality and courtship discussed in the column and, more importantly, to confirm their stances to their peers. Stephanie Newell has argued in her study of readers of popular novels in Ghana that most readers read the fiction as true stories—true in a sense of being applicable to reality (Newell 1997). My interviews suggest that male readers, like their female counterparts, read the letters in the column as true stories; they tended to grasp the essential features of characters and situations and use them to interpret and rewrite their own social experiences. As most of the men who could read and write in the 1960s and 1970s were upwardly mobile, they communally rewrote the letters in order to reflect their adherence to the emerging image of modern men. According to Josiah Mukiri, a university student in the 1970s:

> We read the column to each other [in groups] clicking [clucking, condemning] at men who behaved weak in front of their girlfriends. Surely, a real man shouldn't let a woman control him. And the university women were the worst—the women's lib type. Even if they worked and brought in money, a man and especially an educated modern man was still in charge of the household. So you read the letters and simply clicked and made sure that your friends knew that you would never let that happen to you.[47]

Eric Oshagei, with an advanced-level diploma, noted:

> As a modern man you could not let your parents determine what woman you were going to marry. Such was the habit of illiterate and backwards "bush" people. So you tended to ridicule men who in their letters to Dolly agreed to such things. And you were glad that your friends knew that you weren't going to let that happen to you.[48]

For these men, then, education, the rejection of traditional norms, and the need to control their households, were important components of their definition of a modern man.[49] Reading and discussing letters in the column allowed young men to perform this image publicly, and especially to do so in front of their peers. Their peers in turn legitimated them as "real" modern men (Mutongi 1999). In many ways, then, the reading process helped men confirm and reconfirm their sense of masculinity, and also gave them the opportunity to redefine their identities in accordance with norms they perceived to be more up-to-date.

Conclusion

By exploring courtship as represented in one emerging form of popular media in early postcolonial Africa, this chapter speaks to many of the issues of love and sex raised elsewhere in this volume. Compared to *Bantu World*'s women's pages during the 1930s (Thomas, this volume), *Drum*'s "Dear Dolly" column featured more sensationalistic and sexually explicit discussions of intimacy. The relationship advice offered by "Dolly," however, was far more moralizing and directive than that which has been featured in some Kenyan magazines and newspapers since the late 1990s (Spronk, this volume). "Dear Dolly" indexes some of the intimate issues with which young people grappled during the 1960s and 1970s. The letters, and especially the responses, demonstrate how gender and sexual orientation informed courtship language. Clearly, the discourse in the column privileged heterosexuality over homosexuality. It also stipulated that women assume submissive roles in heterosexual courtship, that men initiate all sexual encounters, and that women alone bear responsibility for the consequences of premarital pregnancies. While men were allowed to use explicit sexual language in verbal conversations with their girlfriends, "proper" women were expected only to write letters to their boyfriends. Women who verbally expressed their feelings for their boyfriends were viewed as having loose morals. Inevitably, then, men tended to shape courtship discourse—largely because they were able to enjoy relatively open verbal conversations. Women, on the other hand, did not enjoy such rhetorical liberties. Since they bore nearly all of the responsibilities that accompanied premarital pregnancies, the editors' correspondence with them assumed a predictably moralistic and didactic tone. For all its supposed open-mindedness, then, "Dear Dolly" more often than not defended a familiar double standard.

ACKNOWLEDGMENTS

This chapter is a slightly revised version of an article (2000) previously published in the *International Journal of African Historical Studies* 33 (1): 1–23. Copyright 2000, Trustees of Boston University. Many thanks to Emmanuel Akyeampong, Alan de Gooyer, Nancy Rose Hunt, Joseph C. Miller, Yaseen Noorani, Lynn Thomas, Pat Tracy, and the anonymous reviewers for this volume for their com-
‧‧er drafts. Earlier versions of this piece were presented at the 1997
s Association Conference in Columbus, Ohio, and at Harvard Uni-

NOTES

1. "Ban on Petting," *Drum*, November 1965.
2. *Drum*'s offices were closed in East and West Africa in 1984, when the magazine was sold to *Nationale Pers*, an Afrikaner publishing house. For details, see Morris (1984). *Drum* continues to be published in South Africa, and the column remains one of its regular features.
3. The column also received wide-ranging publicity abroad. In January and June 1978, for instance, the British Broadcasting Company (BBC), during one of its peak hours, held a section to discuss the "Dear Dolly" column. *Drum*, January and July 1978.
4. While the South African *Drum* has been the subject of much research, no extensive research has been done on the East, Central, and West African *Drum*. For studies of South African *Drum*, see Coplan (1985); Dodson (1974); Lodge (1981); Gready (1990); Woodson (1989); Chapman (1989); Sampson (1957).
5. My efforts to find men and women who were in homosexual relationships during this time, and who could openly talk to me about their reading habits, were fruitless.
6. "What Is Wrong with My Letters," *Drum*, April 1977, 62. All correspondents were asked to send a self-addressed stamped envelope for replies.
7. In the early 1960s, however, most of the editorial material for *Drum* was assembled at the magazine's London office (Morris 1984, 53).
8. For details of Dolly's singing career, see Sampson (1957, 145–52).
9. Examples of studies of representations in African popular culture include Gondola (1999); Barber (1997a); White (1993).
10. For examples, see Barber (1997a); Frederiksen (1997); Fuglesang (1994); and Martin (1995).
11. For examples, see B. Cooper (1997); Jeater (1993); Mann (1985); Parkin and Nyamwaya (1987); Kuper (1982); Meillassoux (1981); and Comaroff (1980).
12. Note that in South Africa print media became popular in the 1930s. See Thomas, this volume.
13. South Africa recently became the only country in Africa to recognize gay rights in its constitution. Scholars and journalists have also paid more attention to homosexuality in South Africa—perhaps because South Africa, compared to other African countries, has been a little more tolerant about same-sex relations. For examples of studies of homosexuality in South Africa, see Moodie, Ndatshe, and Sibuyi (1988); Moodie (1994); Achmat (1993); P. Harris (1990); Epprecht (1998); Porter (1995); Shepard (1987); Amory (1997).
14. More elaborate pictures of Dolly appeared in *Drum* from time to time. For an interesting study of gender and visual advertisements, see Solomon-Godeau (1996, 112–32).
15. *Drum*, January 1963.
16. *Drum*, July 1967.
17. *Drum*, January 1968.

18. Previous studies have attested to the amicable relations between older female relatives (especially grandmothers and aunt) and youth (Schoenbrun 1995).

19. *Drum*, April 1967.

20. *Drum*, March 1978.

21. "I May Drop Dead," *Drum*, January 1967.

22. "How Do I Tell Her," *Drum*, January 1977.

23. "How Can I Win Her," *Drum*, January 1977.

24. *Drum*, March 1978.

25. "Sex before Marriage," *Drum*, June 1967; "Sex and the Single Girl: A Special *Viva* Investigation," *Viva*, March 1976; "The Language of Love," *True Love*, May 1977; "The Love Bond," *Trust*, July 1979; "No Easy Path for Love," *Joe Magazine*, June 1979.

26. *Drum*, May 1974.

27. *Drum*, April 1977.

28. *Drum*, June 1968.

29. *Drum*, July 1973.

30. "Must I Take This Risk for My Boy," *Drum*, September 1972.

31. "I Want to Say Yes," *Drum*, December 1967.

32. "Lovesick in Kisumu," *Drum*, October 1972.

33. For example, see "Should I Leave Her," *Drum*, December 1970; "Will She or Will She Not," *Drum*, December 1977; "My Problem Is My Stay-Away Girl," *Drum*, October 1977; "Does She Love Me," *Drum*, December 1971; "What Does She Mean?" *Drum*, January 1968; "She Is Fooling Me," *Drum*, June 1969.

34. "Girls Love Each Other," *Drum*, January 1965.

35. "Am I a Homosexual," *Drum*, November 1971.

36. "Some families in Zimbabwe have recently had their lesbian relatives raped so that they could conceive" (McNeil 1995). In general, most studies of homosexuality in Africa have tended to concentrate on men. For a discussion of this omission, see Amory (1997).

37. "I Prefer Handsome Boys to My Wife," *Drum*, July 1965.

38. Epprecht has noted that in Zimbabwe homosexual men and not women were likely to be prosecuted because it was easier to prove the physical sexual act between men than between women (1998, 637).

39. "Is He a Homosexual," *Drum*, February 1972.

40. "Is He a Homosexual," *Drum*, July 1975

41. "I Think I'm Gay," *Drum*, January 1978.

42. Amy Kisia, interview by the author, July 12, 1997.

43. Mary Emali, interview by the author, December 21, 1998.

44. Ester Njoki, interview by the author, June 30, 1997.

45. Ester Njoki, interview by the author, June 29, 1997.

46. *Drum*, February 1977.

47. Josiah Mukiri, interview by the author, December 22, 1998.

48. Eric Oshagei, interview by the author, December 19, 1998.

49. For a comparable argument, see Lindsay (1998).

Love, Money, and Economies of Intimacy in Tamatave, Madagascar

Jennifer Cole

It was early in my fieldwork in Tamatave, a large port town on Madagascar's east coast, when I first became aware of the keen interest that young people had in the relationship of love (*fitiavina*) to money.[1] I was sitting with some high-school-age students who had gathered to drink beer in the early evening. As the conversation became increasingly boisterous, one young woman declared, "If there isn't any *sosy* [literally "sauce," slang for "money"] in the relationship, I would just tell the guy to get a job." A young male college student in the group looked dismayed and said, "What, just because a guy is poor, you wouldn't love him?" The girl responded archly: "Guys just make us pregnant. Why go with him if he can't fulfill you?"

The implication was that without money, there could be no fitiavina. Young men would respond to such statements by complaining that girls wanted them only for their money, and that there was, in fact, no such thing anymore as "clean love" (*fitiavina madio*). Yet while in some circumstances girls claimed that there was no such thing as fitiavina without money, implying that giving gifts or money was a part of love, in other circumstances they made sharp distinctions between the two categories. At some moments, fitiavina and money were intertwined; at other times, they were opposed. In an effort to make sense of these contradictory conversations, this chapter offers both a genealogy of the changing semantic field associated with fitiavina and an analysis of some of the social dynamics that have contributed to those changes.

Desacralizing Love

To perform such an analysis, however, it is necessary first to desacralize and relativize the notion of love. In most Euro-American cultural representations, love is deeply intertwined with Christian ideals of humility and self-sacrifice. The Christian image of a God who loved the world so much that he gave his only son to save it captures this ideal. These ideas are closely interconnected with Christian conceptions of an autonomous subject, which entail a self "that must be abstracted from material and social entanglements" (Keane 2007, 55). In the case of love, material entanglements prove the most problematic. One is not supposed to love another to gain wealth or fame. Rather, one is supposed to love selflessly. Likewise, one is not supposed to love God instrumentally. Rather, one learns to love God by taking one's proximate attachments and building outwards from them toward a more encompassing conception of love. Love of God should be modeled on love of kin, but in the name of love of God, one leaves kin behind (Fulton 2002).

This vision of an autonomous subject who can take his or her proximate attachments and generalize them in the name of the common good also underpins the political contract of liberal states, which presuppose a subject constituted through a shared national project. The reciprocal exchange of an affective gaze that has come to define romantic love supposedly makes political identification with the larger nation possible. However, as Povinelli (2002) argues, liberal politics contrasts this kind of non-instrumental love with the love allegedly found in the once-colonized world, a love that is premised in the more local, material and potentially instrumentalist demands of kinship. The tension between instrumental and non-instrumental kinds of love that is a part of Christian thought reemerges here, but this time is distributed spatially across the world.

Povinelli and others have studied love to disentangle the genealogy of these ideas and how they validate some relationships and stigmatize others (Berlant and Warner 2000). Nonetheless, in many cases, culturally conditioned understandings of love continue to shape interpretations of intimate relations in other times and places. Given that the ability to love is an important aspect of how one judges the humanity of others, one may unconsciously measure affective or intimate social relations in other times and places and find them lacking.

Nowhere is this tendency to judge others more likely to emerge than in representations and analyses of Africa. Recent work on African intimacies has repeatedly foregrounded the instrumental, as opposed to the emotional, nature of intimate male-female relations (Arnfred 2004; Dinan 1983; Ashforth 1999; Haram 2004; Mark Hunter 2002; LeClerc-Madlala 2003). Many of these studies emphasize the strategic nature of these relationships either to highlight African agency despite difficult social and economic conditions or to illuminate the underlying logic behind seemingly promiscuous behavior. Nonetheless, the effect is simultaneously to downplay the affective dimensions of these relationships and to give academic credence to a view frequently espoused by African men that they are "used" by African women (see especially Ferguson 1999). Where once European discourse represented Africa as a place where people were so poor and cared so little about their children or other kin that they sold them into slavery, contemporary explanations of transactional sex inadvertently reproduce the stereotype by suggesting that Africans (and particularly African women) are purely instrumental. These arguments are implicitly informed by popular Western ideologies of love, which tend to ignore how emotions and materiality might, in fact, be deeply intertwined. When it comes to questions of economic activity and intimate social attachments, the idea that these domains coexist as "hostile worlds" tends to predominate (Zelizer 2005).

To explain the shifting meanings of fitiavina, my approach draws together work on the political economy of love with studies of money and exchange. Recent ethnographies have shown that economic relations and change influence the meaning and practice of love (Scheper-Hughes 1985, 1992; Rebhun 1999, 2007; Hirsch 2003; Farrer 2002; Collier 1997). For example, in her study of love in northeast Brazil, Linda-Anne Rebhun (1999, 85) argued that as peasants moved from the countryside to the city, they took waged jobs, and women increasingly earned money. In response, women started to talk of their relationships in terms of emotional work, rather than through an idiom of endurance or resignation (see Collier 1997 for a comparable example from Spain). Writing of an impoverished shantytown also located in northeast Brazil, Jessica Gregg (2006) describes how poverty makes it increasingly difficult for men to fulfill gendered ideas of support. Some women respond by rejecting love altogether, embracing a conception of sex as vengeance in its place. Clearly what love means, how it is performed—even whether it is allowed to be a part of sexual relationships at all—changes with economic context.

Studies of the relation between gifts and commodities extend these insights by showing the specific impact of capitalist social relations on affective life. Drawing on Marcel Mauss's famous *Essay on the Gift* (1990 [1950]), scholars have sought to understand how gifts differ from commodities, often implying that gifts and commodities are two opposed kinds of exchange, the one self-interested, the other somehow "free" of self-interested intentions (Mauss 1990 [1950]; Parry 1986). However, as Parry (1986) has shown in his rereading of Mauss, the very opposition between "gifts" and "commodities" is itself an outcome of the emergence of capitalist social relations. "The ideology of a disinterested gift," he writes, "emerges in parallel with an ideology of purely interested exchange" (1986, 458). This line of reasoning suggests that the ideology of a pure gift versus an intrinsically self-interested commodity, of which money is the iconic example, emerged in tandem with the growth of capitalism and modern social institutions. When applied to the domain of intimate relations, this line of scholarship suggests that the dichotomy of love and money, or of pure gift versus interested commodity, is not natural. Rather it is a historical effect of particular economic transformations. Interpreted in this way, the question then becomes not whether love and money are opposed but rather how the divisions between the two are socioculturally produced and managed and what the potential consequences are for intimate relations.

The contemporary moment offers a particularly illuminating time to track the changing nature of Malagasy conceptions of fitiavina because many urbanites believe that the current period demands renewed moral reflection. Over the course of the 1990s, Madagascar's government abandoned the state socialist policy that had governed the country since 1975 and embraced economic liberalization. The once state-controlled media diversified and privatized, bringing a host of new television shows, including programming from France and the United States. The Internet arrived as well, and in most major towns, Internet cafés have sprung up where during the day young men and women look for jobs or chat with friends who have managed to emigrate from Madagascar to Europe. Women also put their names on mail-order-bride Web sites where they hope to find a foreign husband. Young men come to look at pornography, particularly at night. There has been a marked increase in stores owned by foreigners, usually from other countries bordering on the Indian Ocean, and many more commodities—many of them foreign-made—are for sale.

These intensified forms of contact with the commercialized elements of the global north incite urbanites' desires to attain European ways of life. Yet not only have International Monetary Fund reforms devalued the currency to the point that people can buy comparatively little with their money, but rates of unemployment have increased, especially for young men and women just entering the job market (Projet Madio 2001). At the same time, many urbanites continue to maintain their ties to rural areas, whose inhabitants have a different set of ideals and expectations. Riven by the contradictory forces of desire and exclusion, and torn by competing ideas about the nature of intimate relations, Malagasy talk incessantly about love and money, reciprocity and self-interest. What is the proper relationship of love to money? I start by examining how these dilemmas are conceived of and dealt with in rural practice.

Fitiavina in Rural Practice

Like the English word *love*, the Malagasy word *fitiavina* covers a wide semantic field including "to be loved," "to be liked," "to prefer," "to desire" (Richardson 1885). However, the English word *love* is part of a cultural tradition in which emotion is supposed to exist within individuals and where great care is taken to distinguish between emotional attachments and economic interests. By contrast, fitiavina is part of long-standing cultural practices that explicitly treat affect and exchange as mutually constitutive and distributed across social networks. In rural areas of the central east coast of Madagascar, fitiavina and the sentiments that bind people to one another are constituted through the continuous reciprocal exchange of material support and care (Hunter and Smith, this volume, for comparative examples from South Africa and Nigeria, respectively). Villagers both make and express fitiavina through their willingness to contribute goods and labor to another's well-being. To give someone rice that you have produced from your own land; to buy clothes for a lover, a parent, or a child; to pay for a child's school supplies or medical care—these are well-known forms of fitiavina. In a context where people can acquire resources only through the collaborative, labor-intensive activities of farming or fishing, to take resources and put them toward the well-being of another is to nurture, protect, and give of oneself. It is the primary way to create attachment. In fitiavina, love and material support are ideally fused.

To understand how these ideas play out in daily life, it helps to look at how different relationships embody fitiavina. In Madagascar, the relationship between ancestors and descendents serves as a potent master symbol through which other relationships are also imagined. Consequently, the relationship of ancestors and descendents stands as a prototype of fitiavina (see Cole and Middleton 2001). Reciprocity is the central concept underpinning the ancestral-descendent relationship. Ancestors are supposed to love their descendents and bestow blessing on them, and descendents are supposed to reciprocate by recognizing the beneficence of their ancestors in rituals. In fact, a popular Betsimisaraka name for children is *Tiandrazana*, a name that means "loved by the ancestors." The relationship between living parents and their children is modeled on that of ancestors and descendents. Just as parents are supposed to love and bless their children, children are supposed to honor their parents with gifts and other material expressions of attachment. Both proverbs and ritual practice embody this ideal of reciprocity. One proverb has it that "children are like your horns," comparing children to the strength of a bull. When I asked an old man what this phrase meant, he explained, "Whatever you do, you lean on your children. Your children are your protectors, so you say that you have horns. When they're still small you carry them on your back and later [when you are old] they become your horns." Almost every ritual embodies the idea of fitiavina as constituted through reciprocal exchange across generations: The ceremonies carried out on Christmas and Independence Day in which children visit their parents' houses bringing gifts or food, to which the parents respond with food and blessing of their own; the rituals of cattle sacrifice in which guests come bearing small cash contributions in return for which they receive ancestral blessing; and second burials, in which descendents lovingly cradle the ancestors in their laps and give them food and candy, in exchange for ancestral blessing.

In keeping with the idea that the exchange of material support both expresses and constitutes fitiavina, adult villagers constantly talk about their fitiavina for their children in terms of either the labor or the services that their children performed for them. When Ramarie, an old woman, sent her daughter and granddaughter up-country to help a family friend harvest coffee, she was despondent, even though she had urged the girls to go. Waxing sentimental in their absence, she told me that, "Children remove your lice and fleas. To be without children is total poverty, they are your wealth and comfort, and those you raise will always remember you—most especially daughters always remember their mother" (Cole 2001, 94). What she did not say, because she assumed it was self-evident, was that to "remember" (*mahatsiaro*) is a word that villagers sometimes use to indicate the gifts that descendents give to their ancestors. On another day, she expressed the sense of mutual empathy and interconnection embodied in exchange by saying, "Children are like your mirror. You love to see them glitter." Like a mirror in the sun throwing back light, children were ideally supposed to prosper and give material support back to their parents. Bette, a woman who had nine children but lost an eighteen-year-old son when he was killed by a crocodile, was particularly attached to that son because he was such a good fisherman and had given her so much fish.

Although proverbs, ritual practice, and discourse emphasize that parents and children, or ancestors and descendents, are supposed to create fitiavina through reciprocal exchange, villagers recognize how difficult it is to maintain balanced reciprocity as well as the violence and suffering that may ensue when this ideal is not upheld. Ancestors might generously bless their descendents with fertility and prosperity, but they can also be grasping and cruel, demanding sacrifices from their descendents that impose tremendous hardship on the living. Descendents supposedly feel fitiavina for their ancestors, but they are also notorious for failing to fulfill their vows of gifts or cattle sacrifice for their ancestors. Similarly, while local ideology holds that parents are supposed to love all their children equally, everyone who lives in a village believes they know which parent-child bonds are strongest or who loves whom and how much. As evidence, they cite which child or grandchild is held and coddled more than another, who receives the most gifts or material support, or whose fields someone chooses to labor in.

This way of valuing relationships and building fitiavina has two negative aspects. In many contexts, people interpret the failure to offer resources, the inability to reciprocate (because of poverty), or the refusal to receive resources offered by someone else as a refusal of fitiavina and the relationship that fitiavina entails. To be denied fitiavina, or to be unable to offer it, is a deeply humiliating experience, one that cuts to the core of what it means to be a respected human being. In some cases, people will become extremely angry if slighted in this way, and they will let that anger be known, although others may disapprove of them for doing so. As a result, villagers can go to enormous lengths to avoid humiliating others. Many of the small daily rituals that people engage in—for example, certain kinds of greetings or the proverbs that one proffers to guests when presenting food—reflect this emphasis on social recognition.

The other side of the coin is that people who are poor or weak and therefore less able to give services or gifts to others are also less likely to receive fitiavina. So common is the assumption that those who are weak or poor receive less affection (measured in goods or labor) that numerous proverbs remark on this dynamic. As one oft-cited proverb has it, "The thin cow is not licked by his friends." Those who have less to give are also likely to receive less: Their poverty both signals and reproduces a lack of significant connection to others.

By adding the dimension of sexual desire in creating connections and directing the flow of resources, the bond that is supposed to exist between lovers or spouses both builds on and complicates this culturally idealized model of parent-child love. In other words, exchange, sex, affect, and power are intimately linked—what I am calling a sexual economy. The explorer G. Grandidier (1913) described what he considered to be the loose morals of Malagasy women, suggesting that they were entirely motivated by greed and that emotional attachment played no part in their relations with men. While his own cultural blinders likely caused him to miss the affective dimension of these exchanges, his descriptions nevertheless resonate with the kinds of material exchanges that I encountered both in rural areas and in Tamatave. He described matters thus:

> Malagasy use the same word, "mitangy" to say work for wages as a domestic or to have intimate relations with a lover, because it is not only foreigners who give gifts to their Malagasy concubines, but the indigenous men must also give them some small present, which can't be compared to what Europeans normally offer, but nonetheless is a remuneration for their services. (11)

Although Grandidier vulgarized the issue by using the word *remuneration*, he nevertheless captured the basic assumption that in male-female relationships, desire engenders exchange.[2]

Despite the evident importance of both material considerations and personal desire in shaping traditional male-female relationships, villagers talk about marriage in terms of *anjara*, a word that means "fate," "lot," or "portion," but is commonly used to describe one's destined marriage partner. Ramarie observed, "You don't get the one you necessarily want (*tia azo*)—you get the one God has chosen for you. . . . Few indeed are those who realize their dreams! You might like the boy over there, and never stop thinking about him, but it's your anjara you will get!" She told the following story:

> There was one boy I really loved (*tena tiako*). He came through the village with the agricultural workforce. I was his lover (*sipa*) for a night. And he left me money and then came back. I'd hide from my parents and say I'd gone to town to pick up some sewing, and then I'd go to meet him. And he would write me every week and put stamps in the letter so that I could write back. The postman would tease me. "Who are those letters from?" "Ah, my cheri I would answer."[3] I sent him my picture but his wife got hold of it, and it became poison in her hands. His mother . . .

convinced him not to leave the woman he'd already born children with. I only went with him three times, but Zanahary would have blessed that marriage.

Ramarie's story was about a fleeting love affair, but it nevertheless reveals important aspects of how villagers think about love in relation to marriage. In male-female relationships, a man makes fitiavina through gifts to the woman, and the woman returns fitiavina by offering her sexual and domestic services, and labor. Much as Grandidier described for the early nineteenth century, women expect to receive material resources from their lovers (see also Bloch 1989). The amount and regularity of the gifts that they receive embody and represent fitiavina.

The reciprocity in affection and resources that ideally signals fitiavina is much harder to maintain in horizontal relationships than in vertical ones. In vertical ancestor-descendent or parent-child relations, participants to the relationship always struggle over who has given more of what to whom. But these relations are nevertheless enduring because ancestors and elders can use either violence or the threat of violence—for example, causing a descendent to fall ill if one is an ancestor or uttering a curse if one is still living—to extract resources from their juniors. By contrast, it is more diffi- cult to enforce reciprocity in horizontal male-female relations. Given that villagers reckon descent and inheritance bilaterally, women can usually leave an unsatisfactory marriage—typically construed as a marriage where the man starts to give gifts to a lover, causing an imbalance in fitiavina— and return to their natal kin. Consequently, where inequities in fitiavina in ancestral-descendent relationships result in redressing the balance through sacrifice, inequities of fitiavina in horizontal male-female relationships of- ten end in the rupture of the relationship. If the man decides to repent and ask for his wife to come back, he must repeat the process of marriage in miniature: He follows her to her father's house and begs for her to come home to him, offering her a gift (tamby) so that she will consent to do so.[4] But it is much harder to force either party to restore the relationship if they really do not want to.

Christian Influences on Fitiavina and Marriage

Over the course of the colonial period, both Protestant and Catholic mis- sionaries introduced new interpretations of fitiavina. In sermons and pam- phlets, missionaries repeatedly tried to teach Malagasy about the dangers of money and to distinguish desires for wealth from less tangible sentiments like love, which they translated as fitiavina. Missionaries thus drove a conceptual wedge between the intertwined concepts of love and exchange. At the same time, they tried to restructure marriage. Given the missionaries' fear that Malagasy would convert to Christianity to achieve social and material, rather than spiritual, ends, their efforts to remake fitiavina took on a special urgency.

In the early 1930s, the *Fanilo'ny Tanora* (The Torch of Youth), a magazine published by the French Protestant boy scout movement, which had branches in Antananarivo and Tamatave, ran a series of commentaries in which it lectured people about the proper role of money in social life. All of the articles warned that while money is incredibly powerful and useful (It can print books that sharpen the intelligence, it sustains studious teachers . . . Or, it is fast like fire . . .), it belongs to the worldly realm and must be kept separate from the spiritual or emotional dimensions of social life. One article admonished, "Money is the domain of the flesh. . . . Those things that are visible are the domain of money. While money may work to stir the intelligence—books for school, etc.—on balance, money has nothing to do with the mind, especially the emotions and the spirit."[5] By arguing that money could be separated from the affective dimensions of the relationships, these teachings attacked the core of indigenous conceptions of fitiavina.

Writing on fitiavina in both Catholic and Protestant magazines offering marital advice reinforced these messages. These sources emphasized that the foundation of a happy marriage was love—conceived of here as a spiritual, emotional and physical bond between two people. One article published in *Ny Adidy* in 1947, a newspaper aimed at social and moral uplift, was devoted entirely to the analysis of fitiavina. The article described fitiavina in terms that sound very close to contemporary European ideas of love. It argued for a spiritual vision of fitiavina as a "force that comes from within and incites you to action" and makes you fulfill your ideals. It went on to argue that God placed fitiavina in human hearts, and that those who felt this fitiavina would fulfill their duties. The author of another pamphlet, "The Seven Commandments of Homemaking" (*Lalana Fiton'Ny Tokantrano*), combined Protestant teaching with his reading of Malagasy tradition (embodied in proverbs) to argue for a similarly spiritual interpretation of fitiavina. He argued that the first commandment of marriage was that it was the "fruit of love" (*tsimoky ny fitiavina*). Individuals came to feel love because they looked and felt moved by someone, and love awoke in their hearts in response. But he also warned that love must be guarded and kept to the proper path, lest it promote irresponsible relationships. Nowhere do these pamphlets mention that fitiavina might be linked to any sort of exchange of objects or services. Christian missionaries and their converts attempted to purify fitiavina according to a Christian conception of love, which downplayed fitiavina's instrumental and material dimensions. Not surprisingly that this model met with uneven success among Malagasy.

These reinterpretations of the meaning of fitiavina were part of a more general effort by missionaries to reform the practical nature of Malagasy marriage. In the Tamatave region, marriage had often been of short duration characterized by frequent divorce and remarriage. Women were actively involved in work outside the home—whether working in the fields, selling food in the market, or both.[6] Their contribution of labor and material support to the household was part of the enactment of fitiavina as a moral-material and emotional exchange. By contrast, missionaries advocated marriages in which men and women were life partners in the formation of a household guided by mutual respect and founded on the complementary division of labor. This marriage was supposed to be sanctified by both the church and, because colonial Madagascar was secular like France, the state. The man governed the household, but both the man and the woman were supposed to respect each other's wishes and consult each other on how best to run the household. Given that most of these magazines were aimed at aspiring urbanites, the assumption was that the man worked in an office while the woman cared for the household, although women were also encouraged to find appropriate ways to earn money from home, through activities like embroidery or sewing. This division of labor, in which the men were primarily responsible for the generation of income, which they then handed over to the women to manage, potentially created contradictions for women. Families who achieved this model gained prestige because they had attained a lifestyle associated with the French. But at another level, it also undermined women's value within the home by decreasing their material contributions to the household.

If many urbanites aspired to the model of companionate marriage promoted by the missionaries, few actually attained it. For the most part, oral histories about marriage and fitiavina from Tamatavians in their forties, fifties, and sixties do not diverge significantly from the rural practice discussed above. (Indeed, some of the people I interviewed had grown up in the country and then moved to Tamatave, suggesting the porous nature of rural-urban distinctions.) These older urbanites' expectations that fitiavina embodies both affective and material reciprocity are most evident

FIGURE 4.1 (left) Bride and groom on the day of their church wedding, 1935. Over the course of the colonial period, it became fashionable for Malagasy urbanites to display their social status by following French practice. In addition to the traditional ceremony between kin groups, couples also married at church and in a civil marriage recognized by the colonial state. *Photo courtesy of Simone Ralaizonia.*

FIGURE 4.2 (right) Bride and groom on the day of their civil marriage, 1960. This photo is of the son of the man in figure 4.1. Although the celebration of the church marriage was most elaborate, couples who wished to have their union recognized by law also married in a civil ceremony. *Photo courtesy of Simone Ralaizonia.*

in the stories that older women tell about marital conflicts. Bernadette, a fifty-six-year-old woman who lived in Tamatave, asked her errant husband to buy her a house:

> If there is a problem, and the man is caught cheating, you go home, and you don't go back until he comes to get you. . . . When that happened to me I asked for a house! And he went home and wrote a letter testifying that he would build me a house. I pulled in my belt at home to save money for that house, and that house, it isn't shared—it is written (legally) in my name.

Though the house (which we were sitting in at the time) was a traditional one made of thatch, and though she was in fact quite poor, owning her own house nevertheless gave her a permanent foothold in Tamatave, one that was considerably more secure than many. Another woman, also in her fifties, narrated how after his military service in Algeria, her husband became increasingly violent. They kept fighting, and she would return home to her mother's where she would wait for him to come fetch her and coax her back with gifts:

> He came to Tamatave three times to try and bring me home, but I wouldn't go. At first, I told him to buy me a sewing machine. And he said, "Where am I going to get the money to buy you a sewing machine?" That meant that he didn't really love me but was just teasing me. And I decided not to return to him.

Given the period in which they came of age, these women were exposed to Christian discourses about fitiavina and companionate marriage then in circulation. But they continued to speak about fitiavina using the rural conceptions of fitiavina in which affect and exchange are intertwined.

Yet to say that missionary interpretations of fitiavina and marriage had no impact on local conceptions of fitiavina would be a mistake. Listen, for example, to Bertine, a woman who is forty-nine-years-old, married to a functionary, and mother of nine children. When I asked her what marriage had been like in her youth, she remarked:

> Before, love [fitiavina] would order one woman to marry a particular man. Whether that man had money or not she would marry him but if there was a man with money and she didn't like him she wouldn't go with him. And she might dare to kill herself if she was forced.

Bertine made this comment while criticizing the importance of money in contemporary youths' intimate lives, so it is difficult to know whether her view reflects her own experience or is a reaction to contemporary practice that she then projects into the past. Either way, her comment—suggesting an idealized, almost spiritual "true" love—indicates some of the multiple layers of meaning that fitiavina had acquired, meanings that could be foregrounded in particular circumstances.

Fitiavina in Contemporary Tamatave

At first glance, romantic entanglements in contemporary Tamatave appear quite similar to their rural counterparts. Money has replaced labor as a focus of exchange and there is a greater emphasis on the acquisition of mass-produced commodities befitting an urban context where money is more readily available. Nevertheless, reciprocity is still expected. Whether male or female, many young people's narratives about romance and dating convey an enormous sense of pleasure, excitement, and desire, in which money acts as both a motivation to seek fitiavina and an expression of it.

Take, for example, Cathy, a fifteen-year-old girl whose father worked unloading ships at the port and whose mother worked by the side of the road selling food. I asked her how old she was when she started going out with men. She responded that she was twelve and then recounted the following story:

> When I was still little, I already loved money (*tia vola*). But my parents could hardly afford to support that. There was a boy who was the child of a merchant here in the neighborhood. Each time I would see him I would ask him for things. At that time I was already very flirtatious; I loved every boy I saw! And I saw my older sibling having many boyfriends and I wanted to do that too. Often, that boy he would give me chewing gum, or a bit of money, and I'd be overjoyed. In the end, Independence Day celebration came. The boy's parents had gone up to Tana [Antananarivo] for a funeral, and the boy was home alone. It was evening around 4 o'clock, and my mother asked me to buy some salt. When I got there, the boutique was closed. He was sitting out in front, and called to me, "Come here. Let us go strolling about tonight." "Won't you be scolded by your parents?" I asked. "My parents aren't home," he replied. "I'll be there soon," I said, "I just have to change clothes." I ran home and changed . . . and ran back to his house. He was very surprised to see that I'd returned so quickly. "Come in for a little while," he said, "for we'll go out to stroll when it gets dark." I went into the house and we drank cocoa and ate cookies. And we ate rice, and there was meat for our sauce. I looked at him and he was getting closer and closer to me, staring at my breasts. He said, "I love you" (*tiako anao*). Then we started caressing each other. That was the first time I went with a man. At 11 o'clock that night I went home to sleep. The next day there was a party for Independence Day, but I was sick. And my mother asked me, "Why are you sick?" "Malaria," I answered. But it wasn't that at all; I was lying. Starting then, I really loved men (*tia lehilahy*). And I wasn't afraid of them.

In Cathy's narrative, it is almost impossible to tease apart love, sex, and money: The pleasures of one are clearly bound up in the pleasures of the other. In fact, the way she starts her narrative, "When I was still little, I already loved money," even though I had asked about going with men, suggests that loving money and loving men are inseparable. While hers is a narrative of young, fickle fitiavina, it nevertheless suggests many of the sentiments and expectations that young women have when they enter into romantic relationships. The story told to me by Dez, a young man, portrays fitiavina from a male perspective:

> One day, I saw her. She was looking at a dress in the market. She kept looking at it, turning it over in her hands saying, "Oh, I really like this dress." At that time, I was just behind her, pretending to look at shoes. But really I was just watching her. And I asked her, "Why don't you buy it if you like it so much?" She started laughing and said, "I don't have enough money." And I said, "Well, I can help you out if it doesn't bother you. It isn't that I'm showing off that I have a lot of money, but I want to make you happy." And she said, "Is it your heart's will?" "Yes, that is my heart's desire." And I called the salesperson to get down the dress. She thanked me profusely and smiled away. "Think nothing of it" I said and took off. A week later it was Christmas. The 24 of December she came looking for me. "Where are you going this evening?" And I said, "I have no direction, as I don't have a girlfriend like all of my friends. So can I take you out?" She said yes and came to my house at 7.00. She'd even put on the dress that we had bought together. My heart was beating like an earthquake when I saw her. I thought she looked like an angel. And we went off strolling. At that time I took the opportunity to say, "I really like you" (*tena tiako anao*). And she replied that she was willing to go with me. I was so happy and I hugged her really tight. The next day was Christmas, and I was very happy at home but didn't drink any rum. My mother asked me, "Why are you so happy?" And I said, "Oh, I'm happy because it's a holiday today." But I couldn't even eat I was so busy dreaming of her. Starting then we were together. She was fifteen years old, and I was sixteen. If there is nothing that prevents us, then I'll marry her one day in the future, because she is pretty and of good character, and she knows how to bend (*mahay mandefitra*). Even if she knows that I cheat she doesn't mind, and I often feel ashamed and apologize to her. And I'm very jealous of her, because I want no one else to have her. I haven't seen a girl I would trade for her to this day. I really love her.

Dez's narrative, which situates the beginning of romance in a clothing stall at the market, is iconic, given the role of gifts, and especially clothes, in creating and expressing fitiavina between men and women.[7] Not only does it reveal the role of gifts and money in making fitiavina, but it also suggests how fitiavina relates to other ideals that men seek in a spouse. In particular, his narrative suggests the widespread male ideal that women should be "of good character." In addition to the expression "of good character," he also added the qualification that "she knows how to bend" (*mahay mandefitra*), an expression used to refer to the highly prized quality of tolerance and willingness to put others' needs before one's own. In this case, he uses the expression to refer to how he respects and admires her for putting up with his infidelities while remaining faithful to him.

Contemporary Social and Economic Contexts, Strained Intimacies

It would be possible to read Cathy's and Dez's stories as continuous with rural conceptions of fitiavina. To emphasize only continuity, however, would be to miss how the political economy's shifting dynamics have placed new strains on intimate relations. Although state and economic reforms have exposed urban Malagasy to Western media and standards of living, attaining those standards remains difficult for most Malagasy. Young urbanites feel themselves caught between their intense desires to attain Western levels of material comfort, with all the social prestige and moral weight of fitiavina that "having" signifies, and the difficulties that they face in actually doing so. They respond in gender-specific ways.[8] Here I focus on the strategies pursued by young women because it is their actions that Tamatavians privilege in their thinking about fitiavina.

Young women pursue relationships with men, ideally European men, because they see these relationships as a way to gain the money that signifies fitiavina, enabling them to forge their own networks of patronage and exchange (see Cole 2004). To meet these men, they go to night clubs or cafés frequented by foreigners, use the Internet to establish correspondence relationships, and find networks within Tamatave where Europeans, or frequently men from Réunion circulate.[9] When they are able to forge enduring relationships with these European men, they create a substantial flow of resources toward themselves and their families in ways that give them social power. When they fail, they become extremely vulnerable and often end up downwardly mobile, possibly with children to care for. Women's use of relations with foreign men for these purposes is very old, dating back to at least the early eighteenth century. Nevertheless, the sharpening of global inequalities means that the stakes of success, and particularly the stakes associated with finding a European man, have increased considerably (Cole 2008a.). If Christian discourses about fitiavina added a potentially spiritual dimension to local understandings of fitiavina that was primarily restricted to a limited religious domain, the social and economic transformations that have taken place in Madagascar since the early 1990s have broadened the relevance of this bifurcating interpretation in unexpected ways.

The iconic narrative that urbanites of all ages recount to justify why women start to "play at love" (*milalao fitavina*) or use men to obtain resources is one that echoes the interplay between fitiavina and humiliation, giving and taking, social interconnection and isolation that are integral to the dynamics of fitiavina in rural contexts. Recall that in rural contexts, to be denied fitiavina or to be unable to offer it is a deeply humiliating experience, one that cuts to the core of what it means to be a respected human being. The same is true in Tamatave, except that in the urban context, what it means to have fitiavina is complexly bound up with one's ability to signal a modern identity through the possession of certain commodities. Perhaps a young woman is at the water pump and one of her peers mocks her dress, or perhaps she is shamed while wearing rubber thongs, the mark of poverty, at school. Either way, the girl responds by finding a boyfriend— frequently an older man, ideally a European—who showers her with gifts and money. Sometimes I heard the story as a morality tale, in which the young woman is seduced and abandoned, and has perhaps in the meantime given up school, leaving her with few options. At other times, I heard versions of this narrative recounted to other young people to inspire desire and hope, and possibly motivate action. In these accounts, the young woman continues to be supported by her powerful lover and succeeds socially as a result.[10]

Let us look closely at one young woman and how she thinks about fitiavina and her relationships with men. When I knew her, Anita was a pretty woman in her mid-twenties. Born in Fenerive, a town to the north of Tamatave, she had moved to Tamatave to try and earn a living. She worked finding used clothes and selling them in the countryside. In addition, she was the mistress of one of the local political deputies. As she explained,

> It is hard to live in the country, but it is still harder to live here—in the country you can farm and make a living, and that is what everyone does, but here, you see your friends dress up, and you desire to be like them. Life here, it's just about social competition, and so you start doing things you shouldn't do. For example, clothes. If you find money, well my mother, she really suffers—so if you find someone who can help you, then you go with them.

Anita's statement contains a number of different concerns, namely the fact that urbanites feel driven by social competition to keep up with certain idealized levels of consumption, which in turn motivates them to engage in acts that they "shouldn't do," by which she means using men to find money. Her concern to keep up with various fashions and be socially valued is further complicated by her desire to take care of her mother, which she did occasionally by sending money back to the countryside. She went on to explain how she "got things" from men:

> You tell them how you suffer, and you say, "Can you help me?"—well what else can you do? For you want money, even if you don't like the person. But if there is someone you really love, but they can't help you, then it's hard to go with them. The people you want to go with, they have to have money so that they can help you. Me, I search for money with men, I sell, I go to school, and that way I can help my parents.

While Anita clearly used her relationships with men explicitly to obtain resources, she also had a conception of fitiavina that did not depend on the flow of resources:

> There is nothing better than two people who fall in love, but you need money. If you both work, then your life will be easy. But if they don't have money, then it isn't worth it to go with him because you will never be at peace, and you'll just think about cheating on him (to find a man with more money). But for me, I wish we could both work so that I wouldn't think of looking (for money) elsewhere (e.g., with other men). The reason women cheat is that the men can't take care of them. For me, if they have money and like me, then I like them.

Anita was hardly alone, either in her practices of using men to obtain money or in her way of thinking about it (see also Gregg 2003 for comparable attitudes among women in a Brazilian shantytown). What is striking about her narrative is the way she distinguishes fitiavina and money.

Nowhere is this practical division between love and money more evident than in the lives of women who develop relationships with more than one man at a time, typically an older European who gives them money and a Malagasy man who is dependent on them for resources, called a *jaombilo* (see Cole 2005). As the number of Europeans coming to Madagascar has increased and rates of unemployment remain high, some young women have been able to achieve positions of comparative power by forging relationships with European men. Other urbanites view jaombilo primarily negatively because the relationship inverts gender norms in which men achieve a dominant position because the women ideally follows them to live virilocally (Cole 2005). What interests me here, however, is the way these relationships embody the deepening split between fitiavina and money. Claudin, a college student, explained what a jaombilo is:

> When the European supports the Malagasy girl, and the Malagasy girl then supports a Malagasy man, that man is the jaombilo. That is to say, there is a parallel finance system going on (*financement parallel*). The way I see it, the Malagasy man is doing "love for self interest" (*l'amour par interet*—a line from a now celebrated song by Dr. J. B.) to the Malagasy girl. Because he too has another girlfriend [whom] he really likes somewhere else. For example, there is an old Australian man who is married to my cousin. And I see that my cousin only loves him for his money, for my cousin she has a Malagasy boyfriend hidden away, but the old European he doesn't know. Often I joke around with the old man, "You know my cousin she is just using you for money" and he just laughs and says, "That is true."

In the contemporary context, one relationship can no longer fulfill all desires, despite the ideals of reciprocity embodied in fitiavina. Women who had jaombilo emphasize that they need both affective connection and material resources, but it is not always easy to obtain those needs in the same relationship. Like young women in Dakar who seek the "three V's"—*villa, virement bancaire,* and *voiture* ("house, bank transfer, and car") (Nyamnjoh 2005)—or women in South Africa who go in search of the "three C's"—cash, cell phones, and cars (Hunter, this volume)—where their specific desires cause them to cultivate different relationships for different ends, so too, these women start to create some relationships that are only for economic gain, while cultivating others that are based on emotional attachment and physical desire.

It is important to note, however, that while they often talked about their jaombilo as the person they felt fitiavina for, in contrast to the European whom they used for money, in practice these women's relationships with their jaombilo were characterized by complex exchanges of goods and services. For example, in a stark reversal of normative gender roles, jaombilo are known to offer their girlfriends help around the house, to wash the laundry, and to offer them physical protection going to and from rendezvous with other men. Young women who had jaombilo might have talked about them in emotional and non-instrumental ways, and contrasted it to their use of European men to earn money. Nevertheless, they also relied on their jaombilo to perform certain kinds of services—services that suggested that ideally fitiavina was still equally constituted by both affect and exchange.

The Conundrums of Love versus Money

In the contemporary context, Tamatavian women find themselves in the position of using intimate relationships to obtain money in ways that sometimes have little to do with reciprocity, and hence fitiavina. Men often complain that they are being financially used (see also Hunter, Smith, and Masquelier, this volume). In response, young urbanites start to increasingly reimagine fitiavina according to a more familiar Western conception of love that they then oppose to material gain or self-interest. Echoing Parry's (1986) insight that the opposition of gifts and exchange, persons and things is, according to Mauss, a result of capitalist economic relations, James Farrer (1998, 15) has observed that in market-reform Shanghai, "love and material benefits [are] paired rhetorical opposites in which the increased emphasis on one entails the compensatory emphasis on the other, reflecting socially constructed dilemmas ... that youth face in the market economy." Farrer describes how young women in Shanghai seek to negotiate the contradiction between their economic dependence on men, their need to "marry up," *and* their expectations that they will "fall in love." In a context where premarital sex was previously forbidden, women's "pure" as opposed to materially interested motives become an important part of justifying their actions. Similarly, in Tamatave, the emergent, ever-diversifying discourses about love and money that youth develop provide them with new tools for framing affective life and intimate relations, but in still-hybrid ways.

Anita's narrative clearly embodies the increasingly evident opposition between fitiavina and money. Recall that she is frank about how she earns a living as the mistress of a wealthy man: She talks about how she constantly has to choose between men for whom she feels fitiavina and men who have money. In her remark, "There is nothing better than two people who fall in love, *but* you need money," she explicitly made a distinction between fitiavina and exchange. So did many others. Repeatedly in their accounts of what fitiavina meant, young people talked about fitiavina in ethereal terms. As Filiaste remarked, "To me it means the combining of two people's hearts. It means that two people have agreed to be of one voyage together, even as they face bitter times or sweet, and those two people they respect each other and share their troubles."

Like the missionaries who translated fitiavina as love and then proceeded to define it, young people resort to creating new word combinations to express different aspects of fitiavina. On the one hand, they tend to use the term "clean fitiavina" or "fitiavina with a clean heart" (*fitiavina madio, fitiavina madio fo* respectively) to indicate relationships characterized by self-sacrifice. As Bera, a young man who had finished high school but still lived at home, explained, "But clean love (*fitiavina madio*) still exists. For example, my neighbor, she goes out with this boy, and that boy he doesn't give her any money and he makes her suffer. Yet she never breaks up with him, even when he hits her on occasion. For me, that means she really loves that man with a clean heart." On the other hand, they speak of a kind of fitiavina that they fear characterizes most relationships in contemporary Tamatave: not "dirty" fitiavina, as one might expect, but love for self-interest.

While "clean love" appears closer to the Euro-American ideal of romantic love with its emphasis on self-sacrifice, it is also important to remember this conceptualization opens the possibility for violence against women. In fact, "clean love" and "love for self-interest" are mirror images of one another, whose evocation depends on the gender of the speaker. For Bera, the woman who truly loves a man is a woman who will stay with him and receive nothing in return. She will take worse than nothing; she will even put up with abuse. Meanwhile, when a person accuses another of practicing "love for self-interest," it usually means that a woman is milking a man for all that he's worth and giving him little by way of affective commitment in return. From the rural perspective with which I started, both of these extremes represent pathologies of fitiavina. Rather than a reciprocal exchange of affect and resources, one person receives and the other person simply takes. From the contemporary male urban perspective, only "love for self-interest" appears morally wrong.

To explore further how young people think about the relationship between fitiavina and money, I started to tell my informants a particularly dramatic version of an encounter between a Malagasy woman, her jaombilo, and the European man with whom she had a relationship, which one of my informants had recounted. It went like this:

There was a girl in Nosy Be, and she was married to a man. They struggled together. But then one day she found a vazaha (European), and she agreed with her husband that every time the vazaha came she would sleep with him and that was how they would get money. And the Malagasy man agreed and he said, "When that vazaha gets here just say that I am your brother and we'll split the wealth." And the vazaha believed that he was her brother and they had already opened a grocery store, and they got new bicycles and the vazaha even bought the Malagasy man a boat to use for fishing. After two years they got caught by the vazaha who realized they were husband and wife, and he took all of his things. He put the man in prison, but he kept the girl with him. But when the vazaha left for France, the police released the Malagasy man and that is how everyone heard the story.

Given young women's insistence on the necessity of obtaining money through intimate relationships, and given that some young women do create arrangements like the one described above, it is striking that all the young people—whether male or female—who heard the story argued that it indicated a profound perversion of social relationships. In part, the perception of perversion is linked to the way jaombilo embody an inversion of local gender norms, as I mentioned earlier. What interests me here, however, is that young people took the story as an opportunity to reflect on the relationship of affect to exchange that preoccupies them. Regis, a young man at the university, put the issue as follows:

> To me, that story suggests that they need to learn how to distinguish between love (fitiavina) and money. If those two things go together, there are many things that will be ruined and one of them (e.g., love or money) will always have more importance than the other. The way I see that story, money came first, money that they just got like that, without any physical effort, although I suppose the man had to make some mental effort since he gave his wife to someone! But you should feel love for one another before you search for money together—for me love means you suffer together, you rejoice together, and together you search for answers to your problems.

Regis's friend, Olivier, agreed:

> If there are some people who kill themselves for love, then love is something really grand! There is nothing more important in life. Because if you are sick you part with your money to buy medicine, but love makes people kill themselves! For me, that is the highest thing of all. The way I think about that story, he and his wife couldn't really have loved each other. If they really loved each other, that never would have happened.

Not only men reacted negatively to the story. One girl noted, "If I were in those people's place I would never have done that, because I couldn't give my spouse to anyone, he is for me alone. To me, love means desiring good things for those you love."

Clearly, all of these young people think that the jaombilo relationship recounted in the story is problematic because it represents a perversion of fitiavina. But where does that perversion really lie? None of them are worried about the European and the fact that he is being cheated, and none of them even entertain the idea that the Malagasy woman might actually love the European man. Rather, they focus their answers on the Malagasy couple with whom they identify. Their interpretations all suggest that what the couple has done wrong is to act as if money is more important than their marriage, so that the couple allows a relationship through which they obtain money to dictate the terms of their relationship with each other. In theory, the couple has chosen a path that is logical in the context of those local ideas that see affect and exchange as mutually constituted: They take the flow of resources obtained from one relationship and convert it into the flow of resources to another. Nevertheless, their solution to the predicament of poverty remains unacceptable because there is a failure of reciprocity within their relationship.

When read alongside the other examples, these young people's reactions suggest that the more young urbanites rely on their intimate relationships to gain money, the less likely they are to see fitiavina as the reciprocal exchange of affect and material resources and the more they come to see fitiavina as a separate emotion that seems very similar to the Christian ideal of love. What these abstract reflections imply about daily practice is another matter. If we look closely, their narratives are riven with ambivalence, sometimes appearing nostalgic for an older ideal of fitiavina and for the material conditions that allowed men and women to enter into more reciprocal relationships. Arguably, the tragedy of contemporary economic conditions is that urbanites have a harder time entering into the reciprocal relations of exchange through which they have constituted fitiavina. The result is that some young Tamatavians are formulating new ways to think about what fitiavina means.

Conclusion

Born of everyday experience, ideologies of intimate attachments help shape horizons of interpretation and action. For rural inhabitants like Ramarie, fitiavina is deeply implicated in practices of exchange and an ideal of material reciprocity that structures intimate social relations. For the Catholic

Protestant missionaries who worked in Madagascar during the colonial period, fitiavina was an emotion separate from the reciprocal flow of resources that was so crucial to east coast Malagasy understandings. While Christian missionaries were never able to generalize their conception of love to the wider population or beyond the narrow confines of the religious practices associated with the Catholic and Protestant churches, they were able to introduce an ideological wedge between fitiavina and exchange. Today, this split has become multiply reinforced in the context of a consumer-oriented market economy characterized by great scarcity and growing socioeconomic disparities. As they wrestle with their circumstances and use their intimate relations with one another and with powerful foreign men to obtain resources, young urbanites essentially take what was a Christian ideal of love and secularize it, though hardly in the way the missionaries either hoped for or would have wanted.

Consequently, for contemporary urbanites like Anita or Bera, fitiavina has become split and differentiated so that there can be such a thing as "clean fitiavina" where a woman can feel love for a man and get nothing in return or a woman can take resources from one man while "loving" another. In tracing out these different instantiations of fitiavina, I am not suggesting that one stage or version of fitiavina has somehow replaced the other. Rather, each iteration of fitiavina simultaneously partially displaces and reconfigures the previous one, and each manifestation continues to exist as a possibility, to be called forth by particular social actors in particular social circumstances. Like northeast Brazil, where Rebhun (1999, 207) compared discourses of love to a palimpsest because of the way they combined aspects of the European past of New World settlers, cultural elements of the Brazilian experience, and facets of contemporary life, so too fitiavina in Tamatave shares this palimpsestic quality. Words gather history around them, as we know.

The changes that I have traced do not only reformulate the past; they also imply certain possibilities for the future. After all, the transformations that I have described are also part of much larger global realignments of _____ Madagascar, Europe, and North America. This new global _____ ngly common for women to use intimate relation- _____ le 2008b). When they do so, they will bring their _____ vina into contact with the ideologies of love that _____ litics of the French state. From here it is not a big _____ st that since these women are often perceived of by _____ g inadequate conceptions of love based on material _____ e viewed as less worthy of humane treatment at the hands of the state (see also Garrett 2007; Amrhein 2007). The irony is that for those women who stay in Tamatave, Tamatavian men may mobilize the flip side of this ideology, where affect is privileged over exchange, to justify women's self-sacrifice.

ACKNOWLEDGMENTS

I gratefully acknowledge the support of the Fulbright program, the Wenner Gren Foundation for Anthropological Research, and the American Philosophical Society. Without their financial support, this research would not have been completed. I also thank the participants at the joint session of the African Studies and Gender Studies workshops at the University of Chicago in 2007; the anonymous reviewers for the University of Chicago Press; and most especially Judy Farquhar, Maria Garrett, Rochona Majumdar, Danilyn Rutherford, and Lynn Thomas for their helpful comments on earlier drafts.

NOTES

1. The research on which this chapter is based was conducted in Tamatave in 2000–2001, 2002, and 2003, as well as earlier fieldwork in the Mahanoro region in 1992–1994 and again in 2007.
2. Villagers say that physical desire for a member of the opposite sex is natural and spontaneous, explaining that it comes from Zanahary or God. For example, Ramarie's first marriage was to a man who had been married to his older brother's widow, a traditional levirate marriage. The wife bore no children, and so the man decided to remarry in order to obtain an heir. But even Ramarie, who had grown up in a time when the demands of kinship had shaped one of her marriages, talked about how women choose partners in terms of personal preference and desire. As she explained, "Some girls choose lovers for looks, others seek their material comfort." She went on to tell me about how an older man, who was comparatively wealthy by village standards, had come and greeted her, the traditional way that a man seeks to establish sexual relations with a woman. The thought of sleeping with him made her cringe, so she refused the offer.
3. It is not clear to me how she read the letters, given that she was illiterate. It is likely that she had a close kinsperson do it for her.
4. Alternatively, pathologies of reciprocity are talked about in the idiom of love magic: *ody fitia* (from the word *fitiavina*). Whenever a man slavishly gives over all of his material wealth to a woman, whenever he abandons the interests of his kith and kin, his neighbors will assume that love magic is the cause. If fitiavina is constituted through the reciprocal exchange of gifts and labor, then fitiavina gone amok is about the uncontrolled flow of resources and affect in a single direction. See also Graeber (1996).
5. *Fanilo Ny Tanora*, No. 44–45, Juin 1931.

6. At the same time, missionaries and colonial administrators alike worried that Malagasy women, in particular, would be attracted to the glamour and glitter of the new commodities that signaled modernity and gave urbanites social status, without adopting the social forms and proper attitudes that were supposed to accompany them. Over the course of the colonial and early independence period, women's magazines repeatedly warned that women should not pursue men in search of money. Popular moralists blamed women's overweening desire to be fashionable for the imminent downfall of the conjugal household because they assumed that women would inevitably seek out ever wealthier men in their quest for fashion. In 1929, the Malagasy vernacular magazine *Tafa sy Dinika* published a poem entitled "Mihaingo" or "Ornamentation." The poem warned that an excessive love of fashion and adornment led women to use men to gain money, causing them to neglect their moral duty to their families. The last line of the poem, which in Malagasy is written in clever rhyming verse, notes: "The last words I want to say to you, a little advice I give to you, be careful not to overdose on fashion. Because it is as evil and hurtful as tuberculosis." (*Ka ny farateny 'zay tiako hambara, O! Dinika kely sy hafatra tsara. Tandremo ny haingo mihoatra ny daozy. Satria farasisan-tiberkilaozy.*) One magazine, *Loharano Malagasy*, which can be translated, roughly, as "Women, the Fount of Life," had one issue in which the cover itself brought home the critical point. It featured a young, sophisticated woman sporting French-style short hair with "Women are blind" written across where the woman's eyes would be. Below in the right-hand corner, two men, whose Jewish identities are signaled by their beards, carry a pot of money marked "1000." The message, directed at urban Christians, is clear: Women should not be seduced by men's money.

7. For a more detailed discussion of clothing in male-female relationships in Madagascar, see Cole (2008b) and Feeley-Harnik (2003).

8. Young men seek access to resources, sometimes by trying to position themselves as clients of more powerful older men, sometimes by circumventing the law, because it is by dispensing resources that they earn not only power and prestige but also the fitiavina of others.

9. Réunion is an island located to the east of Tamatave, which is still administratively part of France.

10. Another common reaction is that these young women turn to one of the Pentecostal churches for solace. As one older woman who did not belong to one of these churches remarked to me, a wry smile playing on her lips, "The love of Jesus *never* disappoints."

Providing Love

SEX AND EXCHANGE IN TWENTIETH-CENTURY SOUTH AFRICA

Mark Hunter

The AIDS epidemic in Africa is frequently said to be exacerbated by non-prostitute sexual interactions constituted in part by men giving gifts to poorer "girlfriends."[1] This chapter shows how this "transactional sex" is inadequately conceptualized. In the main, scholars have comprehended the supposed ease with which sex is exchanged in African society through one of two narratives: Sex is outside of "traditional" African moral values and therefore easily exchangeable, or the forces of modernity have aggressively individualized, commodified, and casualized African sexual relations.[2] In turn, these viewpoints are given strength by the tendency to portray expenditures surrounding intimate relations in Africa in instrumental terms and therefore juxtaposed to love. For instance, the voluminous literature on kinship and *ilobolo* (bridewealth) tended to present marriage as a mechanical *exchange* of women between kinship groups; according to the famous structural-functionalist anthropologist, Radcliffe-Brown (1950, 46): "The African does not think of marriage as a union based on romantic love. . . ." Affection, he argued, "is the product of the marriage itself. . . ."[3] Not unrelated, the small number of writers who have studied romantic love in Africa tended to see it as a quintessential modern force fighting against restrictive traditions; here, individualistic practices such as the modern companionate marriage or new communication forms such as the love letter undermine the dense kinship bonds that characterized traditional African society (for instance, Little and Price 1967; Little 1973; Vandewiele and Philbrick 1983; Stones and Philbrick 1989). In contrast, this chapter's starting point is the mutually constitutive nature of intimacy and exchange.[4] Pioneering anthropological studies have long demonstrated the constitutive role of culture in material transactions, but to this literature must be added matters of love (see Comaroff 1980 on marital exchanges; Parry and Bloch 1989 on money and exchange).

What do we mean by love? Recent anthropological literature finds a universal form of *romantic passion* realized in diverse cultural settings (Jankowiak 1995). But it is historically based writings on *romantic love* that exert the most influence on the academy: These studies typically locate love's historical transcendence in the rise of companionate marriage and the increase of choice in the selection of marriage partners (Shorter 1975; Stone 1979; Macfarlane 1986). They present modern societies as becoming "progressively more loving"; a teleological position that results in part from a dependence on written sources such as diaries and love letters (Gillis 1988). In response, however, critics have emphasized the way that love is expressed in practical acts such as support, cooperation, and reciprocity that predate literacy (Gillis 1988 drawing from Cancian 1986). It is this expression of love through acts of mutual assistance—practices that are simultaneously material and meaningful, even if they are not articulated in writing—that this chapter argues is crucial to the intertwined histories of love and exchange in twentieth-century South Africa. Specifically, I chart the changing ways in which men have "provided love" in South Africa as love became embroiled with vastly different forms of male assistance: from a position where men were the providers of marital households to one today where men can support multiple unmarried girlfriends.

This chapter begins with a brief discussion of love and marriage in the nineteenth century. Its second section then notes how African men's growing dependence on wage labor helped to engender masculinities whereby men worked in order to provide ilobolo and then support the marital homestead.[5] This shows how, over the twentieth century, ideas of love became embroiled with men's emergent roles as providers. As its third section argues, however, chronic unemployment has now largely undermined men's ability to secure steady work. Crucially, over the last three decades, men's failure to marry and support a family has led to the fracturing of the implicit bargain that rested on men and women contributing to a project of "building a home."[6] Now, indignant at men's unreliability, and with few prospects of marriage or employment, women can actively evoke the provider masculinity justify milking boyfriends for gifts in new ways. Yet these apparently instrumental sex exchanges do not signal the end of love; a more contingent and fragile love remains expressed in men's support, even if this is typically from "boyfriends" to "girlfriends" rather than from husbands to wives.

This chapter focuses principally on the South African province of KwaZulu-Natal and draws from ethnographic, archival, and secondary research. In brief, the study involved living in an "informal settlement" on the north coast of KwaZulu-Natal extensively between 2000 and 2006. During this time, I conducted around three hundred interviews with residents aged between sixteen and eighty (for more details, see Mark Hunter 2005a). In this chapter, I draw mainly from secondary and archival sources, interviews with elderly men and women (generally informants aged over sixty) in a rural part of my research site, and discussions with young women in a nearby township. South Africa is a heterogeneous country, with a rising middle class, but in general, the chapter restricts itself to the poorest South Africans and specifically those categorized under apartheid as "African." Another caveat: The chapter attends to broad historical themes stretching over the twentieth century rather than providing ethnographic thickness in one particular period.

Kinship, Marriage, and Love in the Nineteenth and Early Twentieth Centuries

In nineteenth century KwaZulu-Natal, *imizi* (homesteads) headed by *abanumzana* (male heads of household) were the pivotal institution through which animal husbandry and agricultural production were organized.[7] Since women were responsible for agriculture and therefore producing staple foods such as maize, men gained status not by "providing" for women but by heading a large and successful *umuzi* (homestead), a position that hinged on the cooperation and productivity of a wife or wives. From a young age, men were socialized into a masculine world through activities that included cattle herding, hunting, and stick fighting; their education prepared them for the day when they would assume the role of *umnumzana* (household head). A son worked for his father and knew that ultimately the cattle he herded would be used for bridewealth to secure marriage. If married men did not in this period support women economically, elements of male power were entrenched in the rule that only they—or more accurately their fathers— could initiate marriage through the giving of ilobolo to a bride's father.

Ilobolo symbolized the transfer of women's guardianship from father to husband and men's preeminent role in forming new kinship bonds—but it also reflected women's value in society. On the latter, it has often been noted

FIGURE 5.1 South African wedding ceremony. This photo shows a group bearing gifts on their way to a KwaZulu-Natal wedding ceremony in 1928. The exchange of gifts between families was an integral part of African marriage; at this time, men who lured girlfriends through gifts could be criticized as "bribing" them. *Photo courtesy of Campbell Collections of the University of KwaZulu-Natal (d07-145).*

that ilobolo was granted to a woman's family primarily as an exchange for women's reproductive capacities. Indeed, a wife's infertility could lead to the ilobolo given for her being returned to her husband's family.[8] And among young men and women, ilobolo stirred emotions in part because it necessitated a profound commitment to a new set of gendered expectations and forms of cooperation: Men and women, as adults, would embark on a joint but contested project of building an umuzi, one led by a man but heavily dependent on women.

British colonialists first settled in Natal in the early nineteenth century, and in 1879 they extended their geographical reach into Zululand after defeating the independent Zulu Kingdom. In the early colonial period, settlers exhibited a desperate need for African labor, especially male labor. This hunger for land and labor shaped the view that love was absent from African society. Aware of women's vital economic contribution to umuzi, some settlers blamed loveless gender relations for men's ability to remain idle themselves; uppermost in their minds were the practices of "forced marriages," polygamy, and ilobolo that were said to subordinate women. These concerns contributed to the passing in 1869 of an act on customary marriages that legislated against "forced marriage" by making compulsory the presence of an "official witness" at customary weddings to protect women (Welsh 1971).[9] Settlers' perceptions that the state must free love from the restrictive clutches of African society can be further gleaned from dictionary definitions at the time. To help define the word *uthando* (love), the author of the first Zulu dictionary, Bishop Colenso, used the phrase *uHulemente ute izintombi azitshaye ngotando, zingabotshelwa emadodeni,* which was translated as "the Government says that girls should choose through love, and not be compelled to husbands."[10]

But seemingly rigid controls on marriage in African society in the early colonial period coexisted with strong expressions of passion and choice—categories, it must be noted, that had a different meaning among isiZulu speakers than among settlers influenced by ideas of liberal individualism. Indeed, there was no automatic contradiction between young people having choice in whom they marry and the role of marriage as an instigator of new social alliances, a situation consolidated by the exchange of gifts between kinship groups. Marital choice could lay a foundation for the spousal cooperation necessary to build a successful umuzi and forge stable kinship alliances. While "forced marriage" did occur, many aspects of Zulu society, including the isiZulu language itself, legitimized courting desire and choice.[11] For example, the verb *ukushela* (translated as "burning with desire for") was used when a man proposed love to a woman, and the verb *ukuqoma* (translated as "to choose") was used when a woman responded favorably.[12]

Premarital lovers in Zulu society also engaged in intimate acts that would have shocked Victorian society, especially because of the relative independence of single women.[13] Thus *ukuhlobonga/ukusoma* was a form of "thigh sex" that young men and women took part in with relative freedom, and sometimes with multiple partners, so long as the woman did not fall pregnant. There are also signs of the risks that some young people could take in order to be with their lovers. The most well-known illustration of this point is the case of the *inGcugce* age set of girls who in the 1870s flouted King Cetshwayo's order to marry an older age set/regiment and ran away with their sweethearts, only for many of the young rebels to be captured and brutally killed.[14]

It was to this complex and fluid setting that missionaries and settlers sought to bring an often singular idea of romantic love. Women were expected to be the main beneficiaries of romantic love, and there is no question that some women seized on liberal ideas of choice to counter patriarchal customs such as *ukungena* (levirate marriage, when a deceased husband is replaced by his brother).[15] But Christian ideas of propriety could also restrict women's sexual freedom. In the early twentieth century, African men, the colonial authorities, and missionaries directed increased attention toward preserving African women's "purity" (Chanock 1985; Marks 1989). In part as a consequence, there is strong evidence that women's ability to court multiple lovers—to express intimacy and enjoy pleasure through hlobanga-ing with more than one man—diminished at the beginning of the twentieth century (Mark Hunter 2005b, 2005c). Of course, the sources from this period are limited, and we can only speculate on the meanings that surrounded love. But it is clear that colonialism was not a unilinear force that was simply liberating love and women from the strangleholds of exchange. Rather than existing as polar opposites, love and exchange were actively embroiled. I now turn to the way that wage labor helped to enmesh love in the joint but contested project of "building a home."

Divided Love: Migrancy, Segregation, and Apartheid

In 1910, Natal was brought together with the Cape, Transvaal, and Orange Free State to establish the Union of South Africa, a territory now under the jurisdiction of whites of Afrikaner and British backgrounds. In the early segregationist period, the state entrenched the foundations of white minority control, namely pass laws, racial segregation, and the rule of Africans by "traditional" authorities. As restrictions on African use of land began to bite in the early twentieth century, some African men survived as sharecroppers or labor tenants on white farms or moved semipermanently to urban areas. The majority, however, were restricted to languishing "native reserves" and destined to become migrants in the country's gold and diamond mines and factories. Figures collected in the 1940s suggest that about four times as many men as women in their twenties were absent from rural KwaZulu-Natal (Kark 1950). The vagaries of migrant labor and relative lack of restrictions on women in urban areas (it was only in the post-1948 apartheid era that legislation was passed requiring women as well as men to carry passes) led some women to reject marriage and move to cities. Moreover, a small number of often well-educated women moved temporarily to urban areas before marrying near their rural homes (on female circular migrants in what is today the North West province, see Bozzoli 1991).

But for the most part, women remained in rural areas where they were expected to marry and embark on the project of building a rural umuzi—a project captured by the powerful Zulu metaphor *ukwakha umuzi,* or "to build a home."

Prior to the influence of migrant labor, marriage in South Africa was not a stable, unchanging institution, and extramarital affairs were one sign of this fact (Delius and Glaser 2004). Migrant labor certainly accentuated marital tensions; yet marital rates remained high. The onset of migrant labor, however, did occasion a profound shift in the flow of resources surrounding marriage. Young men's entry into the labor market and ability to save cattle or cash for ilobolo helped to wrest control over marriage away from fathers, a change that increased generational tensions (Carton 2000). The harsh world of migrant labor, which caused lovers to be separated for long periods, therefore somewhat ironically provided an economic basis for ideas of choice central to the ideology of romantic love. By the midcentury, men typically worked for several years in order to pay ilobolo for a wife whom they chose. By this time, economic circumstances meant that few marriages were polygamous, a fact that was also in tune with the deepening penetration of Christian ideas of monogamous "love" marriages.

Marriage raised a man's status to that of household head. But, in contrast to the nineteenth century, a man was required to suffer the ignominy of working for whites to maintain this role, a situation that could involve him being addressed as a "boy." Unsurprisingly, the long absence of men from their rural homes stimulated sporadic domestic conflicts. But men and women also had a joint interest in building a strong productive homestead. The biggest threat to this project undoubtedly came when migrant men or rural women abandoned their rural homes for lives in the city. To discourage men from doing so, both men and women circulated a powerful vocabulary around manliness that sought to condemn absconding (on narratives of "purity" that increased controls on women's mobility, see Marks 1989). The act of a man abandoning his home for the evils of the town was harshly condemned through the verb *ukubhunguka* ("to abandon one's home"). Moreover, *isahluleki* (literally, "a failure") was a damning word used to describe a man who failed to support his marital home. Later, we shall see how this word is now used to criticize a man who does not support his "girlfriend."

This basic life path and resultant masculinities profoundly molded courting and conceptions of love in the twentieth century. When describing their early courting experiences, elderly female informants typically combined a narrative whereby love came from the heart, which suggests that their body drove their mind, with more prosaic accounts about what constituted a good man.[16] Intertwined with emotions, therefore, were more practical considerations. Central to this was a man's ability to marry and then support umuzi at a time when women's agricultural contributions were being undermined by land shortages in rural areas. Without marriage, a woman was a perpetual girl, dependent on her father and unable to give birth to a legitimate child. Qualities that women fell in love with—reliability, industriousness, and thriftiness—became expressed first in men's saving of ilobolo through wage labor, a gift that usually amounted to eleven cows.[17] As one eighty-year-old lady told me, remembering courting: "If a boy would come to me and tell me that he loves me, I would ask him what he can do for me since he says that he loves me." She elaborated that this meant ilobolo payments to her father and not gifts to herself.

The centrality of marriage and "building a home" to men's identity also shaped the way that men fell in love. As already stated, polygamy declined rapidly in the twentieth century. Thus the situation that Bell (1995) describes in Kenya, whereby a man's first wife could fulfill family obligations while subsequent wives could be motivated by passion, rarely occurred. A single spouse was expected to satisfy a partner's many expectations, although extramarital affairs were not uncommon. Elderly men who grew up in rural areas told me they were attracted to women with beauty but also recount how they selected a wife because she was *khutele* (hardworking) and showed *inhlonipho* (respect).[18] In particular, for a woman to be seen as marriageable, she was required to demonstrate *hlonipha* (respect)—to bend a knee when serving food, avert her eyes from men and elders, stoop with both hands on her knees when asking a question, and adopt a generally chaste demeanor. Missionaries and Christian men valued women's purity too. Indeed, they saw this not only as necessary to protect social hierarchies but as a prerequisite for the divine relationship between God and his subjects—an outlook signaled by the phrase "the body is the temple of God."[19]

In large part because of the economic and symbolic centrality of marriage to society, it was not gifts from men to their lovers that stirred the most emotions but the gift of ilobolo that was given to a girlfriend's father, often in installments lasting several years. There is no doubt that increased levels of male migrant labor, growing rural impoverishment, and the introduction of money increased the ease with which sex was exchanged in twentieth-century South Africa, especially in urban areas. This includes "prostitute" relations.[20] Yet this was by no means a universal experience. It appears that if a rural woman was lured to a man through gifts, she could be branded as loose. Her love was not true love, ultimately realized in marriage, but a fast and shallow love symbolized by the city. That sex-gift exchanges were for the most part rare in rural areas is evidenced by Absolom Vilakazi's (1962) rich rural ethnography *Zulu Transformations* and my interviews with elderly informants carried out much later. Vilakazi (1962, 49) reported great shock in the Valley of a Thousand Hills when asking about courting gifts: "The boy would be accused of trying to bribe the girl to love him." He continued: "A girl who accepted gifts from a suitor would impugn her honour and damage the reputation of the girls of her lineage who would then be regarded as women who sell their love and virtue." Interviews that I conducted with elderly rural informants also suggest that for most unmarried rural women, much more important than any short-term gifts a suitor may give her was his commitment to marriage and building umuzi. While some informants said that gifts were given from boyfriend to girlfriend, they were adamant that a woman would not abandon a man if these gifts were not forthcoming. Vilakazi's use of the verb "bribe" (in isiZulu, *gwaza*) suggests that gift giving to attract women would be seen as improper, even immoral, interventions. Similarly, my elderly informants used the word *umkhonzo* to describe gifts given in rural areas. To *khonza* is to pay respects or send compliments (you *khonzela* a chief to show that you are under his authority), which suggests that gifts were aimed at stirring remembrance and not at bestowing material benefit.[21]

In the stage of life before a man started to *lobola* (give bridewealth for) a woman, therefore, rich men could have more girlfriends than poor men, not because they had a larger amount of disposable money for gifts (as is largely the case today) but because they had a greater ability to marry, demonstrated by their father's well-stocked cattle kraal or their success in finding work. Men could have multiple girlfriends—a privilege they sought to deny women—but those who subscribed to ideals of dominant masculinity would deride men as being *isoka lamanyala* if they "played with" too many partners (*isoka* is a playboy, and *amanyala* is dirt or a disgraceful act; see Mark Hunter 2005c). Rather than falling in love with a flashy man who showered her with gifts, women tended to fall in love with men who demonstrated the attributes of hard work, sacrifice, and commitment, values necessary to complete lobola. Yet, and this is a vital point, once men were married, their dependence on migrancy meant that gifts became rerouted to support the homestead and became signifiers of men's continued love for their wives and families. The privileges associated with being umnumzana had become fused with the responsibility to provide for umuzi.

There is, however, some evidence of non-prostitute sex exchanges in parts of South Africa, perhaps most notably the accounts of *amadikazi* women described so vividly by Monica Wilson (née Hunter).[22] Another revealing example of their existence is when certain extramarital affairs involved material exchanges and could be met with guarded social approval. In rural KwaZulu-Natal, women's extramarital relations were talked about through the metaphor of the pot (*ibhodwe*) and the top (*isidikiselo*), the pot being the man "who had paid cows" and the top the secondary lover. An *isidikiselo* was usually described as being more morally defensible than *ishende* (a more derogatory term for "secret lover"). Indeed, the man's family could sometimes connive in securing an isidikiselo for a lonely wife. These types of isidikiselo relations therefore operated in an ambiguous moral space. Though a woman was married and expected to remain faithful, her husband's absence for long periods meant that an isidikiselo's meeting of her sexual and monetary needs could be seen as congruent with the maintenance of an umuzi's integrity. When extramarital affairs supported the umuzi, they could enjoy the sanction of the husband's family; when they were motivated by lust or greed, they could be called ishende.

These forms of exchange, and the melding of ideas of love with support, jostled and were infused with growing values of romantic love. In this volume, Lynn Thomas describes the way in which a missionary-educated elite debated love in the pages of *Bantu World* in the 1930s. Two decades later, the state rapidly expanded the provision of state schooling, albeit at a dismally poor standard. One effect of mass schooling was the introduction of new social spaces and media through which young people could court. The growth of schooling also coincided with the expansion of formal urban townships and the increased acceptance of Christianity. Signaling the rise of an urban literate group was the growing popularity of *Drum* magazine, launched at the beginning of the 1950s. *Drum,* although itself a site of struggle, was in general bold and uncompromising in its belief that courting should be a matter decided between individuals and not kin. *Drum* also helped to circulate a vocabulary of love that included the words *darling* and *sweetie* that were employed in love letters of the time (see Mutongi, this volume, on this trend in East Africa). In contrast to the older *Bantu World,* it also saw penetrative sex as a vital expression of love. Yet if modern ideas and spaces of love provided a site for renegotiating gender relations—in ways that I can barely touch on here—most women did not lose sight of the provider role that an umnumzana was expected to play. A good man—one to fall in love with—was still a committed provider even if he might now be an urban umnumzana (a word that quickly broadened its definition from rural "household head" to also mean urban "gentleman").

Economic Crisis and Sex-Money Gifts

The last three decades have been marked by profound, if rarely recognized, changes in the political economy of sex (Mark Hunter 2007). Marital rates have plummeted, and it is extremely rare to find young men and women setting up a rural or an urban marital home; one-roomed *imijondolo* (roughly, "shacks") in burgeoning informal settlements are the type of household increasing most rapidly in the post-apartheid period.[23] According to the most recent population census, less than 30 percent of African men and women over fifteen years of age are married.[24] These dramatic shifts, coupled with rising unemployment, envelope love in more fragile relations.

In South Africa, a country whose social landscape combines state-of-the-art industrial production and languishing rural areas, gendered inequalities are driven by men's advantageous position in the labor market—although this must be qualified. While men still dominate the highest paying jobs in the formal and informal sectors, many are not employed in stable work and fail to act as providers within marriage. From the mid-1970s, unemployment began to rise dramatically to its current rate of over 40 percent nationally. Educated and employed women have long pressed for marriage on more equal terms and been prepared to forgo wedlock for independence. But the collapse of men's provider role in recent decades greatly accentuated a decline in marriage. A further dramatic change from the mid-1970s is the widespread adoption of biomedical forms of contraception. Cynically implemented by the apartheid state to reduce African population growth (Brown 1987), contraception became a contested terrain, especially between women and elders and men and women (on contestations over fertility in Kenya, see L. Thomas 2003). Most significantly for this chapter, the widespread adoption of contraception served to separate penetrative sex from fertility in ways that greatly facilitated sex for money exchanges.

In the post-apartheid period, these political economic and demographic dynamics have been exacerbated. The middle class is the main beneficiary of the post-apartheid dispensation. Now, an increasingly racially mixed middle class dates in distinctive ways (although still predominantly along "racial" lines), embracing spaces of leisure that include shopping malls, beaches, and restaurants. In isiZulu, the new pursuit of leisure is denoted by the increased use of the verb *ukungcebeleka* (roughly, to "go out"). But for poorer South African women, gifts from boyfriends to girlfriends can provide a vital means of survival. If the apparent struggle between romantic love and "forced marriages" was decisively won by the former, images such as the

FIGURE 5.2 loveLife billboard. Responding to the materiality of sex today, this billboard sponsored by the AIDS prevention group loveLife promotes the "gift of love." Chocolates—gifts closely associated with romance—are an attempt to place gifts within a romantic love paradigm where they are valued as being unique and thoughtful and not simply for their material worth. But, with unemployment in some areas running at 60 or 70 percent, most boyfriend-to-girlfriend gifts serve more immediate purposes. *Reproduced with permission of loveLife, c. 2003.*

loveLife billboard describe an apparent dichotomy today between money and love as material transactions have become vitally important to relationships (see Cole and Smith, this volume). So, has love been squeezed out by money and sex?

THE SEXUAL ECONOMY: WHAT'S LOVE GOT TO DO WITH IT?

Today, men's gifts to girlfriends are one symptom of heightened gendered inequalities in post-apartheid South Africa. In some cases, women's livelihoods depend on gifts, for example when monetary gifts mean access to food. In other instances, however, women can demand consumer goods such as cell phones and flashy clothes. Consumption has long been an indicator of status in South Africa, but in the post-apartheid period advertisers have cleverly realigned consumption with ideas of freedom (Bertelsen 1998). Widespread electrification over the last two decades has meant that most South Africans, especially in urban areas, have access to TVs and are bombarded with Hollywood films and TV programs that embroil love and consumption in a "romantic utopia" (see Illouz 1997 on the United States).

Indeed, love has become something of a metaphor for social mobility in this post-apartheid consumer society; just as "love conquers all," anyone can move from "rags to riches" in the new South Africa. At times during the following discussion with three young women in Sundumbili township in 2003, love is expressed in romantic terms; it suggests feelings, sentiment, and passion, and can be directed toward only one man. But all three young women combine narratives that "money can't buy love" with the view that gifts can foster love, and these gifts can sometimes be consumer items. The provider love that this chapter has traced is now reconfigured in new ways and with a new intensity, as Dumazile explains:

> Dumazile: Some women do these things [take gifts] because they have no money. She loves the one who is already her boyfriend, but the problem is that he does not do anything for her. Then another boy will *shela* [propose love to] her and she discovers that this one has money, so she will love him too.

Qondeni elaborates the way in which multiple partners can be presented to men:

> Qondeni: I don't think there is a boy who would accept the fact that you have many lovers and yet say nothing about that situation. When he comes to me he will ask if I am involved. Then I will either tell him that I am single or that there is someone I am involved with and that he will be the second one. Then to the third one I won't say that he is the third I will say that he is number two. . . .

But the romantic view, the perspective that love conquers all, was expressed when I asked what would happen if the number one boyfriend lost his job. Hlengiwe replied:

> Hlengiwe: If you really love the number one boyfriend truly, there is nothing that can change because you love the others for their money only.

These three young women therefore express a paradox: They claim that men's ability to provide for their girlfriends provides evidence of love, yet they also argue that a more pure love rests tantalizingly outside of material relations.

Consider the sense of betrayal that envelopes many relationships and is rooted in men's inability to provide for and marry women as they did in the past. Even financially supportive boyfriends can be treated with some scorn if they do not eventually pay bridewealth for a woman. One derisory name given to boyfriends who have "done nothing" is *iO*. Township residents were unable to tell me the source of iO, but one said that they were taught at school that *O* meant zero, nothing, and that the men today cannot adequately provide for, or marry, a woman (*O* is also used to refer to a man in Afrikaans). In some circumstances, women can mock boyfriends—although usually not to their faces—by positioning multiple boyfriends through idioms such as the minister of finance (who provides gifts), minister of transport (who has a car), and minister of entertainment (who takes a woman out). At times, women can also seize on the language of "50/50" found in the new democracy to position themselves as equal citizens; they now have the right to play men at their own game of having multiple partners. A generation ago, women fell in love with a man who showed promise of providing love through saving ilobolo and then supporting an umuzi. Now the central question for many women is who will furnish the most generous gifts outside of marriage.

In this regard, women's evocation of the male "provider" masculinity is central to the unfolding of relationships. Men are well aware that unless they can make a case that they are saving resources to lobola a woman at a future date, they must support an unmarried girlfriend with whom they are in love. Despite, or perhaps because of, the contemporary emphasis on gender equality, many women do not discard the patriarchal male provider role but rework it to place new demands on men. If in the past a man provided love through supporting a wife, today he provides love by giving gifts to a girlfriend. The broadening of the meaning of the insult *isahluleki* is strong evidence of these changes: It is used by women today to scorn not only a married man who fails to support his family but also an unmarried man who fails to support his girlfriend. And, as stated, support is thought of not only in terms of survival items; in the post-apartheid period, the quickening beat of consumption is seen when consumer items are presented by men to their girlfriends (for illuminating accounts of the consumption boom and sex-money exchanges in postsocialist Madagscar, see Cole 2004; for an account of Senegal, see Nyamnjoh 2005).

Disposable income and consumption are now vital if men are to attract multiple women, a far cry from the days when women desired thrifty men who would lobola them. Poorer men are often extremely resentful of better off men, not simply because they consume expensive goods but because they are able to secure multiple girlfriends. As a result, while some men can defend the provider ideology that underpins gift exchanges, seeing it as reinforcing "traditional" values of male power, other men can argue that it is no longer appropriate. Women are, it is said, no longer after real love but only money, and some now earn more than men. As the following musical example illustrates, men and women are redrawing the battle lines over provider masculinity. In 2000, the popular U.S. band Destiny's Child released the song "Independent Women." The hit became something of an anthem for many South African women who looked up to the success of the all-women African American group. The chorus begins: "All the women who are independent throw your hands up at me." But a year later, the male South African music stars Mandoza and Mdu produced a strong riposte. Their hit track, called "50/50," deliberately mimicked the rhythm and tune of "Independent Women," though with a chorus that went: "*wonke umfazi oindependent* let's go 50/50" (every woman is independent let's go 50/50). Challenging key tenets of the provider masculinity, the two male artists' lyrics urged women to pay 50/50 if they want equality.

Yet despite the existence of multiple partners, many relationships extend for long periods. Love is embroiled in a set of reciprocal obligations that might include monetary gifts, affection, emotional support, domestic labor, and sex.[25] It can be sustained for many years, or last only a few hours, days, or months. These sets of obligations are embodied in real feelings, and the strength, terms, and duration of the bond evolve over time. And it is during acts of betrayal that the "rules of the game" come to the surface most acutely. When sexual fidelity is central to a relationship implicitly or explicitly, a person cheating can cause stress; at other times, a woman can fall out of love with a man when he fails to support her or their child.[26]

Carefully crafted love letters still circulate (see below) but are usually said to be have been replaced by SMS (cell phone) text messages. Overcoming geographical barriers, cell phones are the most important ways in which lovers keep in touch privately, sometimes with more than one person. Below are five text messages between long-term lovers collected by my research assistant, a woman in her mid-twenties. These suggest the ways in which love is intertwined with expectations of support and assistance as well as physical attraction.

> *Sthandwa ngilambile ngicela uzopheka ukhiye kwanextdoor* see you after work I love u. (my love I am hungry please can you cook the key is next door see you after work I love u.) [young man, thirty, to young woman, twenty-six; two-year relationship]

> Baby *ngithi angikwazise ukuthi ngiyakuthanda, ngicela uziphathe kahle* (Baby, I want you to know that I love you, please behave yourself) [young woman, twenty-three, to young man, twenty-four; six months staying together]

I'm all alone in bed hoping you will join me, naked I'm dying to have sex with u. Reply pls. [young woman, twenty-six, to young man, twenty-seven; one-and-a-half-year relationship]

Angiyeki ukucabanga ngawe you are the most important thing that ever happened to me *ngiyakuthanda* lovey (I am not stopping thinking about you are the most important thing that ever happened to me I love you lovey) [young man, twenty-seven, to young woman, twenty-six; nine-and-one-half-month relationship]

Sthandwa sami anginayo imali yokugibela this week emsebenzini pls help I love you (my lover I don't have money for transport to get to work this week pls help I love you) [young woman, twenty-four, to young man, twenty-four; eleven-month relationship]

There is now an established literature on well-educated, professional, urban women in Africa partially rejecting marriage in favor of relationships with men that involve (but cannot be reduced to) sex-money exchanges (for example, Powdermaker 1962 on the Copperbelt; Schuster 1979 on Lusaka; and Dinan 1983 on Ghana). For sure, in South Africa today, middle-class women are in a strong economic position (as they have been for much of the century) to challenge androcentric ideas of romance and marriage. In one edition of her weekly newspaper column called "Bitch's Brew," for instance, media celebrity Nomakhula Roberts gave forthright advice on how to be a *Nyatsi*, here defined as a high-class mistress to a married man (Roberts 2004). But, in general, if both men and women are more skeptical of marriage, the institution still enjoys a high status. In some cases, ilobolo among central lovers will have begun or will be planned, and a woman who is being lobola'ed tends to be looked on with envy by her peers. Indeed, precisely because of ilobolo's association with men's commitment and respectability, more young women than men often support the custom. It is an unparalleled way to test a man's character and his commitment to "true love," in part because the first ilobolo payment is a significant one (roughly, four cattle or the cash equivalent).

Marriage, the "happily ever after" of romantic love relationships, therefore hovers perennially around modern ideas of love (see Swidler 2001 on the profound associations between marriage and love in the United States). It interacts with expectations of love that allow women to call on men for support and men to call on women to enact the duties of a girlfriend, for instance, sex. The following letter, collected by my research assistant, is from a twenty-four-year-old woman to her boyfriend of the same age, a man who provides her with gifts. It demonstrates how multiple conceptions of love can frame relationships, including those that foreground marriage and the pleasure of sex. The letter was written in large capital letters, and the spellings and grammar are reproduced as originally written.

DEAR SWEETHEART
IT'S A PLEASURE TO ME TO WRITE THIS LETTER TO YOU. I JUST WANT TO LET YOU KNOW HOW MUCH YOU MEAN TO ME BABY. I LOVE YOU LIKE CRAZY SINCE THE FIRST DAY I LAY MY EYES TO YOU FOR BETTER I LOVE YOU, FOR WORSE I LOVE YOU, IN JOY I LOVE YOU, IN SORROW I LOVE YOU. I LOVE YOU WHERE YOU ARE. AND ABOUT LAST NIGHT THANK YOU I CAN'T FORGET IT YOU MAKE ME FEEL LIKE A NATURAL WOMAN. BABY YOU DO SATISFY ME ESPECIALLY IN BED YOU LIKE "O" I CAN'T SAY IT I CAN'T DESCRIBE IT. BUT I LOVE U FOR IT AND ALWAYS WHEN I'M NOT WITH YOU I KEEP MISSING YOU HONEY I WISH TO SLEEP NEXT TO YOU ALL THE TIME. IF I AM A MEN I WOULD ASK YOU TO MARRY ME BECAUSE I DON'T WANT TO LOOSE YOU SWEETY. . . .
YOU ARE THE MEN OF MY DREAMS
ALWAYS LOVE YOU!!!
ALWAYS MISS YOU!!!
PLEASE DON'T STOP LOVING ME
TAKE CARE
ALL MY LOVE

The aggressive pursuit of men for gifts as described in this chapter, however, is only one response by poorer women to social conditions in contemporary South Africa. The HIV/AIDS epidemic in particular casts a deadly and visible shadow over women who exchange sex for gifts and signifies the dangers of materialistic values. Evoking the language and acts of *ukuhlonipha* (respect) to position themselves as "pure," some women can yearn for an old-fashioned love, if not the patriarchy that it comes with. The chapter has already mentioned women's support for ilobolo, a patriarchal custom that nevertheless symbolizes an old-fashioned chivalrous love. Reinvented traditions such as virginity testing, a practice revitalized in KwaZulu-Natal at the time of AIDS, also allow women to differentiate themselves from their peers (Scorgie 2002). The church too is an important site where women can present themselves as respectable, loyal, and chaste. There can be real consequences of doing so: Some women in my research site eschew "transactional sex" and eventually do marry a man who sees them as different and of a higher morality—as still believing in an uncontaminated love.

Conclusion

A number of scholars have elevated examples of sex-money exchanges in Africa to argue that sex is inherently instrumental in African society. But the prevalence of sex-money exchanges today in South Africa—a dynamic often said to fuel the AIDS epidemic—should not be seen as a residue of an instrumentalism ultimately rooted in African "tradition." There is no automatic connection between kinship, marriage, and "transactional sex." Prior to the restrictive morality of Christianity, sex may not have been imbued with a godly guilt; yet it was circumscribed by a definite set of morals. Neither was precolonial love wholly subsumed by patriarchal kinship relations. Yet if love has long been present among isiZulu speakers, meanings of love in the colonial era became increasingly entangled with men's growing role as absent providers. Romantic love—typified by marital choice and the companionate marriage—jostled with and infused the provider masculinity that was to dominate the twentieth century.

In the contemporary period, most men are failing to marry and provide for wives, but many can satisfy a more contingent form of love by supporting girlfriends. Women are active participants in this process, contesting love in new ways. On the one hand, they justify the milking of men because of men's failure to support wives; on the other, they draw on long-standing masculinities that position men as providers to demand gifts outside of marriage. But these gendered struggles are a far cry from Anthony Giddens's (1992) popular account of a wholesale move from romantic love to a more contingent "confluent love" characterized by its existence only as far it suits both parties (see Goody 1998). This perspective is ethnocentric and does not reflect the realities of contemporary South Africa. The changes Giddens describes for the West, which are rooted in women's greater economic and social power, are barely relevant in South Africa, where huge gendered inequality still exists. What's more, these sexual exchanges are not disembodied acts: Embedded in exchanges of obligations, they require an emotional investment and involve moments of deep intimacy and pleasure, as well as at times the physical pain of violence.[27] Sex exchanges in post-apartheid South Africa are a manifestation of profound gender, class, and race divisions, but they cannot be understood without factoring love as a fundamental social force.

ACKNOWLEDGMENTS

Thanks to Jennifer Cole, Lynn Thomas, and the anonymous reviewers for insightful comments on earlier drafts. This research was funded by fellowships from the Wenner-Gren Foundation for Anthropological Research and the International Dissertation Field Research Fellowship Program of the Social Science Research Council with funds provided by the Andrew W. Mellon Foundation.

NOTES

1. For an excellent summary of the inadequacy of the category of "prostitution" to describe many sex exchanges in Africa, see Standing (1992). For a rich critique of prevailing understanding of "sex in development," see Adams and Pigg (2005). I follow these authors in thinking about the changing meaning of "sex" as it comes into tension with "development"; it should be noted that it is for practical purposes that I do not use scare quotes around the word *sex*. In South Africa, a number of ethnographic studies have argued that everyday sex-money exchanges can fuel multiple sexual partners, sometimes across large age differences (see Mark Hunter 2002, 2007; Selikow, Zulu, and Cedras 2002; LeClerc-Madlala 2004). For a review of the broader sub-Saharan literature, see Luke (2003); and for a particularly interesting study in Malawi, see Swidler and Watkins (2005). Quantitative data suggests that sex exchanges may play a part in fueling AIDS: One study in South Africa found that nearly four times as many women as men aged twenty to twenty-four were HIV positive (23.9 percent compared to 6 percent) and that many young women had older partners (Human Science Research Council, 2005). For the argument that sexuality is given too much emphasis in AIDS research, see Packard and Epstein (1991) and, more recently, Stillwaggon (2006).

2. On the inherent instrumentalism of African relations, see, for instance, the Caldwells' widely quoted thesis on an "African system of sexuality" (Caldwell, Caldwell, and Quiggin 1989). Another much-quoted piece argues that "sugar daddy" relations in Ghana result in part from the fact that sexuality was "objective and instrumental" (Dinan 1983). See also, more recently, Chernoff (2003), a popular book on a West African bar girl. There are numerous accounts of how the forces of modernity have dissolved African family relations and led to prostitution; see, for example, the urban South African ethnographies written by Krige (1936a), Hellman (1948), and Longmore (1959).

3. By no means did social anthropology hold a united view on love. The classic structural-functionalist account of the Zulu, Eileen Krige's (1936b) *Social System of the Zulus*, noted elaborate courting rituals. Moreover, Monica Hunter's (1936) *Reaction to Conquest* and Isaac Shapera's (1940) *Married Life in an African Tribe*, both of which embraced the study of social change, are among the best sources on love in the early colonial period. On Schapera and Hunter, see Thomas (this

volume). The recent volume *Love and Globalization* edited by Padilla et al. (2007) is a good source of some of the important new anthropological work on love.

4. See Cornwall (2001) and Rebhun (1999) for important attempts to go beyond the love-money dichotomy in Nigeria and Brazil. See Lipset (2004) for a fascinating account of how modernity did not lead to romance in Papua New Guinea.

5. For recent historical accounts relevant to the arguments here, see Carton (2000), Moodie (1994), and Mark Hunter (2005b, 2005c).

6. On this point in Brazil, see particularly Gregg (2003).

7. For isiZulu-speaking areas, the most influential analysis is Guy (1979, 1987). See also Hanretta (1998) for reviews of some of this literature. The Natal and Zulu-land region formed the basis of what became the province of KwaZulu-Natal in the post-apartheid period.

8. As Jeffreys (1951) put it, ilobolo represented "child price" and not "bride price." The return of cattle because a woman was "without issue" is illustrated in many civil court cases; see, for example, *Vanganye v. Makanyezi* (Durban Archives, 1/ESH 2/1/1/2/1, 1907).

9. The idea that at this time British society itself exhibited free choice in marriage must be questioned. Around this time, Engels (1972 [1884]) was penning his famous *Origin of the Family, Private Property, and the State* that characterized Western bourgeois marriages as marriages of convenience.

10. This was contained in the second edition of the dictionary (1878) but not the first (1861). The colonial voice was by no means unitary: Bishop Colenso himself rebelled against many elements of mainstream settler thinking, particularly the view that Africans should not be allowed to convert to Christianity unless they withdrew from polygamous marriages. On the extraordinary career of Colenso, see Guy (1983), and on colonial conflicts over marriage and ilobolo, see Welsh (1971).

11. Evidence for "forced marriages" is contained in the accounts of some women who arrived at early missionary stations; see Etherington (1978).

12. For instance, see Bryant's (1905) dictionary.

13. That apparent Victorian silences around "sexuality" amounted to not simply "repression" but an enactment of modern discourses that in fact produced "sexuality" is described by Foucault (1978).

14. See Hanretta (1998) for the claim that we must be cautious in interpreting this episode since Cetshwayo may have had political reasons for wanting to destroy the *inGcugce* age set. Another example of human sacrifice in the name of love comes from Mpondoland where Monica Hunter (1936, 189) describes a cliff called *iNtombi nenDoda* ("the girl and the man"), named after the tragedy of a girl who, being forced to marry a man she did not love, bound herself to her true lover and flung herself over the edge.

15. Thomas McClendon (2002) explores tensions around ukungena rooted in Christianity. From contemporary testimonies of elderly informants, I got a sense of the deep unpopularity of the practice with most women.

16. It was not only in South Africa, however, that passion was melded with more

practical ideas of marriage. Ann Swidler (2001) argues that Americans combine a "mythic" movie image culture of love with a self-conscious "realist" understanding of love. Moreover, ideas of men as providers are common in many settings. Beth Bailey (1989) shows the growth of dating in 1920s America with the expectation that men take responsibility for the financial side of dates. Some writers now stress how in parts of the West men's provider status is under threat as a consequence of women's movement into the labor market; see, for instance, McDowell (2003).

17. Ilobolo is one of the most revered traditions in KwaZulu-Natal, but the customary payment of eleven cattle (this typically being ten for the bride's father and one for the mother) was actually set by the colonial administration in 1869 to limit the cost of marriage and thus allow more men to enter wedlock (it was not set at a fixed amount elsewhere in South Africa). See Welsh (1971).

18. Bryant (1949, 566) noted that "to such physical beauty must too be added the moral virtues of gentle submissiveness and willing service, agricultural and domestic diligence, and healthy generative organs."

19. See Gaitskell (1982) on Christianity and domestic femininity.

20. As a consequence of migrant labor, prostitution became more prevalent in urban areas, and migrant men's income could be distributed through sexual liaisons in rural areas (see, for instance, Van Onselen (1982); Bonner (1990) in urban areas; Spiegel (1981) in rural areas).

21. I am not giving a great deal of attention here to urban areas. Nevertheless, I do not believe that there is evidence of substantial sex-money exchanges among *never married* women in urban areas. Laura Longmore's (1959) account showed many examples of poor married women dependent on men; yet she also suggests that in South African townships there was a trend whereby young *unmarried* women could give gifts to *unmarried* men in the 1950s (1959, 26). Other accounts show that men could attract young women through gifts but also describe gifts from women to men. In an East London township, Pauw (1963) notes that gift giving was generally reciprocal, and multiple partnered relations were often avoided since women feared boyfriends' denials of paternity and men were concerned about losing control over relationships. Similarly, Levin (1947, 22) discussing Langa township reports mainly reciprocal gifts: *"During courtship men try to win the favour of girls by giving them presents such as slabs of chocolate, jewellery, and scarves. Women, in turn, are said to give their boyfriends presents, such as ties and socks."* It appears that, compared to today at least, the importance of gifts in premarital relations in urban areas was relatively minor.

22. Hunter (1936) suggests that although not explicitly trading sex, this group of women could benefit materially from sexual relations, including with married men. But, we must note, the amadikazi women were comprised of particular groups, namely women who were divorced, widowed, or bore children before marriage; in rural settings, these lived at their fathers' homesteads. They were largely ineligible for marriage as first wives, generally the most prized outcome for a young woman.

23. From 1996 to 2003, the number of informal dwellings rose by 688,000 in South Africa, despite the existence of house building projects funded by the state (Pressly 2006).
24. According to census figures, the number of married people above fifteen years was as follows: 1936 – 56 percent; 1951 – 54 percent; 1960 – 57 percent; 1970 – 49 percent; 1980 – 42 percent; 1991 – 38 percent; 2001 – 30 percent (author's calculation from various census reports, Statistics South Africa, Pretoria).
25. The reciprocal nature of "gifts" (often opposed to single acts of commodity exchange) has been at the heart of a long-standing literature in economic anthropology rooted in the work of Mauss (1990 [1950]). For useful discussions, see Gregory (1982), Bloch and Parry (1989), and Piot (1999).
26. One step a person can take to promote love, even if their practical acts refute it, is to use love potions. Although these might be seen as remnants of premodern love, they are perfectly in step with modernity; there is often not seen to be a conflict between love potions, which can work through *amadlozi* (ancestors), and the more modern, rational ideas of romantic love. For a previous account of love charms in this area, see Bryant (1949).
27. I do not consider the question of violence here, although exploring love and violence together can produce important new insights. On sexual violence in South Africa, see Wood and Jewkes (2001); for an account that links sexual violence to some of the themes in this chapter, especially changing household structure, see Niehaus (2005).

Managing Men, Marriage, and Modern Love

WOMEN'S PERSPECTIVES ON INTIMACY AND MALE INFIDELITY IN SOUTHEASTERN NIGERIA

Daniel Jordan Smith

When Ifeoma recounted why she agreed to marry Chibueze, she emphasized that they were in love.[1] She told nostalgic stories about their courtship, recalling birthday presents, holiday cards with adoring inscriptions, and a romantic walk at Nike Lake, a resort catering to the growing middle-class tastes of young adults in Igbo-speaking southeastern Nigeria. At the time of our conversation in 2004, Ifeoma had been married almost fourteen years. She had four children; was the proprietor of a small shop where she sold soap, skin lotion, and other cosmetics in the market of her urbanizing village; and served as the secretary of the women's group of her church. Chibueze worked in the nearby town in a white-collar clerical job in a government office. They had built their own modest house and lived near but independently from extended kin. By all appearances—with four healthy children, her own small business, a house, and a respectable reputation in her community and church—Ifeoma had achieved the ideals of modern Igbo womanhood.

But we were talking because Ifeoma had agreed to speak with me about her husband's regular infidelity. It was not easy to get Ifeoma—or any married woman—to speak openly about her husband's extramarital sexual behavior. Prior to our meeting, I had spent several months interviewing men and women in two communities in southeastern Nigeria about their marriages. The focus of the study was to understand the relationship between transformations in marriage—especially the rise of what might be called "love marriage"—and women's risk of contracting HIV/AIDS from their husbands.[2] Because the primary mechanism of women's infection is believed to be sex with their spouses (Glynn et al. 2003)—who are generally suspected of contracting the virus through extramarital relations—much of my research centered on understanding the social organization of men's extramarital sex in the context of prevailing patterns of gender inequality. While my previous work has focused on understanding men's behavior, in this chapter my primary aim is to situate women's perceptions, experiences, and reactions to male infidelity in the context of the rise of romantic love as a relationship ideal for modern marriage.

The two communities I studied in Nigeria were Ubakala, a semi-rural but rapidly urbanizing community several miles outside the city of Umuahia, the capital of Abia State, and Owerri, a city of about 350,000 people that is the capital of Imo State.[3] Typically, I interviewed husbands while female research assistants interviewed women, on the theory that people would converse more comfortably about intimate subjects like marriage, sexuality, and infidelity with someone of the same sex. Indeed, I seemed to have little problem getting most men to tell me quite a lot about their extramarital relationships by the time we reached a third hour-long interview. Some men were more willing to talk about their past infidelities, denying that they were presently cheating on their wives. But many men spoke easily about their current extramarital relationships, indicative of a form of a masculine culture in which men talk quite comfortably to each other about such topics (D. Smith 2002, 2007b).

Married Igbo women, however, were extremely reluctant to discuss personal stories of infidelity in peer-group settings, much less with a prying anthropologist or his assistants. In our interviews with twenty-two married women, not a single one admitted to having an extramarital sexual relationship. Even more significant, only a handful reported that their husbands had ever been unfaithful, and none said she thought that her husband was currently cheating. This contrasted with reports from the same women that male infidelity is extremely common in the community and their remarkable willingness to tell stories about *other* women's problems with cheating husbands. My own interviews with the men not only contradicted women's assertions that their husbands were faithful, but in many cases revealed that, despite what they said in interviews, many women knew about, or at least suspected, their husband's infidelity.

In this chapter, I situate women's perspectives and behavioral responses to men's cheating in the context of continuities and changes that characterize contemporary marriage in southeastern Nigeria. While much of the literature, including this volume, focuses on the tensions and interconnections between intimacy and exchange in individual relationships, in looking at married women's experiences of their husbands' infidelity, I consider the contradictions that arise in marriage between love as a relationship ideal and the imperatives of social reproduction. As in many settings around the world, in southeastern Nigeria intimate spousal communication, mutual sexual pleasure, shared decision making, and trust seem to be more valued and more openly discussed in Ifeoma and Chibueze's generation than in the past (Ahearn 2001; Hirsch 2003; Hirsch and Wardlow 2006; D. Smith 2001). In some respects, it appears that the rise of romantic love as a privileged rationale for choosing a spouse and assessing the quality of a marriage is in tension with the notion that marriage is a form of social exchange, between families and communities and also between husbands and wives. But as recent research attests—including chapters in this volume (e.g., Cole and Hunter)—intimacy and exchange are not always and not inherently opposed (Cornwall 2002; Rebhun 1999). In the context of marriage, the dynamics between intimacy and exchange are shaped not only by the unfolding of individual relationships, but also by the collective project of social reproduction, a fact that can both exacerbate and help reconcile the conflicts that result from infidelity.

With regard to African marriage, the tendency has been to emphasize the rise of romantic love as conflicting with and displacing marriage's function as a mechanism of exchange between kin and communities (Harrell-Bond 1975; Little and Price 1973; Mair 1969 [1953]), often with the implication that these changes contribute to or are the result of women's empowerment (Hollos 1997; but see van der Vliet 1991). Relatively little scholarship on marriage in Africa has approached modern marriage as a site where affect and exchange can be in varying ways opposed and mutually constitutive, the perspective I adopt here. I show that as married Igbo men and women navigate the complex terrain of intimacy and exchange, the continued primacy of the fertility and family and the reputational imperatives of social reproduction shape negotiations about love, money, and infidelity.

Women's responses to male infidelity provide a revealing and instructive lens through which to examine the complex connections between economics, romance, and gender, particularly in marriages where couples see themselves as having modern relationships premised on romantic love. Even as Igbo women in southeastern Nigeria feel betrayed by a husband's unfaithfulness, they are able to manipulate a range of gendered cultural expectations about marriage to manage sometimes problematic relationships both publicly and privately. After tracing the rise of love marriage and the continuities and changes that it has entailed, I examine the intersection of intimacy and exchange as they are experienced by men and women prior to marriage, a range of experiences that both sets the stage for marriage and contrasts with marital experiences in significant ways. I then explore the gendered contours of modern Igbo marriages and explain why men cheat. Finally, I focus on understanding the reasons Igbo women mostly choose to tolerate and even help hide male infidelity. The argument explicates the continuing primacy of marriage and parenthood for the attainment of socially recognized personhood. I suggest that intimacy in marriage is heavily inflected by people's concerns about the social perceptions of their marriage and can best be understood as a kind of negotiated exchange between husband and wife. Finally, I try to show the paradoxical ways in which love marriages are both liberating and shackling for Igbo women.

Love and Marriage

In Nigeria, as across Africa, evidence indicates that people are increasingly likely to select marriage partners based, at least in part, on whether they are "in love" (Obiechina 1973; Okonjo 1992; D. Smith 2001). The emergence of romantic love as a criterion in mate selection and the increasing importance of a couple's personal emotional relationship in marriage should not be interpreted to mean that romantic love itself has only recently emerged in Nigeria. When I asked elderly Igbos about their betrothals, about their marriages, and about love, I was told numerous personal stories and popular fables that indicated a long tradition of romantic love. A number of older men and women confessed that they would have married a person other than their spouse had they been allowed to "follow the heart." Scholars have documented the existence of romantic love in Africa long before it became a widely accepted criterion for marriage (Bell 1995; Plotnicov 1995; Riesman 1972, 1981). Uchendu (1965) confirms the existence of passionate love in his study of concubinage in traditional Igbo society. Interestingly, both men and women were reportedly accorded significant socially acceptable extramarital sexual freedom and a related proverb survives to the present: *uto ka na iko* ("sweetness is deepest among lovers"). As Obiechina notes:

"The question is not whether love and sexual attraction as normal human traits exist within Western and African societies, but how they are woven into the fabric of life" (1973, 34).

Exactly when Nigerians in general and Igbos in particular began to conceptualize marriage choices in more individualistic terms, privileging romantic love as a criterion in the selection of a spouse, is hard to pinpoint. In some parts of Igboland and in many parts of Nigeria, the social acceptance of individual choice in mate selection is still just beginning. Certainly these changes occurred first in urban areas among relatively educated and elite populations (Marris 1962; Little and Price 1973). Obiechina's (1973) study of Onitsha pamphlet literature indicates that popular Nigerian literature about love, romance, and modern marriage began to emerge just after World War II. Historical accounts suggest that elements of modern marriage began even earlier in the twentieth century (Mann 1985). By the 1970s, a number of monographs about modern marriage in West Africa had been produced (e.g., Oppong 1974; Harrell-Bond 1975). Most of these accounts focused on relatively elite, urban, and educated populations.

In contemporary Igboland, the ideal that marriage should be based on romantic love has spread well beyond urban elites. Young people across a wide range of socioeconomic statuses increasingly value choosing their own spouses, and individual choice is widely associated with the notion that marriage should be based on love. It is important to recognize that ideas about what constitutes love are culturally inflected and individually variable. But in southeastern Nigeria, it is fair to say that when people talk about the importance of love for marriage, they are generally signaling the value accorded to the personal and emotional quality of the conjugal relationship. People recognize that strong bonds can develop in more traditional marriages not premised on romantic love, but when people talk about marrying for love—as they frequently do—they mean a kind of love that is associated with being modern.

As part of my dissertation research in 1996, I interviewed a village sample of just over 200 married women of reproductive age. Over 60 percent of these women reported that their marriages were choice marriages rather than arranged marriages, and, not surprisingly, the percentages were higher among younger women. The expectation of choosing one's spouse is almost universal among young people still in school. In a sample of 775 students drawn from nineteen secondary schools in the Umuahia area during the same year, over 95 percent said they expected to choose their marriage partners themselves, and the expectation was universal among 420 students I surveyed at Abia State University. Although my more recent research did

FIGURE 6.1 Nigerian wedding banner, 2004. In southeastern Nigeria, commonly displayed banners announcing an upcoming wedding ceremony frequently reference the ideals of modern marriage. *Photo by Daniel Jordan Smith, 2004.*

not entail sample surveys, every indication from participant observation and popular culture is that the ideal of love marriage has continued to grow.

The nature of social transformation driving these changes in marriage is too extensive to fully account for here, but intertwining factors include economic diversification and labor migration, urbanization, education, religious conversion, and globalization. Contemporary economic strategies hinge on rural-urban migration. As larger numbers of families move to the city in search of better education, employment, and other economic opportunities, family structure is changing. Modifications in family organization induced by economic and demographic transitions have been complemented by moral, ideological, and religious trends that also affect the institution of marriage.

The modern marriages of young couples in southeastern Nigeria are clearly different from their parents. Describing the differences between her marriage and her parents' marriage, a thirty-year-old woman married for three years said: "My father had three wives and fourteen children. Often it was every woman for herself. My husband and I have a partnership. We decide things. There is love between us." Perhaps the most concise way to contrast modern Igbo marriages with the past is to note that young couples see their marriages as a life project in which they as a couple are the primary actors and where the idea of being in love is one of the principal foundations of the relationship, whereas their parents' marriages were more obviously embedded in the structures of the extended family. The differences are most pronounced in narratives about courtship, descriptions of how husbands and wives resolve marital quarrels, and decision making about contributions to their children's education and well-being. In each of these arenas, people in more modern marriages tend to emphasize the primacy of the individual couple and their personal relationship, often in conscious opposition to the constraints imposed by ties to kin and community. For example, a forty-three-year-old teacher reported:

> For me and my wife our marriage is our business, whereas in my parents' time everything was scrutinized by the extended family. If they had any little problem everyone might become involved. We try to keep things within the married house. If we have any problem we handle it ourselves and maybe pray over it, but we don't go running to the elders broadcasting our problems here and there.

But it is important not to exaggerate these trends. Even in the most modern marriages, ties to kin and community remain strong, and the project of marriage and child rearing continues to be a social project, strongly embedded in the relationships and values of the extended family system. Scholars of West African society have long recognized the pronounced social importance of marriage and fertility in the region (Fortes 1978; Bledsoe and Pison 1994; Feldman-Savelsberg 1999). People's stories about courtship, the resolution of marital disputes, and decisions about child rearing reflect the continued importance of marriage and fertility in the community and couples' concerns about social and familial expectations for their relationships. The choice of a future spouse based on love is, in almost all cases, still subjected to the advice and consent of families. The fact that modern marriage in southeastern Nigeria remains a resolutely social endeavor creates contradictions for younger couples, who must navigate not only their individual relationships, but also the outward representation of their marriages to kin and community. Most couples seek to portray their marriages to themselves and to others as being modern, but also as morally upright. The tension between being modern and being moral is crucial to explaining the dynamics of intimacy in marriage, the motives for men's extramarital sexual relationships, and married women's responses to their husbands' infidelity.

No Romance without Finance:
Learning about Love and Exchange

Most Igbo men and women enter marriage with premarital experience in romantic and sexual relationships. With later age at marriage, a changing sexual culture that has become more accepting of premarital sex, and high rates of rural-urban migration that place unmarried young people farther away from the moral gaze of their parents, their extended families, and their communities, opportunities for premarital relationships are common. Further, sexual and romantic relationships before marriage are widely seen as markers of being modern (D. Smith 2000) but also as a sort of rehearsal for marriage (D. Smith 2004).

Of course there are many different kinds of premarital relationships, and whether they serve as a precursor to marriage depends partly on the nature of the relationship. For example, a young woman in a relationship with an older married man would almost never think of displacing the man's wife. The age and life course position of the individuals are crucial in situating the purpose, meaning, and possible outcomes of a premarital relationship. A young woman beginning university would be less likely to be "looking for a husband," as Nigerians like to say, than a woman in her late twenties, whom society views as quickly approaching the end of her marriageable years. Regardless of whether sexual relationships progress to marriage, premarital experiences create expectations that both set the stage for and contrast with the gendered division of labor that is characteristic of marriage. Of particular interest here is the dynamic between interpersonal intimacy and material exchange—or, more crudely, between love and money.

The intertwining of intimacy and exchange is colloquially captured in the widely recognized saying that there is "no romance without finance." In Nigeria it can be deployed differently by men and women to advance individual or gendered agendas, but it is also used as a kind of discourse of complaint. In addition, it stands for a more subtle reality in which the very expression of love involves gifts, economic support, and a range of material exchanges that both solidify and build on the sexual and emotional dimensions of intimate relationships (see Cole and Hunter, this volume).

Young unmarried women use the phrase "no romance without finance" to signal to their female peers that they are savvy about men and their motives and to assert agency by announcing plainly that they intend to benefit materially from any man with whom they have sex. Young women in southeastern Nigeria commonly complain that men will make promises they do not keep—particularly with regard to love and fidelity—in order to persuade women to become their lovers. Particularly in the context of urban educational institutions such as secondary schools and universities, young women commonly criticize each other's sexual decisions in terms of whether someone gave herself too easily to a man. A university student, passing judgment on her friend's recently failed relationship, voiced a strand of discourse I heard frequently with regard to the material dimension of premarital sexual relationships: "All he gave her was soap—ordinary soap. She was swept away by all his rubbish talk about love. But he was just playing her. She did not benefit at all."

Young women are collectively skeptical about men's pronouncements of love, knowing full well that many men will use the allure of romance not only to secure sexual access, but to skirt the widely shared expectation that a man should provide material support for his lover. Sometimes women seek emotional satisfaction in one relationship and economic support in another. A common situation—and certainly the common story in everyday discourse about unmarried girls who keep more than one lover—is that a woman will have an older (often married) lover from whom she seeks mainly monetary support and a younger man (perhaps a fellow student) for whom she has romantic feelings.

But it is not simply between kinds of lovers that emotion and economics compete; it is also within specific relationships. Many young women have only one boyfriend. In their relationships, men and women frequently engage in both subtle and fierce negotiations about the relative importance of love and money. At its simplest, love can often make up for a lack of material support and vice versa.

Seeing feelings and finances as in competition or as substitutable elements in sexual relationships, however, obscures the extent to which they are—in most relationships and in most people's minds—inextricably intertwined. As the introduction to this volume suggests, and as other chapters attest, love and material exchange cannot be easily separated in practice. One particularly Nigerian example is revealing. When young women in southeastern Nigeria speak of the way that men deceive them in sexual relationships, they commonly use the phrase "he played me 419." "419" is an expression connected with Nigeria's notorious scam industry, which depends on deception (D. Smith 2007a). Applied to the arena of sex and romance, it implies that a man did not deliver on his promises of love and material support. Young women can tolerate less money if there is more emotional support and affection and little or no emotional intimacy if there is a lot of money. But ultimately almost every woman wants both. Love is perceived as real only if it is backed up by a man's best effort to provide material as well as emotional support.

Women's premarital experiences prepare them for the negotiations over love, money, and fidelity that will unfold in their relationships with their husbands. But as I will suggest below, the gendered division of labor (both economic and emotional) changes in marriage, and with it the dynamics between love, money, and infidelity are also transformed. More and more women marry for love, but not only for love. They expect their husbands to be good providers, responsible fathers, and socially competent men who represent their marriages positively to the wider community. While a man's infidelity undermines a woman's hopes that romantic love is the enduring foundation of their marriage, women must navigate a number of intersecting goals, values, and social expectations in crafting their responses to a cheating husband. Before exploring women's perceptions and reactions to men's extramarital sexual behavior, it is important to understand why men act as they do.

Modern Marriage and Men's Infidelity[4]

The prevalence of married men's participation in extramarital sex in Nigeria is well documented (Karanja 1987; Orubuloye, Caldwell, and Caldwell 1991; Lawoyin and Larsen 2002; Mitsunaga et al. 2005). Conventional scholarly understandings and explanations for the phenomenon are not persuasive, however, because they tend to reproduce common stereotypes, often ignore the diversity and complexity of these relationships, and overlook the ambivalence that sometimes accompanies this behavior. As in many societies, people in southeastern Nigeria commonly attribute men's more frequent participation in extramarital sexual relationships to some sort of innate male predisposition, and this perspective is well represented in the literature (Isiugo-Abanihe 1994; Orubuloye, Caldwell, and Caldwell 1997). Some men and women interviewed in the marital case studies articulated this view. In response to a question about why married men seek extramarital lovers, a fifty-four-year-old civil engineer in Owerri repeated a pidgin English phrase heard frequently among Nigerian men: "Man no be wood. It's something men need, especially African men. You know we have a polygamous culture. This practice of marrying only one wife is the influence of Christianity. But men still have that desire for more than one woman." Only a piece of wood, he implies, lacks an outward-looking sexual appetite.

The notion that men naturally want or need multiple sexual partners is reinforced by gendered norms that produce and perpetuate a double standard about extramarital sex. Over the past two decades, I have spent scores of evenings in settings in southeastern Nigeria where married men entertain their unmarried girlfriends or talk with their male peers about their extramarital sexual experiences and partners. I remember asking a particularly colorful older Igbo man who was quite blatant in his philandering about the consequences of extramarital affairs for men and women. He replied, quite boastfully, "If I catch my wife, she is gone; if she catches me, she is gone too." In other words, not only was it unacceptable for her to have extramarital sex, it was also unacceptable for her to object to his having extramarital sex. As I will show below, while this man's claim of male privilege in the realm of extramarital sex is generally reflective of a prevailing double standard, it reveals little about the real contexts of how men and women navigate marriage and infidelity.

Despite their currency in popular and scholarly accounts, explanations of male extramarital sexual behavior in terms of innate male need or privilege are insufficient because sexual desires do not emerge or operate in a vacuum. Men's extramarital sexual behavior is socially produced and organized. From interviews with men about their extramarital relationships, from listening to men's conversations among themselves pertaining to these relationships, and from observations of men interacting with their extramarital partners in various public or semi-public settings, a number of patterns in the social organization of extramarital sex become apparent. Three sociological factors are particularly important for explaining the opportunity structures that facilitate men's participation in extramarital sexual relationships: work-related migration, the intertwining of masculinity and socioeconomic status, and involvement in predominately male peer groups that encourage or reward extramarital sexual relations.

MOBILITY AND MEN'S EXTRAMARITAL SEX

Of the twenty men interviewed in the marital case studies, fourteen reported having extramarital sex at some point during their marriages, and of the six who said they had not engaged in extramarital sex, four had been married less than five years.[5] Approximately half of all the cases of extramarital relationships described in the interviews occurred in situations where work-related mobility was a factor. Men whose work takes them away from their wives and families are more likely to have extramarital relationships, and they regularly attribute their behavior to the opportunities and hardships produced by these absences. A forty-seven-year-old civil servant whose postings regularly took him away from his family explained a relatively long-term relationship with a woman in one of the places he was transferred: "I stayed a long time without my wife. But eventually this woman befriended me. She was a widow and a very nice woman. She cooked for me and provided companionship. Later, I was transferred back home, and it was over. It was like that." While men's representations of hardship as a justification for extramarital sex contradict the realities of male privilege in Nigeria's social order, they nevertheless reflect many Nigerians' experience that labor-related migration creates not only opportunities but also pressures to become involved in extramarital relationships.

Further, extramarital relationships in the context of work-related migration can be more easily hidden from wives, family, and neighbors. Every man in the sample who admitted to having extramarital sex expressed the importance of keeping such relationships secret from their wives, but also from their extended families and their local communities. Men's motivations for keeping extramarital relationships hidden included not only a desire to maintain peace and uphold the appearance of fidelity for their wives, but also a clear concern over their own social reputations. The same man who described his relationship above explained: "I am a mature man with responsibilities in my community—in the church, in various associations. I hold offices in these organizations. I can't be seen to be running here and there chasing after women. My own son is almost a man now. How can I advise him if I am known for doing this and that?" To the degree that male infidelity is socially acceptable, it is even more strongly expected that outside affairs should not threaten a marriage, and this mandates some discretion. Many men were ambivalent about their extramarital sexual behavior, but in most cases men viewed it as acceptable given an appropriate degree of prudence so as not to disgrace one's spouse, one's self, and one's family.

MASCULINITY AND MONEY

In the vast majority of cases described in the interviews, issues of socioeconomic status, and specifically the intersection of economic and gender inequality, featured in men's accounts of their extramarital relationships. Most often, a man's relationship to his female lover included an expectation that the man provide certain kinds of economic support. Men frequently view extramarital relationships as arenas for the expression of economic and masculine status. Indeed, it is necessary to understand the intertwining of masculinity and wealth, and gender and economics more generally, to make sense of the most common forms of extramarital sexual relationships in southeastern Nigeria.

In popular discourse, the most common form of economically driven extramarital relationships is said to be so-called sugar daddy relationships, wherein married men of means engage in sexual relationships with much younger women with the expectation that the men will provide various forms of economic support in exchange for sex. While many Nigerians, including many of the participants in these relationships, view sugar daddy relationships in fairly stark economic terms, a closer look at these relationships suggests that they are much more complicated than portrayed in the stereotypical image of rich men exchanging money for sex with impoverished girls (Cole 2004; Cornwall 2002; Mark Hunter 2002, 2005b; Luke 2005). Young women frequently have motives other than the alleviation of poverty. Indeed, typical female participants in these sugar daddy relationships are not the truly poor, but rather young women who are in urban secondary schools or universities, and who seek and represent a kind of modern femininity. They are frequently relatively educated, almost always highly fashionable, and while their motivations for having a sugar daddy may be largely economic, they are usually looking for more than money to feed themselves. For married men, the pretty, urban, educated young women who are the most desirable girlfriends provide not only sex, but the opportunity, or at least the fantasy, of having more exciting, stylish, and modern sex than what they have with their wives. At a sports club in Owerri where I spent many evenings during fieldwork, and where men frequently discuss their extramarital experiences, a fifty-two-year-old businessman described a recent encounter with a young university student to the delight of his mates: "Sometimes you think you are going to teach these girls something, but, hey, this girl was teaching me." Married men who have younger girlfriends assert a brand of masculinity wherein sexual prowess, economic capability, and modern sensibility intertwine.

CHEATING HUSBANDS AND REWARDING PEERS

Masculinity is created and expressed both in men's relationships to women and in their relationships with other men (Connell 1995). In male-dominated social settings such as social clubs, sports clubs, sections of the market-place, and particular bars and eateries, Igbo men commonly talk about their girlfriends and sometimes show them off. Male peer groups are a signifi-cant factor in many men's motivations for and behaviors in extramarital relationships.

While it is not uncommon to hear men boast about their sexual exploits to their peers—frequently alluding to styles and practices that are considered simultaneously exciting and modern, sometimes another strand of discourse emerges when men explain their motivations. Many men reported that they enjoyed the feeling of taking care of another woman, of being able to provide her with material and social comforts and luxuries. In a candid discussion with several men over beers about men's motives for extramarital lovers, a forty-six-year-old man known among his peers as "One Man Show" for his penchant for keeping multiple young women, explained: "It's not only about the sex. I like to buy them things, take them nice places, give them good meals, and make them feel they are being taken care of. I like the feel-ing of satisfaction that comes taking care of women, providing for them." Masculinity proven by provisioning a girlfriend parallels the way men talk about taking care of their wives and families. It foregrounds the connec-tions between masculinity and money and between gender and economics more generally.

It is clear that men with money have easier access to and, it seems, more frequent extramarital sex. But poorer men engage in extramarital sex as well, and their relationships with female partners also typically include some form of transaction, whether it is paying a sex worker or giving gifts to a girlfriend, albeit at lower financial levels than more elite men (Mark Hunter 2002; D. Smith 2002). While there is no doubt that the desire to forge and present a modern masculine identity combines issues of economics and gender, not all men's extramarital relationships can be easily explained in these terms. Although nearly all men noted the importance of keeping affairs secret from their wives, in the marital case study interviews many men emphasized discretion more broadly. They hide their extramarital relation-ships not only from their wives, but from virtually everyone. In such cases, it is not easy to attribute men's motives to their desires to appear mascu-line and economically potent to their fellow men, although men's more pri-vate relationships may still be internalized expressions of masculinity and status.

Some men had occasional extramarital sexual liaisons that appeared to be about little more than sex. In a few cases, men seemed genuinely unhappy in their marriages, and in rare instances, men fell in love with their extramarital partners. But by and large, men tended to see their extramarital relationships as independent of the quality of their marriages, and in their minds, extramarital relationships posed no threat to their marriages so long as they were kept secret from wives and so long as men did not waste so many resources on girlfriends that they neglected their obligations to their wives and families.

Women's Responses to Men's Infidelity

The ascendance of love as a basis for marriage, or at least as an aspect of the marital relationship that is increasingly privileged in assessing the quality of the conjugal connection, intersects in potent and sometimes contradictory ways with the fact of prevalent male infidelity. How Igbo women react to their husbands' cheating depends on a complicated mix of contextual factors that are powerfully inflected by the idea of love. Whether a woman acknowledges or ignores her husband's extramarital sexual behavior; whether she confronts it in private or through various more public means; how it makes her feel; and what sorts of emotional, moral, social, and material means she feels equipped to deploy in order to corral or punish (or cover up) her husband's unfaithfulness—all must be understood in relation to the varying ways that love is intertwined with other dimensions of marriage. While the ideal of romantic love is undoubtedly more widespread with regard to Igbo expectations about marriage than it was one or two generations ago, other elements of marriage remain highly valued and shape women's experiences with, perspectives about, and responses to men's infidelity.

In the following sections, I examine major elements of marriage that intersect with love to produce women's understandings of and reactions to men's unfaithfulness. The overall argument is that for Igbo men and women, marriage is as much an economic, social, reproductive, and reputational project as it is a sexual and emotional endeavor. Indeed, the priority given to these socially pragmatic aspects of the marriage relationship resounds clearly in the narratives of the married couples we interviewed. As the ethnographic evidence demonstrates, married women are in some ways complicit in enabling men's extramarital sexual behavior. In order to understand women's position and behavior, it is necessary to map and explain the interests they have in marriage that frequently trump their aspirations for love and their wish for a faithful husband. Further, and perhaps ironically,

FIGURE 6.2 Nigerian young couple and their four children, 2004. For young Nigerian couples who report that they married explicitly because they were "in love," parenthood remains a paramount objective and becomes an important basis for the durability of marriage in the face of male infidelity. *Photo by Daniel Jordan Smith, 2004.*

as love has become more highly valued as a basis for marriage than in the past, new social expectations about women's domestic roles exacerbate the difficulty of addressing men's infidelity.

"I AM MARRIED TO MY CHILDREN"

Many women described a dramatic change in their relationships with their spouses after marriage, regardless of whether they were willing to talk about their husbands' infidelity. Most commonly, women directly contrasted the period of courtship with the longer-term patterns unfolding in their marriages. The perception of a contrast between courtship and marriage was most pronounced for relatively younger women, who recalled that before marriage their husbands were more attentive and more willing to do the sorts of things that they associated with romantic love—for example, saying affectionate things, buying gifts like jewelry or perfume rather than commodities for the household, or helping out with domestic work that is socially defined as female. Some women attributed these changes to the relative shift in power that occurs at marriage. During courtship, a woman has two authoritative vetoes: She can deny sexual access and she can refuse to marry. In contrast, once a woman is married, the ability to opt out—of either marriage or marital sex—is dramatically reduced. Divorce is highly stigmatized, and women are expected to be sexually available for their husbands.

Ogechi was in her late thirties when we interviewed her. She had five children who were between the ages of twelve and nineteen. Her marriage was one of the most unhappy that we encountered. The fact that she stayed married in the face of her marital experience is powerful testimony to the importance of wifehood and motherhood as social identities and the taboos that surround divorce in southeastern Nigeria. Her husband, sporadically employed as a bus driver, physically abused her, was widely known to take young lovers, and squandered most of his meager earnings on alcohol. Asked about the transition from courtship to marriage, Ogechi reported:

> Before we were married my husband was very sweet. He bought me gifts, he played with my younger brothers, and he made lots of promises to my mother [her father was deceased]. We were very poor and I was so young [she married at seventeen]. I didn't know anything. I believed all the rubbish he was saying. And my mother encouraged me. She thought he would help train my juniors. At first he tried. But not long after I had my first child things began to change. He was drinking and messing around. It's a long time he has not supported us the way a man should.

Ogechi had long ago given up on the idea that her marriage would be happy, and she negotiated her relationship with her husband mostly by putting pressure on him to take responsibility for supporting his children. In this, at least, she could count on the backing of kin and community, though without much success. Her husband drank so much that he was more willing than most men to flout collective pressures to be a good provider.

Ogechi felt she had little or no support in checking her husband's extramarital sexual behavior. Like most women, she felt it was shameful to publicly disclose or complain about her husband's cheating because local ideals of modern marriage are often interpreted to blame women for their husbands' infidelity. Further, the idea of divorce was largely unthinkable, especially since she had five children. She had on several occasions during the worst of times left her husband's compound and returned to her natal home to seek refuge. Her male kin spoke with her husband, admonishing his neglectful and abusive behavior, but in the end they always encouraged her to go back—for the sake of the children. She always did.

I knew from other women in the community that Ogechi's husband sometimes forced himself on her when he was drunk. She had complained about it to her closest friends. While her husband was roundly condemned as a beast by Ogechi's friends and relatives, his behavior was tolerated because they were married. Indeed, there is no conception of marital rape in southeastern Nigeria, at least not in the communities where I worked. We asked all of our interviewees about rights of sexual access. While most men and women concurred that sexual intercourse should be based on mutual consent, and most people thought that both men's and women's sexual pleasure was important, nearly everyone also shared the belief that a woman should be sexually available to her husband except during menstruation and after childbirth. The vast majority of people found the notion of marital rape an oxymoron. Once married, a woman's obligations as a wife and a mother superseded notions of individual or personal wishes and preferences.

While Ogechi's case was extreme, many women experienced changes in their relationships after marriage. They emphasized that after marriage the duties of being a wife and mother subsumed most of their time and effort and interfered with and often eclipsed any attempts to make spousal intimacy a central feature of married life. Some women lamented these changes, but most saw the duties of being a wife and mother as inevitable. They tended to judge their husbands more in terms of whether they contributed their share of resources to enable the couple to fulfill their ambitions for successful social reproduction—which, in contemporary southeastern Nigeria, means establishing a household (and building a house) independent of one's kin, educating one's children to the highest level possible, participating respectably (including financially) in the local institutions through which social reputations are established (such as one's church and hometown association), and engaging in appropriate amounts of conspicuous consumption and redistribution during key rituals of the life course, such as at weddings and funerals.

Chetachi, a thirty-four-year-old mother of four, was representative of a lot of younger women in her account of marriage. She described significant changes in her relationship with her husband since they married, but on the whole had a much happier experience than Ogechi. In some ways, Chetachi lamented that marriage and parenthood encroached on the quality of her emotional relationship with her husband, but in other ways she relished the benefits and social recognition of being a wife and mother. Asked about the changes she experienced between courtship and marriage, she said,

"When I married my husband I used to worry all the time about him. Was he happy? Did he still love me? Was he following another woman? Sometimes I would get very jealous, even when there was no reason. See [pointing to the baby on her breast and the three older children playing nearby], now I am married to my children." Chetachi never openly admitted that she knew her husband sometimes had extramarital sex, but I learned from my interviews with him that he did and that she knew. It was also clear that, like many men, Chetachi's husband viewed his family as his highest priority. Because of this, he was discreet about his infidelity. Despite admitting that he had not always been faithful, he also asserted, "I would never allow anything to interfere with taking care of my wife and children." Chetachi and her husband seemed to have a tacit agreement that as long as each played gender-appropriate roles in raising their family in a socially respectable fashion, their marriage would be okay.

Although most women noted how the domestic duties of raising a family could interfere with marital intimacy, the desire for love did not disappear with marriage and parenthood. Many women expected their husbands to continue to express love and invest in the intimate dimensions of their relationship. These women wanted their husbands to be communicative, emotionally supportive, and sexually attentive. And many men complied willingly. Several couples in the sample talked about time they carved out to talk in private. They spoke quite openly about efforts they made to assure their mutual sexual pleasure. And they reported many practices that can only be interpreted as intimate and affectionate. Two men told me, for example, how they lovingly washed their wives (people in this community wash from a bucket since there is no running water)—a practice that I would never have guessed that married Igbo men engaged in. Certainly men did not admit such behavior to their male peers because men still gain points in peer groups for showing their domination over women and their relative disdain for intimate behaviors associated with femininity. But, revealingly, both men who performed these intimate services for their wives also acknowledged that they had cheated on their spouses. For many men, there is absolutely no contradiction between being a good father and husband (and even a loving husband) and having extramarital sex. This fact plays into the ways that women deal with male infidelity.

WOMEN'S LEVERAGE IN LOVE MARRIAGE

Women employ a range of strategies to deal with men's infidelity. Although most women did not talk easily about their own husband's infidelity in the formal interviews, over time we were able to identify eight women who were willing to speak more informally (without a tape recorder and a questionnaire) about their responses to their husband's extramarital affairs. Women's efforts to address male cheating included a range of tactics, appeals, and punishments. Some women drew on the idea of romantic love, reminding their husbands in various ways of their emotional commitments. With Christianity being almost universally observed in southeastern Nigeria and many families being highly observant, religion and allusions to the Bible were common referents in women's confrontations with philandering spouses. Other women appealed to men's sense of material responsibility for their families. Despite the general expectation that wives should be sexually available to their husbands, women frequently punished their husbands when they discovered or suspected infidelity by withholding emotional and sexual intimacy, or by neglecting cooking and other household labor and material support that are typically considered women's duties. Although seemingly less common than in the past, a few women appealed to their kin or their husbands' kin to help persuade a man to stop an extramarital affair. Most women resorted to more than one of these tactics—appeals to romantic love, Christian values, a husband's sense of obligation as a provider, and help from kin—simultaneously or serially, but certain patterns seemed to emerge, reflecting the varying influence of romantic love in modern Igbo marriages.

Amarachi, a twenty-nine-year-old married mother of three young children, described her rage when she discovered that her husband, Chukwuma, had a girlfriend. "I discovered my husband had another lady he was interested in. I confronted him and told him I would not tolerate that sort of business. For almost two months I stopped everything. No road. We had no [sexual] relations at all. For a long time I did not even serve him food. He became sober [meaning "serious"]. He sent friends to beg me. He even recruited my sister to plead for him. Eventually I forgave him, but I put him on notice that I would not stand such nonsense." In the extended conversation with Amarachi and in my discussions with Chukwuma, it was clear that this couple saw themselves as being in a love marriage. When Amarachi spoke about her sense of Chukwuma's violation, it was in visceral, emotional terms. She was hurt. While she resorted to some time-tested tactics like withholding domestic services, in her depictions of her intent it was clear that she saw his infidelity as a betrayal of love, trust, and intimacy. Chukwuma's eventual rehabilitation in Amarachi's eyes depended on his renouncing any intimacy associated with the affair and pledging anew his emotional (and sexual) fidelity.

But appeals to love are not the only or even always the most effective means for women to control or punish men's extramarital relations. Indeed, sometimes the fact of a man's infidelity is evidence that romantic love is no longer (or was perhaps never) the primary foundation of a marriage. Even in cases where love remains part of the language of the relationship, women can find it effective to call on other aspects of men's obligations as husbands. Many men who cheat are nonetheless concerned about their social reputation, and although, as explained above, certain kinds of male peer groups can reward men for their extramarital dalliances, in other social arenas men can be very sensitive to the negative connotations of infidelity for their reputations. For example, in church-related settings, men would openly acknowledge that they cheat. Women take advantage of this. They appeal to their husband's Christian faith to remind him of the biblical message about adultery. While this does not seem to prevent most men from cheating, it certainly contributes to their discretion. In addition, I heard about women in the community who actually exposed their husbands' affairs to the pastor or openly confronted their husbands in front of fellow parishioners. Such acts are highly scandalous and are seen as the resort of a desperate woman. Indeed, in local discourse a woman who is reduced to such a publicly humiliating tactic often becomes the object of greater criticism than her philandering husband.

In addition to appealing to the exclusivity promised in a love marriage or the faithfulness required by Christianity, women commonly call on dominant cultural ideas about men's material duties as husbands and fathers to criticize and curtail extramarital sexual behavior. Even in marriages where there is little pretense of romantic love, or in situations where women find the appeals of emotional betrayal risky or ineffective, women are able to tap into a cultural model of masculinity that says men should, above all, be responsible fathers and husbands. This strategy is most effective when a woman can demonstrate that she and her children are suffering because of her husband's infidelity—that the man does not provide enough money to cook, that the children's school fees are overdue, or that the man has absented himself from the household to the point where his basic masculine duties as head of the family are being neglected. This kind of strategy on the part of a woman is typically associated with reaching out to kin— his or hers—and is more likely to win collective support than concerns about love and intimacy. Even male peers can be mobilized to intervene if a man's extramarital behavior is seen as undermining his ability to provide for his family.

While many women whose husbands cheat work hard to prevent, punish, or minimize this behavior, I would be remiss if I did not also point out that some women seem to be relatively unconcerned about their husband's extramarital behavior. In none of these cases could one accurately describe these marriages as being based on romantic love—at least not by the time we did our interviews. Several women described an evolution in their marriages from a relationship premised on romantic love to a sort of negotiated arrangement where each spouse fulfilled key social expectations about the gendered division of labor in marriage, but without great expectations for emotional intimacy. This often meant that women were relatively tolerant of men's infidelity, so long as they were discreet and continued to act as social husbands, providing resources to the household, acting as fathers, and respecting the women's role of wife in public. For example, Ukachi, a forty-four-year-old mother of five, described the current arrangement with her husband and the diminution of intimacy in her marriage in this way:

> My husband and I are more like partners in managing of the family than sweethearts now. When we first got married he was more attentive and I was more demanding. The love between us was strong. The first time I thought he kept a girlfriend I was furious. At first he denied and then apologized. But eventually it became a habit. And with the children, what could I do? Men are like that. I know he still sees them [other women], but I make sure he gives me the respect as a wife and does not mess up with his responsibilities.

Certainly no woman thought that a cheating husband was a good thing, but many women were willing to tolerate it so long as the man continued to take responsibility for provisioning his family, accorded the wife social recognition by treating her properly in public, and was discreet in his infidelity.

Generally, women who seemed resigned or relatively unperturbed about their husbands' infidelity were older and had enough economic support to be secure regardless of men's outside relationships. In some cases, this was because the husband himself provided his wife with enough resources; in other cases, grown children provided well for their mother; and in still others, women had their own successful businesses and did not have to rely on anyone for support. Divorce is so highly stigmatized in Igbo-speaking southeastern Nigeria that these women felt they were better off in terms of social reputation by simply staying married. Many women felt about their cheating husbands the way one fifty-year-old woman expressed it in pidgin English "I just de manage am" ("I am just managing him").

Conclusion

Most Igbo women found men's extramarital sexual relationships problematic—all the more so in marriages that women self-identified as love marriages. Even women who made no pretenses about romantic love in their marriages experienced male infidelity as threatening because extramarital relationships channel men's attention and resources away from their households and children. Perhaps ironically, women in love marriages seemed to be most likely to keep silent—at least publicly—about their husbands' behavior.

In love marriages, women have multiple reasons to remain silent about suspicions or evidence of their husbands' extramarital affairs. In these more modern marriages, where couples conceive of their relationships as occurring by choice, where romantic love is frequently an important reason for marrying, and where the conjugal unit is viewed as the primary locus of family decision making, women risk undermining whatever leverage they have with their husbands by openly confronting infidelity. Further, in love marriages women are less willing to call on their kin and in-laws for support in the face of male infidelity, not only because these marriages are more independent from extended families, but because of the ideology that in such marriages a man's happiness (and, thus, his proclivity to seek outside women) is directly related to the capacity of his wife to please him.

What this means for many Igbo wives is that a woman risks not only losing her husband's support if she confronts his cheating, but also possibly bearing the blame in the eyes of her community (including her female peers) for allowing (or even pushing) her husband to stray (Mutongi 2000; Wardlow 2006a; Thomas, this volume). Many women described a common dilemma. A thirty-eight-year-old married mother of four put it well: "In this our society, when a man cheats on his wife, it is often the wife who will be blamed. People will say it is because she did not feed him well, she refused him in bed, or she is quarrelsome. And it is often our fellow women who are most likely to blame the wife."

All this suggests that love is less than liberating for Igbo women. While the ideal of romantic love certainly creates expectations for a degree of interpersonal equality in marriage with regard to spousal communication, mutual sexual satisfaction, and household decision making, in the context of wider continued gender inequality, women often find their expectations for conjugal love to be both disappointing and disempowering, especially vis-à-vis men's infidelity. This should not be read as a simple one-sided story. Many couples we interviewed described themselves as having loving relationships. Marital love can be a source of joy for both men and women, and a point of leverage for women in the face of other dimensions of gender inequality. But in a context where being (and staying) married remains a reputational requirement, the idea that marriage should be based on love puts women in the position where they often must tolerate, and even find themselves covering for, their husbands' infidelities.

In the era of HIV/AIDS, women's silence and complicity in keeping men's extramarital sex secret has potentially devastating implications. The ultimate irony is that for women in the most modern marriages, where the conjugal relationship is primary and romantic love is often an explicit foundation of the relationship, the possibility of confronting a man's infidelity may be more difficult, and insisting on condom use is impossible (Hirsch et al. 2007; D. Smith 2007b; Wardlow 2007). In such marriages a woman challenging her husband's extramarital behavior or asking for a condom may be undermining the very basis for the marriage and threatening whatever leverage she has with her husband by implying that the relationship itself has been broken. For many Igbo women, calling on men's sense of responsibility as providers has proven to be a more effective strategy than appealing to love. In this way, they broaden the network of social actors who are willing to intercede on their behalf, whereas in love most everything is left to the couple to negotiate and the woman to bear. Love is often not enough to manage men and marriage.

NOTES

1. All names in the text are pseudonyms.
2. Most of the data presented in this chapter was collected while working on a five-country comparative ethnographic study, "Love, Marriage, and HIV: A Multisite Study of Gender and HIV Risk," funded by the National Institutes of Health (grant 1R01 HD 041724).
3. These two research sites have been described in greater detail in other publications (D. Smith 2007a, 2007b).
4. See D. Smith (2007b) for a more complete analysis of men's extramarital sexual behavior in southeastern Nigeria. Material in this section is drawn directly from that article.
5. We interviewed twenty-two married women but only twenty of their husbands because two men were long-distance migrants who did not return home during the entire period of research.

Media and the Therapeutic Ethos of Romantic Love in Middle-Class Nairobi

Rachel Spronk

The film *Save the Last Dance* is about a white middle-class ballet dancer who meets the love of her life, a black lower-class hip-hop guy. In 2001, it was a huge hit in Nairobi. According to Sereti, twenty-five years old then, the film was a beautiful love story, and watching its larger than life images and hearing its overpowering sound produced a blissful experience. The film also made her fantasize about her own love life. In a society where affection is generally expressed in covert ways, graphic images of emotional indulgence and intimacy made a powerful impression. Representations of such love not only entertained her, they also provided the impetus for her to reflect on and reenvision her own life and intimate relations.

Sereti then worked as a project coordinator in an international non-governmental organization and lived with her mother and older sister, who worked as a flight attendant for Kenya Airways. Her parents had both worked as civil servants. Her father had died five years before, and Sereti had decided to live with her mother for the time being: "My mother is very liberal. I can do what I want and come back home any time. She leaves me to live my own life." She used to go swimming twice a week to keep fit, and she liked to have a beer or two after work. On Fridays and Saturdays, she would go out with friends for drinks or dancing. In 2001, she went on a holiday to Kampala—a remarkable thing to do as most Nairobians spend their vacations at home. That same year, she started studying for a master's degree in business administration in the evenings through the University of Nairobi. Sereti often talked about "real love" and anticipated that she would find it in a relationship. In 2001, she was briefly involved with David to whom she lost her heart. With him, she saw her dreams come true: "David is IT, like he walked out of the movies to find me, Sereti, his princess," she said, giving me a wink, after it became clear they were becoming more and more committed. After a couple of months, they became *the* couple of their friends' circle: "They are the example of what so many women want. He is awesome," Sereti's friend Esther once sighed. Quite suddenly, David broke up with Sereti, and she did not know why. When we spoke again in 2004, she was still preoccupied with what had happened and said, "There were signs I guess, sometimes he could turn moody and he would ask me to leave [him alone], without an explanation." After David, she had a few affairs, but she did not talk extensively about them: "They mean nothing, it's not out of love. What can I say, a woman has her needs [meaning sex], isn't it?" she remarked.

A small group of female and male young professionals in Nairobi, such as information and communication technology professionals, accountants, and junior nongovernmental organization staff, share many of Sereti's experiences and concerns. They represent a minority social group that, though not clearly defined, is nonetheless recognizable in the urban landscape. Like previous generations of school-educated and middle-class Nairobians, these young professionals see themselves as explorers and creators of what they perceive to be modern African lives. They embrace cosmopolitan attitudes and believe that their careers are crucial markers of their identities. When it comes to their personal lives, young professionals seek to forge intimate relations rooted in romantic and progressive ideals. Their aspirations are in line with other young women and men around the world who take up the ideal of companionate marriage as a way to demonstrate their modern individuality (Hirsch and Wardlow 2006).

Passionate love in courtship and marriage is not new to Kenya, as many folktales, songs, life histories, and narrative fiction attest. Nor is the ideal of romantic love new (see Mutongi, this volume). Popular music from the early postcolonial period onward has often foregrounded romantic themes—one thinks, for example, of the famous love song "Malaika" ("angel" in Swahili) (Kidula 2000, 409). Over the same period, Hollywood blockbusters, Hindi films, and locally produced popular novels featuring romantic love held strong appeal, and popular magazines included extensive discussions of how to recognize true love and how to ensure that love marriages triumph over arranged ones (Fuglesang 1994; Odhiambo 2003; Strobel 1979). There also has been—and still is—a rich tradition of students exchanging love letters (L. Thomas 2006). What is new about romantic love in contemporary Kenya is the sheer volume of representations and debates about intimacy in the public domain and the introduction of a therapeutic ethos into those discussions.

The implementation of structural adjustment policies beginning in the 1980s and the reintroduction of a multiparty political system in 1992 led the government to liberalize press restrictions. Increased programming with romantic and sexual content offered by independent media outlets coincided with the elaboration of HIV/AIDS education and prevention campaigns to place issues of sex and intimacy squarely in the public eye. Young professionals have engaged these public representations to reflect on and shape their own relationships (see also Masquelier, this volume). Specific media outlets, in turn, have offered forums for readers and listeners to pose questions and discuss intimacy, thereby enabling new understandings of romantic being and knowing, or what Mark Liechty has called "new epistemic understandings" (2003, 181) of love.

Although young Africans have used various forms of media to reflect on their intimate relationships for generations now, an important shift has occurred with the introduction of a therapeutic ethos. Writing about this ethos in the United States, Eva Illouz (1997, 198–99) defines its core propositions as "relationships can be divided into 'healthy' and 'unhealthy'"; intimate relations are "open to study" and can be "evaluated by experts"; and people can acquire knowledge about romantic relations "through work and the application of appropriate strategies and techniques." Rather than accepting didactic and moralizing advice from others, the therapeutic ethos insists that the solution to romantic problems lies in self-knowledge and reflexivity. Although the precise moment of this discourse's entry into the Kenyan public sphere is difficult to discern, it appears to have arrived during the 1990s amid the liberalization of media.

In this chapter, I explore how young professionals' expectations and practices of intimacy are shaped by postcolonial transformations, consumer capitalism, and engagement of this therapeutic ethos. In particular, I focus on how young professionals consciously seek lessons about love and relationships from magazines and films, and from premarital counseling classes offered by middle-class churches. Although sociologists who have analyzed the development of a therapeutic ethos in Western societies have differed in dating its emergence (locating it anywhere from the late nineteenth century to the post–World War II period), they have concurred in identifying it as a predicament of modernity. Some have argued that secularization, consumer culture, and the growth of expert knowledge have combined to encourage members of the middle class, in particular, to judge their relations according to quasi-clinical notions of what is "healthy," in ways that may foster feelings of victimization (Furedi 2002; Lears 1983; Nolan 1998). As Furedi (2002, 24) argues in his critique of a therapeutic ethos, subjects become docile objects of disciplinary knowledge, "where empowerment means little more than knowledge of voluntary resignation to authority" (Furedi 2002, 24). My argument for contemporary Kenya is different. I argue that a therapeutic ethos helps young professionals in Nairobi, who are experiencing rapid changes in marriage patterns, to understand and *act* on their love relations.

The Young, the Hip, and the Ambitious in Postcolonial Nairobi

Nairobi is the regional headquarters of international banks, nongovernmental organizations and transnational corporations and a major site for accounting, legal, and informational services. Office developments, shopping malls, and hotels dominate the cityscape while white-collar employment and residential areas for the middle class and wealthy elite are expanding, alongside a growing impoverished population. Media and entertainment centers are part of these developments—Nairobi is a site reflecting the effects of a "stylisation of consumption" (Mbembe 2004, 400). The lifestyles of young professionals manifest a new cosmopolitanism that unites the cultural, financial, and political flows within and between non-Western and Western societies (Appadurai 1996).

Transformations in marriage patterns, gender roles, and sexuality are, of course, highly complex processes that occur within individuals and groups, and tend to take place slowly over generations. The grandfathers of many of the people in this study worked during the colonial period as laborers on white settler farms or for the government on road building and construction projects. Their wives, for the most part, remained behind in rural areas where they maintained family homesteads. Practically speaking, women took over male work such as preparing fields for planting or clearing forests, as well as household and certain community responsibilities (Nyaggah 2003). Men, in effect, went from being active heads of households to largely absent breadwinners. This shift caused major changes in conjugal relationships, sexual patterns, family life, and community participation.

In addition to creating a cash economy and widespread labor migration, colonial rule introduced schooling. By the mid-twentieth century, many families eagerly sent their sons and daughters to mission schools. These children, the parents of the young professionals in this study, gained skills that enabled them, after Kenya achieved independence in 1963, to gain white-collar employment in private companies or as government civil servants and teachers. Steady urbanization and migration continued over the first decades of postcolonial rule. These processes further altered family organization, gender relations, and authority structures. As Lynn Thomas has noted of this first postcolonial generation, "schooling, salaried employment and monogamous aspirations . . . catapult[ed] young adults into a world in which elders carried less influence" (2003, 132–33). Nevertheless, most Nairobians still maintained connections with their rural homes, visiting relatives, giving a helping hand, participating in local organizations, and even building and leasing rural homes.

Over time, however, these bonds weakened as these people's children— the young professionals of this study—were incorporated less fully into the activities of rural homes. Their parents invested heavily in their education and often, for example, spoke only English to their children to ensure their success in the English-dominated school system. This emerging urban middle class gave rise to heated public debates about the possible loss of African culture. These debates also encompassed long-standing concerns about the decreasing influence of patriarchal and gerontocratic controls on women and young men (Mutongi 2000; Robertson 1997; L. Thomas 2003; White 1990). Contemporary young professionals thus grew up as part of a society in transformation. Born and raised in Nairobi, they garnered the advanced school education necessary to take advantage of postcolonial opportunities and to pursue professional careers and middle-class lifestyles.

The term *young professionals* applies to a relatively small socially mobile group of young adults that is not part of the political-economic elite. They come from backgrounds ranging from lower to upper middle class, though these differences tend to be leveled once they enter their professional fields. While during the late colonial and early postcolonial periods, middle-class and white-collar workers were largely employed by the state, today—in the wake of the scale-back of state bureaucracies inaugurated by structural adjustment policies—young professionals mainly seek careers in the private or nongovernmental sector. Another defining feature of these young professionals is that many, including Sereti, do not speak an ethnic language since their parents spoke to them in English or in Kiswahili (the lingua franca of East Africa) from childhood onwards. Among themselves they speak English, Kiswahili, and *Sheng*—a youth subculture slang made up of different (ethnic) languages. The basis of their social life is interethnic, and so are their neighborhoods, churches, and professional lives. However, within their families, they are less vocal about such attitudes since their parents tend to be more monoethnically oriented.

The majority of young professionals are unmarried, preferring to delay marriage until around thirty years of age. Female young professionals differ from their mothers and grandmothers in their tendency to postpone childbearing to later ages. Delaying marriage and reproduction enables them to focus on their careers, to save in order to start their married lives in middle-class style, and to postpone the responsibilities that come with married life. Such delays prolong dating and the maintenance of casual relationships. Dating, in fact, is an important element in their lives, and they actively date people of different ethnic groups and nationalities. Though unmarried, they are often financially independent from their parents due to their relatively stable and lucrative jobs. This independence enables them to live on their own and enjoy consumer lifestyles. Familial relations are not unimportant, but generally young professionals make their own decisions and then try to convince their parents to respect those choices, rather than involving them directly in the decision-making process.

Leisure is crucial to young professionals' lifestyles. Although not all of the young professionals that I knew went out on a weekly basis, a majority did. An enjoyable evening out can include roasted meat and pounded maize meal in an open-air residential restaurant, to be followed by dancing in one of the many clubs. Others like to dine at one of the restaurants and continue on to a bar or watch a late-night movie at the cinema. Often, people meet after office hours to have a drink and then go to clubs, bars, or sports centers where they hang out in groups. A significant majority work out in gyms to stay fit or swim in one of the many pools of the international hotels. Through their leisure activities, young professionals engage in global cultural forms to craft a cosmopolitan identity with a particular Kenyan flavor. Their tastes in music, fashion, humor, and social concerns signal their appreciation of multiple modes of being (Nyairo 2005). They are cosmopolitans not because of a cultural orientation to the West, but because of their self-conscious interweaving of global and local perspectives.

Dating stands out as among the most significant symbolic practices of these middle-class cosmopolitans. As Illouz (1997, 14) has argued for the culture of romance in the twentieth-century United States, capitalism has located love amid the twin spheres of consumption and mass media. The media present leisure activities such as dating as constitutive of romance and intimacy. The imbuing of romantic love with associations of money, commodities, and happiness has meant that for Kenyan young professionals, too, dating links love to the consumption of media and commodities. Valentine's Day, for instance, has become a day for young professionals to pay special attention to their relationships (see also Masquelier, this volume). In 2001–02, quite a few people I knew had a Valentine dinner, delivered bouquets, or surprised their loved ones in various ways. In response, others criticized such celebrations as too Western. Young professionals defended their embrace of Valentine's Day by affirming a cosmopolitan identity. Sereti, for instance, explained: "Yaah, it has this association of wanting to be Western ... but if I want to express my love for David as such and if I am very clear about me being an African woman, why not? They also celebrate it in China."

As such comments suggest, the fact that young professionals' lives differ from the lives of their parents and the majority of other Kenyans does not go uncriticized. Although they are respected for their social mobility, they are also accused of acting too Western and being un-African. Accusations of Westernization cut deep, as young professionals ultimately see themselves as modern Africans, people who have moved beyond Kenya's debilitating ethnic rivalries yet who are critical of the economic and cultural influence of the West that they label new imperialism. While such responses to young people's embrace of what are perceived to be Western customs have a long history throughout Africa (Cornwall 2005), these reactions are, perhaps, particularly common amid contemporary global influences. As Peter Geschiere and Birgit Meyer have argued, "People's awareness of being involved in open ended global flows seems to trigger a search for fixed orientation points and action frames, as well as determined efforts to affirm old and construct new boundaries" (1998, 602). This tension is abundantly clear when it comes to young people's intimate relationships.

While generally disagreeing with charges that they are too Western, several young professionals told me that, as a group, they suffer an identity crisis. In an earlier draft of this chapter, I referred to such statements as an extreme explanation. After reading that draft, one young professional named Laura responded with the following e-mail:

> Finally, what people describe as an identity crisis is not at all an extreme expression of what I feel or what many of my friends feel. It's really the most accurate way to describe all this mixed up feelings. It describes the feelings of disconnection, guilt, that we betrayed something, our sense of in-authenticity, the fact that we are confronted daily in Nairobi with the fact that we are NOT the average Kenyan, gives many of us a sense of standing outside history. It makes us unable to truly imagine ourselves as agents of cultural transformation, because we feel like we don't own our culture in the first place. We fear that we are not part of it, but at the same time we hope that we are not part of it. (June 4, 2003)

Laura's message powerfully captures young professionals' sense of ambivalence. Their desire for a modern and cosmopolitan lifestyle that foregrounds practices deemed Western exists in tension with their criticism of Westernization as a new kind of imperialism.

During my research, many young professionals explained their choices regarding courtship and marriage in relation to, and sometimes in opposition to, the lives of their parents. Many described their parents' marriages as old-fashioned. Both female and male young professionals emphasized how they desired more egalitarian and companionate relationships. For example, Dorcas (aged thirty in 2001) explained that "we all have to accept that my generation of women is not like our mothers' generation." She had just ended a difficult relationship with a boyfriend who had urged her to accept domestic subservience by invoking her obligation to "African womanhood." Her ex-boyfriend's behavior reminded her of her father's domineering presence and her mother's subdued manner. Men expressed similar desires to craft relationships different from their parents'. I met Maurice (then aged twenty-seven) at a moment when he had just been approached by a woman who offered to be his second girlfriend, outside of his committed relationship. Some of his male friends encouraged him to take this opportunity. He, however, explained he could not start an affair with another woman because of his love for his girlfriend Nyambura: "We, the men of these days, have to make choices. We cannot live anymore like our fathers. I believe it's not right to be polygamous."[1]

Young professionals differ in two ways from their parents' generation. For their parents, marriage entailed a lifelong commitment, not only to a spouse but to an entire family. By contrast, a defining feature of young professionals' vision of love is that emotional investment and sexual intimacy in relationships is a means of individual development and self-fulfillment. Second, whereas their parents identified themselves mostly through family relationships and ethnicity, they define themselves through lifestyle choices. Young professionals are inclined to enter relationships that center on the pursuit of similar lifestyles (see also Smith on Nigeria, this volume). According to Wardlow, the companionate ideal of romantic love is about more than only marriage itself. It is about a certain lifestyle and a certain kind of personhood that requires certain practices (2006a, 57). In Nairobi, the companionate ideal serves to inspire these young people to make symbolic and practical relations between women and men more egalitarian. Their families, however, have not provided them with models for crafting such relations (see also Mlanga 2006). Moreover, as they also tend to delay marriage and reproduction, many of their relationships are temporary and relatively unstable. This situation foregrounds matters of love, gender, and sexuality as pressing concerns and frequent topics of debate and discussion that are taken up in the media.

The Public Emergence of the Intimate

Before the 1990s, various media such as films and soap operas provided Kenyans opportunities to observe the ins and outs of others' love lives, a phenomenon that clearly has long roots and draws from different traditions (see Thomas and Fair this volume; see also Fuglesang 1994; Behrend 1998; Larkin 1997). Besides visual media, popular magazines such as *Drum* and *Viva* offered forums to learn about the blessings and burdens of love and sexuality in a more educational way (see Mutongi, this volume). They often featured basic articles on family planning methods, and their advice columns urged young people to avoid unwanted pregnancies and premature relationships through premarital abstinence. Other media addressed issues of love and sexuality in either veiled or religious terms for fear that explicit talk of sex would actually encourage unmarried people to have sex (Njau 1993).

While this fear of explicit sex talk in public still holds sway in many regards, the liberalization of media restrictions in the early 1990s significantly altered public discussions of intimacy in Kenya. Over the past fifteen years, independent radio and TV stations have emerged to compete with state-run media, though the government continues to exert a fair amount of control over the sector by refusing permits to aspirant newspapers, television corporations, and radio companies. Besides Western productions, Latin American, a few South African, and, since the 2000s, more and more locally produced soap operas and talk shows are being featured. Print media and radio programs have risen in numbers and more directly address local audiences. The new media outlets, together with consumer culture more broadly, promote romantic love as a defining concern of contemporary youth. Young professionals are both an important inspiration and a significant market for the circulation of such media because they embody a middle-class lifestyle identified as hip. In Kenya today, as elsewhere in the world, media play an important role in the styling of middle-class identities; "Mass media relates to and helps produce emerging middle class culture" (Liechty 2003, 183).

Since the early 1990s, media discussions of love have also been shaped by the HIV/AIDS epidemic. While early in the epidemic, most media addressed HIV/AIDS and sex in moralizing and medicalizing terms, more recently, various media outlets have sought to broaden the discussion of these issues by addressing subjects including love, trust and distrust, passion, attraction, and arousal. Such discussions of love and sexuality are both a reaction to the earlier and narrower discussions of the HIV/AIDS epidemic and a response to a new generation's desire for practical information about relationships, love, and sex.

There are two major differences between contemporary media discussions of love and sex and those of the 1960s and 1970s (Mutongi, this volume; see also L. Thomas 2006). First, love has become more tightly entangled with consumer lifestyles. Colin Campbell (1987) has argued that the spirit of modern consumerism is linked to an eagerness for new experiences, a hedonistic orientation, and infinite desires. The power of consumerism is that it works via the registers of pleasure and intimacy, placing love and sexuality at the center of consumption. This entanglement was present, though nascent, in the early postcolonial period, but the increased size of the social group that can afford leisure activities and luxury commodities has combined with new media, giving the intersection of romance and consumption greater resonance. In Kenya's burgeoning commercial and mass media sectors such as newspaper gossip and advice columns, radio talk shows, and soft porn magazines, the topic of love and sexuality spice up programs, attracting larger audiences and providing entertainment and instruction.

The second defining feature of contemporary love talk is the emergence of a therapeutic ethos that I mentioned earlier. Illouz (1997) argues that the emergence of this ethos in the United States was related to the confluence of middle-class U.S. values with the growth of an integrated rationalized market and scientific discourses across the twentieth century. As a result, therapeutic discourse became an important part of self-formation. Sociologists have associated the growth of a therapeutic ethos with processes of individualization (Furedi 2002; Lears 1983; Nolan 1998). An important undercurrent of the therapeutic ethos, Furedi (2002) argues, is the belief that one's emotional well-being is vulnerable to social influences. Illouz's work examines how therapeutic discourse has reconfigured approaches to romance within the context of twentieth-century consumer capitalism and its ally mass media.

While there are strong similarities between the therapeutic ethos of romance described by Illouz and processes in contemporary Nairobi such as the close alliance between mass media and consumer culture, there are also significant differences. According to Illouz (1997), the therapeutic ethos appeals to middle- and upper-class U.S. couples because it suggests that they can control intimate relations and fix romantic problems. Moreover, the explanatory function of the therapeutic ethos offers reasons for why things are the way they are. By contrast, the attraction of therapeutic discourse for middle-class Nairobians lays not only its explanatory power but also in its potential to provide an alternative relationship epistemology. To wit: By the time therapeutic discourse became widespread in the United States following World War II, it was broadly accepted among all social classes that people should chose their own marriage partners. As a result, in that context, therapeutic discourse became a tool that couples could use to fix their relationships rather than to justify their formation or existence. By contrast, in contemporary Nairobi, therapeutic discourse, with its emphasis on self-understanding and reflexivity, offers young professionals a new way to understand the very foundation of their relationships. Young professionals in Nairobi engage a therapeutic ethos to reflect on their personal aspirations and decisions, and to gain skills necessary to enact lives that they hope will be different from their parents' lives.

As therapeutic discourse entered the Kenyan public sphere in the 1990s through media liberalization, editors and programmers developed new approaches for presenting and communicating information about relationships, love, and sexuality. According to Mutongi (this volume), the male staff of *Drum* who authored the magazine's "Dear Dolly" advice column in the 1960s and 1970s offered off-the-cuff advice that aimed to be both didactic and witty. In contrast, today's editors problematize love and sexuality, and rather than offering clear-cut advice and condemning practices such as premarital sex, they encourage self-reflexivity and greater communication within relations. Whereas previously advice—whether from elders or the media— was directive (Njau 1993; Nzioka 1994), nowadays media experts encourage self-reflection as the most important first step to solving love problems.

The oldest and most popular locally produced magazine in 2001 was the

FIGURE 7.1 *Saturday Magazine* cover, January 2002. Since its inception in 1999, the *Saturday Magazine* has become one of the most popular lifestyle magazines in Kenya. With articles about building healthy relationships and cultivating self-reflection, the *Saturday Magazine* seeks to overcome moralizing discourses on intimacy and instead promote a therapeutic ethos. *Photo source:* Saturday Magazine.

Saturday Magazine, a pullout from one of the main English-language newspapers, *The Daily Nation.*[2] Covers feature stylish models who look like young professionals and use catchy headlines such as "Romantic Space," "The Condom Debate," and "Stalled Weddings."[3] In 1999, editor Rhoda Orengo received the assignment to produce a lifestyle magazine. In my interview with her, she explained that they decided, based on market research, to produce a magazine geared toward professional urbanites between twenty-five and thirty-five years of age, both married and unmarried, addressing all kinds of social concerns.[4] Orengo explained the *Saturday Magazine*'s goal as follows:

> R.O.: We intend to be inspirational by providing information about all kinds of life situations like relationships, health, and so on, but we also want to break up silences about, for example, divorce, single motherhood, sexuality. Also . . . we want to play into people's . . . desires like traveling, a fashionable house, you know, things that are not so common in Kenya but that are becoming part of our lives. . . . We *have to* [her emphasis] write about relationships between men and women because that is what preoccupies people most. I believe we play an important role because people don't talk about the problems in relationships, but they are there so we write about it. We make people face their own situations, like . . . sometimes people don't realize they are in an abusive relationship and when we have an article about it we always receive letters from women who say we helped them to understand their situations.
>
> R.S.: How many letters do you receive on a weekly basis?
>
> R.O.: Well . . . too many, I guess tens every week. Sometimes people come to the office to ask whether they can talk with an author, we have to send them to Amani [a well-known counseling center].[5]

The *Saturday Magazine*'s inspirational approach has proven successful, which is also shown by the popularity of two of its columnists. In 2001, Catherine Awuor and Oyunga Pala, who had been writing for the *Saturday Magazine* since its inception, were two of the most well-known columnists in Kenya. Initially, they were assigned to write about relationships and gender issues. Awuor writes informative columns in a humorous manner, whereas Pala's columns are more sarcastic. Together, they seek to provoke discussions, write about sensitive problems, and generally inform people about that which cannot be said. In the letters that Awuor receives (on average, thirty responses by e-mail per week, and sometimes as many as eighty, in 2004), people often say they are struggling with the topic she has written about and then describe their personal experiences or ask for further advice.[6] I read a few letters that Awour had received, and most took the form of confessional narratives. Pala also receives ten to sixty letters per week. Awuor's opinion that columnists like she and Pala have become advisers resonates with my experience: Local magazines play a major role in providing information and knowledge about personal issues and, thus, create space for discussion of and reflection on emotional and relational problems.

Shanti Parikh (2005) similarly describes how radio and print media offer advice on intimate issues and interpersonal relations in Uganda and how these sources have replaced the traditional sex educators–paternal aunts.[7] Social change has affected not only gender and sexuality but also the social bonds responsible for educating people about love and sexuality (see also Ahlberg 1994; Prazak 2001). While traditionally certain family members, particularly aunts, educated children about relationships, these roles are no longer followed. Many civil society groups or institutions—such as churches, women's groups, and universities—as well as the media attempt to address these lacunae.[8]

Personal narratives in the form of confessional stories or real-life events printed in such magazines have become a major way to learn about others' lives. Testimonies of enduring love in the face of opposition, coupled with discussions about trust and cheating elicit much debate and reflection. These magazines devote a good deal of attention to sensitive issues such as bride-wealth, multipartner sexual relations, sexual abuse, depression, AIDS, financial problems, abortion, and alcoholism. To illustrate the complexity of such situations, personal confessions or revelations often precede discussions.

The naming and defining of problems, emotions, and experiences is an important element of these magazine discussions. Articles weigh modern or supposedly common sense—also sometimes defined as African—perspectives on these issues against customs, old beliefs, or allegedly unrealistic perspectives. They show how people have responded differently in similar situations; let experts such as medical doctors, psychologists, and pastors speak rather than lecture; and provide possible advice for readers to consider. Many times they posit honest communication as key to overcoming relationship challenges. Besides the print media, there are a few local radio and TV programs that reach out to the public in a similar way. Significantly, all these media deploy a discourse that encourages exploration of love's meaning and purpose for (inter)personal well-being.[9] Together, they have introduced a "mode of hermeneutic self-reflexivity" which is fundamental to the therapeutic ethos (Illouz 1997, 203). This ethos empowers young people by providing them alternative ways to think about their relationships.

"Working" on Relationships, or How Young Professionals Incorporate Media Lessons

After Sereti and I left the cinema having watched *Save the Last Dance,* we went to have a drink in the cinema bar, a dark red velvet-carpeted, pleasant space. She renarrated the story of the film, referring to the film characters and what they had experienced. Gradually, while figuring out why the characters had acted as they did, she began to speak in the second person: "But suppose he does that to you, one is inclined to react . . ." After a while she analyzed her relationship with David while referring to the film and, later, to the latest column of Oyunga Pala that dealt with "the danger of being too much of a gentle-man" (Pala 2001). The subtle shift from speaking in the third person when discussing the film, to speaking in the second person about relationships in general, and eventually shifting directly to her own life shows how processes of intertextuality work. Sereti used representations from the media as interpretive frames through which to make sense of her own life.

Bodil Frederiksen states that in Nairobi "global media [have] provided powerful narratives that are used by people in local settings as sounding boards for reflections on how to conduct everyday life and human relations" (2000, 209). She pinpoints exactly what is at stake: Rather than copying, Nairobians make use of media to reflect on their personal lives by looking at, reading about, and imagining different modes of being. These reflections involve complicated identifications that cut across familiar and unfamiliar racial, cultural, and national lines. Discussing Stephanie Newell's work on Ghanaian popular fiction, Karin Barber states that popular romance narratives in Ghana are "read as 'true': not in the sense of being mimetic representations of reality, but rather true in the sense of being *applicable* to reality" (1997b, 357, emphasis in original). It is this applicability to reality that interests me. According to Liechty, the power of film realism—and that of other media, for that matter—lies in convincing people that representations are possible; it is "not some representation of 'reality' but a representation of plausibility" (2003, 180).

In Sereti's view, she needed to explicitly conceptualize ideas of love because, as she put it, "our generation has . . . modern relationships [in contrast to our parents]." She explained how she wanted to be "intimate, not only sexually but also emotionally." In her relationship with David, she tried to bring into practice an idea of love that emphasized being close to another person—"sharing thoughts" and "showing feelings." Real love, for Sereti, was based on companionship and emotional closeness, in which she understood sexual intimacy as a kind of emotional glue. She defined her parents' relationship instead as defined by a love that is more like respect, one forged through predetermined cultural norms rather than consistent communication (see also Hirsch et al. 2006 on Mexico). After watching *Save the Last Dance*, Sereti said that David was not as responsive to her as the man in the film had been to the woman and accordingly analyzed what their relationship was lacking: "I think David and I don't talk, so we don't know what the other thinks, or feels, or wants. We don't talk because we don't share quality time." The notion of quality time was a buzzword in 2001–02 in Nairobi; it was considered a prerequisite for true companionship. According to Sereti, David was acting too much "like the man" whereas she expected them to be on an equal footing. She was criticizing David's articulations of a hegemonic notion of masculinity by using the actor's behavior as a possible alternative. She believed a different kind of relationship was possible because she saw more egalitarian ones around her and because more and more men expressed their desire to engage in such relationships. Nevertheless, this shift toward more egalitarian and companionable relationships is not easy. Both women and men have to come to terms with the fact that existing gender structures mean that men occupy multiple roles in women's lives as lovers, friends, and future husbands, but also as figures of authority and social control (Spronk 2005a, 2005b).

Sereti's account is similar to the experiences of many people with whom I spoke. Both women and men who went to the cinema or read magazine articles expected or hoped that their boyfriends or girlfriends would behave toward them like people did in the films and, even more, in real-life stories from magazines. Several men told me that if there was something they wanted to discuss with their girlfriend but did not know how, they dealt with the issue by suggesting that their partner read a particular article or column. Eric (aged twenty-four in 2001) explained how he tried to persuade his girlfriend to be less constrained when having sex:

> OK. . . . She [Mary] was a little passive; I thought she could not enjoy sex as much because she was passive. So then I decided to get a few copies from *Parents* for her to read. . . . I couldn't talk to her about it, so one day I gave her the copies and asked her to read them. Then I left. . . . You know, when you love each other you should both enjoy sex.

For both Sereti and Eric, media representations of love and sexuality provided them with a sense of what is possible. While Sereti's attempts to learn lessons from the media in her life illustrate the sharp difference between ideals and implementation, she and others continued to look at their own conflicts in the light of how similar conflicts were articulated and resolved in different media. Representations of love and sexuality thus provide models for a new kind of individuated subject that feed into young professionals' search for alternative forms of gender relations. By probing the plausibility of these models, they are engaged in a process of simultaneous self-distancing and self-recognition that is fundamental to the therapeutic ethos and becomes an "important source of the formation of the self" (Illouz 1997, 198).

The media's foregrounding of personal narratives highlights how middle-class Nairobians have shifted away from interpreting marriages as familial unions. By embracing therapeutic discourse, they emphasize the need to choose partners on the basis of companionship, egalitarian relationship, emotional investment, and mutual sexual satisfaction rather than familial, ethnic, or reproductive considerations. The question, of course, is to what extent this new perspective will lead to significant changes. This particular group of young professionals was rather ambitious and, perhaps, idealistic. It is quite possible that when they get older they might grow into more normative patterns. Yet, the fact that therapeutic discourse has been adopted in institutional settings, particularly in churches as I discuss below, suggests that its influence might be far-reaching and lasting.

In a country where almost everybody belongs to a church or mosque and where, as John Lonsdale states, contemporary culture is "soaked in Christianity" (Berman and Lonsdale 1992, 217), the adoption of therapeutic discourse by churches is significant. In October 2001, I attended, with my partner, the premarriage counseling class of the Nairobi Chapel, a Baptist church with a middle-class membership. These classes are organized twice a year for couples intending to get married. Although we had no such intention, after explaining the goal of my study, I was allowed to participate provided that my partner accompanied me. All of the participants appeared to be successful professionals. In general, the women were aged under thirty, while the men were near to or above thirty. An older couple, around forty years old, supervised the twelve-session class that concluded with a weekend at a holiday resort near Lake Naivasha. Every session had a theme such as "what is love?," "love and sexuality," "marriage and money," "managing conflicts," and "relatives and in-laws." According to Mr. Njuguna, one of the leaders of the group, the problem with young couples is that they operate in a "vacuum" because they are left to themselves: "There are no aunts and uncles to advise them and even the parents do not address their children anymore. Young couples live in a vacuum because they have not been told how to make their marriages work."[10] The goal of the class was to expose them to the unavoidable obstacles in marriage and to prepare them for dealing with those obstacles.

The class sought to present young couples with a middle-class way to forge progressive or modern relations and to avoid older or immoral modes of being. To my surprise, the examples given to the class did not specifically focus on their lives as Christians. Rather, the small nuclear family in which fathers play football with their children on Sundays was presented as the icon of contemporary happiness. Similarly, husbands were defined as companions and warned not to take their authority within the household for granted or to make decisions without involving their spouses. The class leaders instructed men to earn their respectability by being responsive and caring fathers and husbands, by being open to emotional and personal engagement with others, and by sharing their own preoccupations and thoughts. Despite the church's Christian theology that figured men as heads of households, in the classes, male privilege was not encouraged. Moreover, the ideal of husband as provider proved unrealistic for these couples as wives often earned equal or higher salaries than their husbands. The classes redefined men's household role from being the authority figure to being responsible for the emotional well-being of their families and being companions to their wives. Christian ideologies and practices thus also portray love-based unions as an essential part of modern personhood (see also Wardlow 2006b on Papua New Guinea).

Class leaders promoted communication as a key concept. The teachers encouraged men, especially, to learn to speak their minds and share their preoccupations with their girlfriends. We were given life stories of couples' conflicts to think about and discuss in small groups, and were asked to understand both sides of the conflict. Then we were made to act out a drama, speaking offensively and then nonoffensively. The leaders also presented honest communication as a way to avoid conflicts that were often caused by misunderstandings and ignorance. Moreover, communication was presented as the key to a loving relationship. Participants responded to the class with unequivocal enthusiasm. The women were generally satisfied with the setup of the classes, stating that it was good preparation and that they had gained much from it. The men generally admitted to having been anxious, but claimed that they had gained an understanding of certain topics or had learned the importance of talking without becoming offensive. One man said he had never realized that "communication is a skill on its own and extremely necessary in a marriage." "You know," he continued, "I always thought communicating is talking, but I learned the importance of listening." Although men were more unfamiliar with these skills, their positive response suggests that they were persuaded by the therapeutic approach, which explained how love is enhanced through communication and how communication is central to make one's relationship work.

The notion of working on one's relationship resonates with older notions of marriage as cooperative—if not egalitarian—partnerships. Tom Odhiambo, drawing on Laura Kipnis, argues that 1970s Kenyan novelists explained adultery by the fact that marriage itself was understood as work: "as labour for which the spouses need to be compensated either affectively or materially, and in the absence of which marital intimate transgression may occur" (2003, 434). According to Odhiambo, the dramas of adultery and their reasons were generally understood as private and personal affairs and were not recognized in the larger public discourses, and that is why they were told in popular fiction. Two decades later, these personal narratives of love and its perils have clearly entered the public domain. More important, public discourse promotes a therapeutic ethos that influences the private lives of people such as the young professionals in this study.

Among young professionals, women discuss love more explicitly than do men. Women reflect on love when assessing their relationships, in the way that Sereti did. She turned the idea of love over in her mind, asked her friends' opinions, came back to David with a few proposals, and later evaluated her attempt to make her relationship work. The question "what is love?"—how does it affect partners' behavior—is something that women ponder. According to Modleski (cited in Abu-Lughod 2002, 117), the narrative structure and close-up shots of soap operas favored by women viewers provide them with examples of how to feel and behave. The same is true for young female professionals' engagement of a wide range of media. The majority of men, by contrast, see love as a self-evident notion. If I asked them why they did such and such, they typically said, "Because I love her." More men than women found it difficult to answer my questions about what love meant. Tom (aged twenty-six) desperately called out at one point: "Oh! You and your difficult questions! I just loved her [the girlfriend with whom he wanted to have a child]! It means that I cared for her, that I supported her, that I respected her ... basically that I wanted our relationship to work." For men, it was often more difficult to articulate what a love relationship was like because they were raised to be self-reliant and to not talk about personal issues. As a consequence, men overall are less engaged in therapeutic discourse, which is in fact part of an overall global trend (Whitehead 2001, 156–58). Moreover, young professionals grew up amid profound social changes that reconfigured on-the-ground gender relations but left gender ideologies largely intact: "Socio-economic change left men with a patriarchal ideology bereft of its legitimising activities" (Silberschmidt 2001, 657). Patriarchal ideology thus continues to inform men's sense of self.

It is easy to fall into the cliché—as did many of my male and female informants—that "men want sex while women want a good conversation." Men acknowledged that they lacked the skills that women possess to speak about intimacy. They explained that confiding in a woman is contrary to remaining autonomous; hence, they feared betrayal or exposure. Whereas the fear of exposure inhibited some men from opening up to their lovers, others responded differently. Therapeutic discourse insists that equality and companionship are central to contemporary love relationships. Some men endorsed this conception by stating that friendship was the most important element of an intimate relationship, and they distanced themselves from the hegemonic notion of masculinity. Alex (aged twenty in 2001), for example, compared himself with his brothers, whom he claimed "were only looking for the sexual aspect of a relationship," while he "also want[ed] intimacy." Such men regarded themselves as different because they made an effort to reflect on love and justified themselves by claiming entitlement to a modern persona. Since most of the men were not in committed relationships when I interviewed them, they did not have much opportunity to engage in an un-guarded manner with women as they perhaps wished. This does not mean, however, that these men do not seek this kind of intimacy. For instance, while explaining that he had multiple partners at the same time, Ongeri (then aged twenty-nine) stated that he enjoyed being "homely" with only one of them, Atieno. By this he meant that he liked to cook for her, watch TV together, and chat about the things that preoccupied him. His behavior implies a closeness and familiarity that indicates intimacy or sharing quality time. Such men, however, were reluctant to engage in therapeutic discourse to undertake their relationship as a project to "work on." Nonetheless, be-cause the media that young professionals consume present companionship, love, and sex as interconnected, the therapeutic ethos is becoming more influential. I believe that slowly men are beginning to engage this ethos to express their experiences and expectations and, together with their partners, to make their relationships "work."

Media and the Skills of Being and Knowing

Young professionals' engagement of a therapeutic ethos in relation to ro-mance reveals the social transformations that have taken and continue to take place in postcolonial Kenya. These Nairobians occupy an ambivalent situation. They are, in many ways, the successful products of postcolonial opportunities, but they do not want to conform to conventional relation-ship norms and expectations. Their differences from lower-class Kenyans are obvious: their cosmopolitan lifestyles, their frequent inability to speak an ethnic language, their lack of engagement with relatives in rural areas, and their desire for new forms of conjugal relations. Whereas many of their parents sought conjugal compatibility in familial and customary as well as personal terms, young professionals are much less preoccupied with the former concerns. Kenyans and non-Kenyans alike often understand young professionals' lifestyles and engagement of a therapeutic discourse of romance as expressions of a shift from a "traditional" to a "modern" way of being. Rather, their lifestyles are modes of practical action in a contemporary urban and consumer landscape. Generational and class dynamics encourage young professionals to turn to the media as a sounding board in their quest to create lives that are different from those of their parents and the majority of their compatriots. Moreover, as others have argued, consumer lifestyles fit well with romantic conceptions that equate love with happiness and emphasize "intensity" and "fun" as a crucial part of intimacy and modern lifestyles. In other words, socioeconomic changes have combined with new media to generate a fresh understanding of courtship and marriage that is particularly appealing to young professionals.

Whereas previous discourses of romantic love presumed a durable emotional tie between two people premised on qualities intrinsic to the tie itself, the therapeutic ethos offers the knowledge and skills to build durable ties. Young professionals actively seek knowledge about reliable relationships, the art of emotional openness and intimacy, and how to manage their relationships. The power of visual media lays in their ability to graphically represent love, whereas print media by making use of interviews, personal letters, and local surveys play an important role in representing and responding to people's immediate experiences. As a result, print media give more concrete advice on psychological well-being and interpersonal relationships. Young professionals reflect on and try out the versions of love and sexuality presented in the media. In turn, romantic self-expression and intimacy become important to their identification as modern or cosmopolitan people. The media, then, subtly work at personal and interpersonal levels to popularize new modes of subjectivity and new discourses of personhood.

Women articulate therapeutic discourse more often than men. The frames of plausibility offered by various media speak more to professional women's concerns because they experience more directly the constraints of patriarchal ideology. By asserting themselves in the realm of work, they are rejecting the idea that to survive women must marry. They look to marriage more as a source of emotional fulfillment than economic security. For men, shifts in gender relations imply a more thorough redefinition of masculinity, and men fear being criticized for compromising their masculine identity. Nevertheless, many young professional men are responsive, in various degrees, to therapeutic discourse. An important defining ideal of this group is that they relate to women as equals, whether they are colleagues, lovers, or friends. Young professional women and men are engaged in a joint project because of their distinctive position in society. They see themselves as a Kenyan avant-garde committed to forging more "modern" relationships. Most men justify their embrace of greater gender equality by explaining that they are modern men. As a result, both female and male young professionals strive toward more egalitarian relationships. Young professionals recognize the challenges of achieving such relationships and thus are keen to spot success stories whether reported in the media or by individuals. In 2002, Sereti sent me the following e-mail:

> And you see the Kenyan population take in what they read and see. Oyunga [Pala] now is a point of reference in men's opinions, guys take him seriously. This kind of assimilation in magazines and movies just flows in and affects society in one way or the other. I think that one culture cannot remain the same and I think that Kenyans are trying to find a balance. We all want a relationship like that of a movie or soap opera on TV but we know it doesn't work that way . . . we have to find our own way, but that is not easy as you know. Do you remember I told you I didn't know a couple that could be my example? I found them, finally. I liked him at once when he handed over the car keys to her to drive when they were leaving church. Real love changes a man eh?! (June 2002)

ACKNOWLEDGMENTS

I conducted fieldwork on love and sexuality among middle-class Nairobians between February 2001 and February 2002 and between January 2004 and March 2004 (see Spronk 2006). I gratefully acknowledge Jennifer Cole and Lynn Thomas, as well as the anonymous reviewers for the University of Chicago Press, for their comments on previous drafts.

NOTES

1. Although many young professionals believed that their lives and relationships diverged sharply from those of their parents, it is likely that when their parents were young they believed similarly. As argued in the introduction to this volume, passionate love has likely long been a source of intergenerational tension. Mothers of young professionals with whom I spoke explained that they had departed from their mothers' generation by embracing romantic ideals and expecting more egalitarian marriages.
2. In 2003, the *East African Standard* introduced a similar pullout on Saturdays, which was clearly inspired by the success of the *Saturday Magazine*.

3. See http://www.nationmedia.com/dailynation/nmgmagazine.asp?categoryid
=32&todaysdate=9/3/2005 for the *Saturday Magazine* that was the only one of
its kind in 2001–02.

4. The *Saturday Magazine* employs a format with recurring topics that typify the
importance of an up-to-date lifestyle. Regular columns are about travel, house
furnishing, the "Lonely Hearts Club" for dating advertisements, "Eating Out,"
"Medical Notes," "Image Matters," "Relationships," and letters to the editor.
Every edition has several longer articles on various topics ranging from fashion,
body maintenance, and gender issues to family matters and societal issues. Every
edition shows a local female beauty as the cover model with her name, surname,
interests, and hobbies.

5. Rhoda Orengo, interview by the author, January 20, 2004.

6. Catherine Awuor, interview by the author, January 19, 2004.

7. However, she describes a particular trend in which sex is presented in a savvy
and capricious manner where the focus seems to be more on portraying carefree
sex rather than on responding to people's experiences. This style is also present
in Kenya, but I concentrate here only on the media outlets that focus more on
involving their audience.

8. Catherine Awuor also mentions the disappearance of the aunt as adviser: "I
think we have taken the role of advisor because . . . the family as it used to be
is not taking that role anymore, like the aunties used to advise you." The idea
of the role of aunts as counselors for their teenage and young adult nieces and
nephews is often expressed as the most desirable way to deal with important life
changes. However, not many people I spoke with had been counseled by their
aunts. Some parents took it upon themselves, some organized parents' meetings
to speak collectively to their teenagers, while in other families such counseling
was largely absent. During the two pre-wedding showers I attended, we waited
eagerly for the arrival of some aunts to come and speak to the future bride. Unfortunately, in both instances the aunts could not make it.

9. The circulations of international magazines like *Elle, Marie-Claire,* the South
African edition of *Ebony,* and *Men's Health* have increased steadily according to
street vendors, while more and more locally published magazines have emerged.
Eve, for example, the first Kenyan woman's glossy, was launched in 2001.

10. Ms. Maxwell, interview by the author, November 7, 2001; Mr. Njuguna, interview
by the author, October 21, 2001.

Lessons from *Rubí*

LOVE, POVERTY, AND THE EDUCATIONAL VALUE OF TELEVISED DRAMAS IN NIGER

Adeline Masquelier

Rubí is a gripping Mexican television serial centered around the poor but beautiful and ambitious Rubí and her obsessive determination to achieve wealth. A melodramatic story of tangled passions and thwarted ambitions, of friendship, loss, and betrayal, it quickly captivated Nigerien audiences when it started airing on national television in early 2006. In the provincial town of Dogondoutchi, the show enjoyed unprecedented popularity, eclipsing other foreign television programs. So great was *Rubí*'s appeal that people took pains to schedule evening activities around the show so as to be done with daily chores before it came on. When the power went out one October evening minutes before the show, some sixty people packed themselves into the home of one of the few men in town who owned a generator. Dozens more stood outside his crowded house, hoping to catch, if not images, at least bits of the dialogues emanating from his generator-powered television. Unlike British or U.S. teledramas, Latin American serials run a set number of episodes and end on a dramatic, though happy, note. *Rubí* aired three times a week on three consecutive nights. Though the show's heroine is not kind (as is typically the case), it was nonetheless a stereotypical teledrama, with love triangles, cases of forbidden attachments, and climactic revelations in each episode to sustain viewers' interest.

In the way that it tracked the lives of the ruthless Rubí and her cohort of rivals and lovers, *Rubí* was seen by many as mirroring the struggles between interest and sentiments that routinely play themselves out in the context of local courtships and marriages. That the characters were white, wealthy urbanites operating in a Christian culture while local viewers were overwhelmingly poor, Muslim, rural-based Africans did not seem to matter. *Rubí* was an instant hit among local, literate, and semi-literate youths for whom love is one of the central, if not the central, preoccupations of the moment. As they saw it, the foregrounding of class tensions in *Rubí* enhanced the realism of the teledrama, contributing to its appeal: Although elders and Muslim preachers routinely warn youth not to marry above their station, young girls from poor households and with little or no schooling dream of emulating Rubí and securing a wealthy—or at the very least, salaried—husband.

By the time I arrived in Dogondoutchi in late 2006, the show had just ended. It nevertheless remained a staple topic of conversations among youths who made frequent allusions to the heroes of the story when discussing how to treat the object of their affection, or conversely what to avoid doing so as not to end up like the lovelorn Rubí. Although a gendered division of interpretation operated—young women looking for feminine models of conduct, young men for masculine ones—all remained captivated by the world of heightened emotion and drama brought to life by *Rubí*.

Through their increasing exposure to televised dramas, both national and foreign, audiences everywhere are coming to understand romantic love as the ideal basis for marriage (Abu-Lughod 1995; Ahearn 2001; Birth and Freilich 1995; Spronk 2002; Verheijen 2006; Wardlow 1996; Zeff 1999). Yet if viewers in Niger, Egypt, and elsewhere link the narratives of courtship and bourgeois conjugality projected on their television screens to ideologies of modern progress, it hardly means that current discourses and practices of love can be analyzed as an inevitable by-product of development (Wardlow and Hirsch 2006). Instead, we must recognize how popular engagement with televised romances is part of a wider strategy through which people position themselves in relation to what they take to be tradition and modernity.

In this essay, I explore how in Dogondoutchi, Latin American *feuilletons* (teledramas) are centrally implicated in the emergence of an ideology of love through which youth assert a modern identity. Foreign television dramas, I suggest, are seen as a medium of development by impoverished youth looking for moral instruction as well as training in the language of love. Youths say that far from triggering unhealthy delusions or encouraging immorality as local critics claim, *feuilletons* provide useful models of romantic behavior that help them become morally responsible individuals, better prepared to face life's challenges.[1]

There is a growing literature on the impact of media in society, much of it originally informed by Baudrillard's (1988) claim that television does not belong to life's reality. Through the production of images that come to constitute a "hyperreality" that overshadows reality, television ultimately dissolves the distinction between reality and representation. From this perspective, media-produced images are seen as global products having no organic connections to the life worlds of local audiences (Honneth 1992). The problem with such formulations is that they provide tantalizingly few details on the desires, concerns, and sensibilities of media consumers. Studies have shown that far from passively ingesting globally produced images, audiences everywhere selectively appropriate content for their purposeful and localized consumption (Abu-Lughod 1995; Ang 1985; Das 1995; Meyer 2003). Moreover, the presence of electronic images does not end once the television shows are over. Instead they become the object of conversations and ruminations, acquiring in the process "a life of their own" (Das 1995, 171). In this vein, Larkin (1997) suggests that the popularity of Indian films among Muslim audiences in northern Nigeria derives from their capacity to create an alternative modernity to both Western modernity and Hausa traditionalism (see also Fair, this volume). Characters in Indian films must negotiate the tension between traditional values and what are perceived as modern values in ways that northern Nigerian viewers, living under comparable postcolonial conditions, can identify with.

Following Ang's (1991, 162) recommendation that we ask how "people encounter, use, interpret, enjoy, think, and talk about television," I explore how the relation between screen events and real life plays itself out in an impoverished West African town where the message conveyed by television dramas is often at odds with Muslim-based notions of virtue and modesty. Through a discussion of how local youth in search of a sentimental education used *Rubí* as a pedagogical resource, I highlight the dynamics of gender and generation at work in the consumption of foreign televised programs and the ways that these programs encourage new kinds of sensibilities (Abu-Lughod 2002). While much has been written on the role of cinema and television in the making of gendered modernities, in these works the appeal of mediatized images of modernity is generally articulated in term of a generational paradigm shift and little else. A more productive line of inquiry might be opened up if we consider what it means for youth to watch television and, more specifically, to "consume" television programs. In a discussion on consumption, Miller (1995, 1) notes that

> to be consumer is to possess consciousness that one is living through objects and images not of one's own creation. It is this which makes the term symptomatic of what some at least have seen as the core meaning of the term modernity. . . . This sense of consumption as a secondary relationship takes on a particular importance within an ideology which espouses not only the aesthetic ideal of authenticity through creation, but its more mundane philosophical counterpart of a notion of natural ownership through labor. Within such a dominant ideology the condition of consumption is always a potential state of rupture. Consumption then may not be about choice, but rather the sense that we have no choice but to attempt to overcome the experience of rupture using those very same goods and images which create for many the sense of modernity as rupture.

Miller's notion that modern consumption is about transcending rupture by using the very images that create the experience of modernity as rupture in the first place highlights the predicament of the young Nigeriens whose ruminations on love I discuss here. Like other young Africans who are powerless to buffer the devastating impact of a continent-wide economic crisis, youths in Dogondoutchi are routinely enticed with the allure of a modernity they cannot hope to access except through fantasy (Ferguson 1999; Friedman 1994; Weiss 2002). Far from being a trivial concern that has no bearing on social realities, I argue that romantic love is the point of entry for translating fantasies about the West into new social identities. By focusing on the power of fantasy to create meaning in contexts of dire poverty, I explore how romantic love has become an empowering emotion through which youths in Dogondoutchi imagine the possibility of a future.

Rubí: A Tale of Love and Betrayal

Like other rags to riches tales imported from Latin America (*Marimar* and *Escrava Isaura* are two that come to mind), *Rubí* focuses on a young woman who escapes poverty by marrying well. Where it differs from telenovelas like *Marimar* or *Escrava Isaura* is in its depiction of the heroine as a deeply flawed, brash, and ultimately self-destructive character. Set for the most part in Mexico City among the well-heeled and the powerful, the televised drama opens with young Rubí Pérez attending university on a scholarship. There, she befriends Maribel de la Fuente, the daughter of a rich man. Maribel, who is lame as a result of an accident, becomes Rubí's conduit to affluence and privilege. She is engaged to Hector Ferrer, a successful architect. After she introduces Rubí to Hector's best friend, Alejandro Cárdenas, it is love at first sight for Rubí and Alejandro. Rather than the prosperous doctor Rubí thought he was, however, Alejandro is a poor medical student. Sacrificing her happiness for the sake of financial security, Rubí jilts him for the wealthy Hector. They elope to New York and marry. But Rubí cannot forget Alejandro.

Fast forward a few years. Alejandro is now an accomplished surgeon. After he operates on her injured leg, Maribel falls for him. But Alejandro is married to Sonia. Meanwhile, Hector and Rubí's marriage is on the rocks. After they meet again, Alejandro and Rubí's romance is rekindled. They make plans to start a life together. Conveniently, Alejandro's pregnant wife Sonia accidentally dies. Initially inconsolable, Alejandro eventually recovers with Rubí's help. Then Rubí, who is pregnant, loses the baby in an accident. She tells Alejandro she miscarried after her husband hit her.

Hector finds out that the baby Rubí was carrying was not his and that she accused him of causing the miscarriage. Before he can tell Alejandro that Rubí has deceived them both, he dies after being hit by a car. Alejandro nonetheless learns the truth. He sees his lover for who she really is—a calculating and selfish woman—and leaves her. While running after him, Rubí falls over a stair banister and sustains terrible wounds. Disfigured and crippled, she can no longer use her beauty to manipulate men. Meanwhile, Alejandro marries Maribel. Years pass. Bitter, but not vanquished, Rubí lives for revenge. When Alejandro returns to Mexico after years of living abroad, Rubí sends her niece Fernanda to seduce him. Fernanda is Rubí's instrument of revenge. She is beautiful, sly, and unscrupulous, just like Rubí from whom she learned her tricks. Alejandro's son falls in love with her. When he first lays eyes on her, Alejandro, too, is overwhelmed by her beauty. Fernanda looks just like young Rubí. The final scene ends with Alejandro and Fernanda kissing passionately as a hidden cameraman records their embrace.

There is a large cast of characters revolving around the four heroes and whose own dramas thicken the main plot and keep audiences engaged. Yet it is Rubí, Maribel, Alejandro, and Hector and the love triangles their respective relationships form that are the focus of viewers' attention. "I still remember the night that Hector died," a twenty-seven-year-old teacher told me. "Me and my friends, we were so shocked. We were obsessed with the show. That night, I didn't sleep. Hector was dead, I felt awful." If Hector aroused sympathy, the most conflicted emotions converged around Rubí. "Rubí is mean, she loves money too much. I don't want to be like her, yet I also like her. She is very beautiful," a nineteen-year-old woman confided.

As the ambitious heroine ultimately undone by greed and selfishness, Rubí is the perfect embodiment of love and betrayal—two key ingredients of success in teledrama recipes. Latin American serials (together with the popular *soyayya* dramas, a product of the burgeoning Nigerian film industry[2]) are known by French-educated Nigeriens as examples of *amour et trahison* ("love and betrayal"). From these foreign melodramas, audiences learn that there is a moral code governing not only social conduct, but also amorous relations. Not everyone abides by the code, however, which is why love and fidelity are regularly under threat. By presenting all that can happen in the tense encounter between romance and materialism, teledramas bring confirmation that sentiments can be powerfully shaped by interest. Yet they also provide the idiom—romantic love—through which youth in Dogondoutchi can transcend the limitations of the present and give shape to their imagined futures.

Love and Marriage in Dogondoutchi: Past Practices, Present Dilemmas

Traditionally, prospective brides, raised as they were in a strictly gender segregated society, did not expect to spend much of their time with their husbands, even if, paradoxically, courtship absorbed all their attention (Callaway 1987). Husbands and wives did not socialize together and did not engage in joint activities—except during the farming season. The rules of avoidance they followed dictated that they eat separately, avoid interaction, and not call each other by name. If young people today are putting increasing emphasis on romantic love (*soyayya*, from *so*, "to want, to desire, to like, to love") as the cornerstone of marriage and the prerequisite for a successful life, it does not mean that *soyayya* is a new concept. Baba, an old Hausa woman, told Mary Smith in 1949–50 that while she "did not love Duma" (1954 [1981], 112), her first husband,[3] and married him at fourteen only because her father forced her to, she "love[d]" her second husband and he "love[d her]" (1954 [1981], 159). Baba's loveless first marriage is a predicament that young Nigerien women still faced in the 1980s. As a means of building alliances between lineages, matrimony was too serious a matter to be left to young people in the throes of passion; instead, marriage arrangements were handled by elders, well positioned to assess the benefits of certain matches and to protect the interests of the lineage.

While Baba's story exemplifies the tension between love marriage (*armen so*, "marriage of desire") and arranged marriage, it also suggests that there was a place for romance and desire in Hausa society, and not just in the popular love stories that were part of oral tradition. Romance was not associated with first marriages, however. It was only once women divorced the older men they had been forced to marry as young girls that they, like Baba, could personally choose their next husbands. Men, too, spoke of favorite wives who received preferential treatment. Given the strict gender segregation that was practiced, spouses were traditionally "distant from each other's emotional lives," and they "seldom cross[ed] each other's paths outside the bedroom" (Callaway 1987, 42; Cooper 1997). If gender segregation does not exclude the possibility that couples experienced deep affection for each other, it does imply, Callaway (1987, 40) notes, that love and romance were strictly Western concepts that "ha[d] little real meaning in this [Hausa] culture." Romantic love, Cole and Thomas (this volume) remind us, is a discursive construct that emerges at a particular place and time. It cannot provide an adequate gloss for the forms of affect and intimacy that women such as Baba experienced even as they claimed to love and be loved by their husbands.

Whether they speak of love as an emotional form of intimacy, an intense physical attraction, or a vulnerability akin to sickness,[4] most youth today insist that they want to marry for love, thereby deliberately positioning themselves in contrast to their parents and grandparents for whom marital relationships were subject to collective surveillance—and often structured around the principle of polygyny. Marrying for love implies committing to an exclusive relationship. When I asked whether polygyny was compatible with love, young men and women would often chide me gently: "You can love only one person truly," they would point out. To add weight to his pronouncements, a young man invoked the Qur'an, which advises men to remain monogamous if they fear they cannot love several women equally.

Developing alongside this ideology of marriage-as-love is the realization that monetary considerations matter greatly, so much so that they can take precedence over sentiment in courtship. Young men and women, disillusioned by experience, frequently answered my questions on romance by alluding to the commoditization of love. They spoke of the poverty that drove some to forgo love. Over the last two decades, the hopes that followed Niger's move toward democratization have been dashed by a pervasive economic crisis and growing social inequalities. A decade after independence, Niger enjoyed a period of relative prosperity thanks to uranium revenues. With the 1985 collapse of the uranium market, however, affluence ended. Unable to support its newly expanded infrastructure, Niger has experienced financial woes ever since, a predicament that neoliberal reforms—mandated by international lenders to ensure debt repayment and economic restructuring—have only exacerbated. Today the country exists in a state of virtual bankruptcy. Past demographic growth has translated into growing numbers of job seekers who can no longer be absorbed by a labor market that has shrunk with the implementation of structural adjustment policies. Consequently, the unemployment rate has skyrocketed.

The economic problems the country faces at the dawn of the twenty-first century have given rise to diffuse anxieties about the moral and material basis of social reproduction, anxieties that have often translated into renewed concern about the predicament of youth. Parents complain about rising immorality, idleness, and criminality. At the same time that they worry about the increasing number of youth who postpone marriage, they wonder how unemployed young men will provide for future dependents in this era of chronic job scarcity (Masquelier 2005). Like numerous other young men on the continent (de Boeck 2002; Diouf 2003; Ferguson 1999; Hansen 2005; O'Brien 1996), local youth faced with dwindling resources and inflated marriage costs have been forced to delay marriage—and by implication, social maturity since it is by marrying that one crosses the threshold of adulthood. Farming, which traditionally provided the basis for subsistence, is no longer an adequate source of income. Many youth have to migrate to the city on a seasonal or even permanent basis. Those who stay behind complain that there are no jobs and no means of escaping poverty. As the forms of social advancement (financial independence, marriage, and so on) that previous generations took for granted become increasingly difficult to guarantee, young men find themselves struggling to secure a place in society.

Even schooling, which had originally produced a literate elite ready to fill the ranks of an emerging bureaucracy at independence, now seems to lead nowhere, save for a minority able to draw on private resources or personal connections. Frustrated young people now blame the state for their ruined youth. Like their uneducated counterparts, they occupy a precarious position in the new world order, which the recent commoditization of love has only exacerbated. In contexts where "the will to consume outstrips the opportunity to earn" (Comaroff and Comaroff 2000, 317), they complain that romantic relationships are more often than not mediated by money. To prove their interest and affection, men must impress women with gifts of cash and commodities. Meanwhile, despite the high premium placed on virginity, young women feel pressured to provide sexual reciprocation in return for the financial commitments made by their suitors.[5]

Like young men, young women hope to marry and aspire to economic prosperity. Because they can often choose a husband from among several suitors—when they do not simply attach themselves to a "sugar daddy"—they appear to negotiate more successfully the multiple hurdles of the marital economy than their male counterparts. Lifestyle and access to consumer goods play a significant role in their choice of marriage partners and in the notions of marriage and womanhood that they entertain. This is especially true for those who wish to escape the rugged, peasant world they come from. Like the Senegalese case described by Buggenhagen (2004, 25), young women in Dogondoutchi are beginning to see marriage as a means to access bourgeois domesticity and to obtain "the kinds of goods through which they would construct their own personhood and their relations to others." Men who cannot help pay for the array of furniture, appliances, and decorative items with which brides fill their domestic interiors cannot be seriously considered as potential marriage partners. In a society in which polygynous marriages remain the norm among wealthy men, it is not uncommon for young women to marry considerably older men with several wives. Impoverished youths who must compete against successful businessmen for the attention of marriageable women are at a distinct disadvantage, even if they champion monogamy and privilege emotional closeness. If young men feel victimized by a matrimonial market that encourages young women to contract hypergamous marriages, it hardly means that young women fare much better. Except for a limited few, most of them struggle in their quest for the bourgeois domesticity they now associate with marriage. Because of the difficulties young people encounter in their search for social advancement, marriage is on everyone's mind.[6]

Despite a widespread recognition that the material and emotional dimensions of romance are inextricably connected, many hold on to the hope of finding "true" love—*l'amour passion,* as they call it. Countering peer claims that finance drives romance (see also Smith, this volume), they speak of having "relationships," building romance based on mutually enjoyed pastimes, and connecting deeply with the object of their affection. As is the case elsewhere (Cornwall 2002; Lewinson 2006; Okonjo 1992; D. Smith 2001; van der Vliet 1991), these notions of companionate marriage and enduring connections have affected the process of spouse selection. In contrast to members of the previous generation, some of whom engaged in *gidan arme* ("cousin marriage"), they tend to marry nonrelatives,[7] similar in age to themselves. Youth also resist parental authority when their choices of partners do not coincide with parental expectations.

I was chatting with Abdou and his friends, as the high school student was preparing a batch of *shai,* the heavily sweetened green tea that has become a necessary ingredient of good conversation for idle youth looking for answers to life's problems. We were discussing the importance of marriage and the virtues of companionship when Abdou proclaimed, "Marriage, it's the foundation of my life. If I fail my marriage, I fail my life." The marriage that Abdou had in mind was based not on parental expectations of what would be a socially appropriate union for the two households involved, but on what could be defined as an emotional connection between two autonomous individuals. In a word: romantic love.[8] From Abdou's perspective, privileging romantic attraction and individual choice was the recipe for marital success. Aside from pointing to the centrality of the conjugal bond in youthful understandings of what it takes to be modern, Abdou's comment betrays the anxiety many youths experience at the prospect of choosing a consort. As Wardlow and Hirsch (2006, 3) point out, "It is one thing to marry for love and another to stay married for love." Once they are married, the personal connection the two partners share must often compete with other familial ties, generational obligations, and social expectations—when it does not simply fizzle in the face of poverty or gender asymmetry (see Bastian 2001; Rebhun 1999b; D. Smith 2001).[9]

Love, Materialism, and Betrayal

If they glorify *soyayya* as an ennobling and enabling sentiment, youths paradoxically acknowledge that building a long-lasting marriage on the basis of an affective bond is not easy. In an era of sharpening economic inequalities, growing numbers of young people allegedly end up marrying for *ku'di* ("money") rather than *soyayya*. Because strategy rather than romance drives their unions, they are decried as cynical individuals who sacrifice love for the sake of economic stability. Even as they contrast *soyayya* to economic interest, their more idealist counterparts admit that it is sometimes hard to disentangle one from the other. As they see it, a major hurdle attending the quest for love involves learning to distinguish *masu son ku'di* ("those who love money," also known as *les matérialistes*) from the genuine person who will love them for who they are. Conversely, those who yearn for the "real thing" must try not to become engulfed in materialistic desires—a temptation that girls, as the traditional recipients of their suitors' largesse, reportedly face more than boys. As was implied in Abdou's remark on love as the measure of life, this hurdle can be a significant source of anxiety, foiling any attempt to build meaningful rapport with members of the other sex: "Women, they are all bitches!" a young man blurted out in response to my question about the problems he and his classmates encountered in their romantic relationships.

He was not alone in casting women as morally corrupt temptresses, unworthy of their suitors' affection. For many of the youths I met, talk of love was tempered by a suspicion of women's materialistic motives, which led to betrayal and broken hearts. "Girls, they want money. Love is not enough," a high school student observed. Indeed, young men are finding that access to money and the ability to shower one's beloved with gifts have increasingly become a sine qua non of romantic relationships. "Girls today," twenty-two-year-old Nasser explained, "they don't love for nothing!" At a time when consumption has become the sole indicator of success, the pursuit of material comforts has taken center stage, eclipsing love for the sake of love and transforming romance into a hypercommodified experience: According to Nasser, "When you have money, women call you *'chéri.'* When you are broke, they want nothing to do with you."

If their voracious appetite for consumer goods is not satisfied, *les matérialistes* reportedly compel their boyfriends to pursue illicit profit-making ventures or abandon them altogether to look for more suitable providers.[10] Although not all of these relationships entail sex, many do, and this despite the strict Muslim prescription against premarital sex. Others allegedly keep several suitors to cater to their different needs (see also Cole and Hunter, this volume).[11] Putting aside modesty and sexual discipline, they combine a boyfriend (handsome, but poor) with an older, wealthier man known as *le bailleur de fonds* ("lender"), who unknowingly helps support his young mistress's "true" love. In such contexts, coming by a faithful girlfriend whom one can trust and eventually marry is, many concede, a near impossibility. "Materialist women are never in love. They are only interested in material things," according to Boube, whose girlfriend had left him for another more prosperous suitor. "For them, betrayal is a way of life."

Betrayal is not a female monopoly, however; young men are routinely described as unfaithful partners who "want to sample other women." For young men who speak of their additional girlfriends as *roues de secours* ("spare tires"), assertive masculinity is intimately bound up with the experience of sexual conquest. In the end, there is widespread consensus that while men cheat on their sweethearts to fulfill irrepressible sexual urges, women do so to satisfy their lust for material goods.

To summarize, young men and women perceive love and marriage with much ambivalence. On the one hand, they see love as the stuff that dreams are made of: in its pure, unadulterated expression, love transcends material issues. On the other hand, the notion that love coexists with betrayal and is continually undone by it routinely emerged in my conversations with youths. While they insisted that money could not buy love, young people nonetheless recognized that money often dictated the terms of courtship and marriage aside from the fact that one could not survive on love alone. Poverty, I was told, is what makes young girls opt for wealthy suitors with deep pockets (see Nyamnjoh 2005). Parents turn a blind eye when their daughters come home with expensive clothes or with money to pay the electricity bill. The issue of whether disparities in wealth and education matter in marriage is subject to much debate. It is also a central axis around which the plot of *Rubí* developed to create a tense yet intensely appealing drama that spoke to youthful concerns about the price and pleasures of love.

Besides drawing attention to the relations between poverty and consumerism, the forms of polyandry that are emerging to complicate conventional marriage arrangements point to the limitations of approaches that use gender as a "shorthand for an oppositional imbalance of power in which women are inevitably the losers, and that fail to make sense either of women's agency or identifications" (Cornwall 2002, 968).[12] In the end, new understandings of affect and intimacy have done little to help economically impotent men reassert their masculinity by facilitating marriage and by creating more enduring bonds. Regardless of whether youth speak of love as money, love of money, or love or money, emotion and materialism in all their permutations "reflect the perceived fragility of contemporary heterosexual relationships as well as the tensions within them" (Cornwall 2002, 977). Surviving the emotional, moral, and economic contradictions of life thus requires a minimum of savoir faire that is not available from traditional educational sources. Although elders largely disagree, youth argue that their situation is far more problematic than their parents' ever was thanks largely to the widening gap between social aspirations and economic realities and the threats posed by the AIDS pandemic.

Of late, Latin American *feuilletons* have become a major source of infotainment for young school-educated Nigeriens yearning for the emotional intimacy that constitutes the necessary prelude to marriage. Given the often contradictory way that social, religious, and economic pressures shape the experience of love, youth find it difficult to achieve the emotional connection they long for. As they see it, finding and nurturing love requires finesse—as well as discernment and maturity. While this kind of affective know-how— together with the conviction that *soyayya* is the legitimate basis of marriage— cannot reportedly be acquired from one's elders (for whom marital relations are about social and sexual reproduction), it is widely available on television. Indeed, one of the main reasons youth in Dogondoutchi watch Brazilian and Mexican telenovelas is to develop the requisite sensibilities for successful romance and long-term, fulfilling relationships.

Youth who attend French-type schools and consider themselves *éduqués* ("educated") universally expect to choose their own spouses based on mutual attraction and a shared sense of what conjugality entails. Newly emerging representations of marriage as companionship are circulating widely thanks in part to the ever-widening spectrum of teledramas available for consumption on Nigerien television. Because they explore the exciting intimacy of modern love in its complex and contradictory dimensions, Latin American televised dramas have become especially popular among school-educated youths in the throes of courtship. These young people see teledramas as a valuable source of learning and inspiration. Halima, a twenty-year-old student, explained:

> At home, we do not speak of love. There is shame. At school, they teach us about sexuality and STDs but we don't talk about marriage. The only people I discuss all that with are my friends. Together, we watch *feuilletons* like *Muñeca Brava, Rubí,* or *Café.* I like watching [them] because they are about love.

As Halima's testimony suggests, teledramas provide both a discursive space and a physical place—ideally away from one's parents—where youths can ponder the problems of love and the possible forms that marriage can take. Not all households own a television, but among those that do, the set is brought out in the evening so that everyone, occasionally including neighbors, can watch. Because teledramas deal with issues (love, sexuality, and so on) that are conventionally taboo subjects, watching them with one's parents can be a source of deep embarrassment. "You can't watch television when your parents are there," Halima noted. "When [the actors] start kissing and you're standing next to your father, you feel such shame you just want the earth to swallow you!"

Learning the Language of Love

Four decades or so ago, it was cinema—and in Anglophone Africa, locally produced pamphlets and magazines (see Mutongi, this volume; Obiechina 1973; Whitsitt 2003)—that brought images of romance to African communities so that young people could master the terms and techniques of love in their pursuit of middle-class modernity (Comhaire-Sylvain 1968). On the Rhodesian Copperbelt, cowboy films taught audiences "how to fight others and how to win lovers" (Powdermaker 1962, 261). In Dogondoutchi, where until recently the only cinematic pictures were occasional martial arts films from Hong Kong, it was largely through the consumption of Indian videos in the 1990s that youthful audiences were introduced to on-screen romances and the attendant dilemmas facing lovers torn between competing systems of values. Today, it is Latin American televised dramas that play a key role in the sentimental education of young people. In part because they create an imagined community (Anderson 1983) of viewers joined in their consumption of the worlds depicted on television, these foreign dramas serve as symbolic anchors for youth who, by virtue of their poverty, feel otherwise disconnected from the world at large.

Televised dramas "educate us," eighteen-year-old Salamatou explained. "They teach us how to conduct ourselves in society, and how to deal with our boyfriends." "I learned about love by watching how they do it on television," Lawali, a twenty-two-year-old economics student, told me. He added:

> Just as music nourishes you and educates you about things you know nothing about, so *feuilletons* inform you on the evolution of the world. They teach you how to live well in our society. You learn about different ways of life and about everything that a couple needs.

Teledramas "show us that love is a necessary ingredient in the search for happiness," his friend, a carpenter, added. Aside from learning how to negotiate the ups and downs of relationships, young lovers are taught what is morally acceptable from what is not:

> A character in the *feuilleton* who behaves appropriately, we'll try to follow his lead, we'll act like him. There's always one [character] who's bad and one who's good. For women too, *feuilletons* provide good [role models]. They see that money is not love.

Although they are watched by audiences who do not understand French, *feuilletons* are most avidly consumed by French-educated youth who see in them both the world they inhabit and the distant world they yearn for. While male viewers find that they deliver practical tips on how to love and grapple with love, telenovelas are especially popular among young women: so much so that young men have complained to me that girlfriends will not greet them if they visit them when their favorite show is on. By promoting new ways of loving and living, television serials help articulate increasingly gendered modes of affect and intimacy.

At a time when overwhelmingly Muslim Niger is undergoing a religious revival and Muslim clerics are condemning foreign television programs for their corrupting influence, youth justify their fondness for Latin American television serials by invoking their pedagogical dimension. In the context of public debates about *armen dole* ("forced marriage"), polygyny, and early marriages, *feuilletons* have become forums for exploring the forms that romance and matrimony should ideally take and for imagining what it means to belong—that is, to be part of the world out there—in contexts where youth are frequently denied real agency. To conservative Muslims, however, these representations of courtship and conjugality are based on understandings of intimacy that are antithetical to proper notions of gender, authority, and sexuality. Youths, who have embraced foreign media—and the supposedly new ideas they convey—in their attempt to gain a purchase on the stark realities of life in the Sahel, are not deaf to the message of Islam. They occasionally admit being troubled by the fact that respect for maraboutic ideologies (the ideologies promoted by Muslim preachers and Qur'anic teachers) is dwindling in the face of rampant consumerism and modern ways. As they indulge their passion for popular culture by watching telenovelas or listening to popular music—activities condemned by Muslim clerics—youths frequently invoke their immaturity to justify their actions. They also point to the ways that things have changed, usually for the worse, for the young people of Niger, a situation that has lately forced them to develop new strategies for survival (selling drugs, stealing, or romancing a woman with a sugar daddy) and to explore alternative modes of consumption (buying knockoffs instead of original brands).

Some residents insist that programs featuring kissing and sexual intimacy should be banned because by exposing adolescents to what they perceive to be immorality, they push them into prostitution and delinquency. In their sermons, Muslim preachers condemn televised "scenes of debauchery" that lead to the sexual arousal of young men and ultimately contribute to the rise of pregnancy among unmarried girls. There is also concern in conservative Muslim quarters that foreign television encourages youthful disobedience by providing dangerous models of individualism: Youths defy the authority of elders, young wives display insubordination, and ill-matched lovers ignore parental advice. Countering such claims, youth insist that *feuilletons* help them "expand their knowledge" by sensitizing them to the problems that lovers routinely face in real life. Far from corrupting them, *feuilletons* enlighten them.

Aside from helping youth refine their French at a time when overcrowded, understaffed state schools can no longer provide adequate language instruction, teledramas also teach the language of love and romance: "To seduce a woman, you must know how to talk to her; you have to be a poet. Women like to be flattered. *Ma petite,* I told her things I learned from *feuilletons,*" Hamidou, a high school student explained. Girls cherish the poems, cards, and other tokens of affection they receive from suitors. Of late, sending one's paramour a store-bought card with a romantic message on February 14 has become de rigueur among educated youths in the throes of love (see Spronk, this volume).

For poor but educated young men, the language of romance and flattery is the only weapon they can wield to outdo wealthier competitors on the romance market. Prosperous merchants with no schooling are said to treat their wives and lovers "like ornaments." While they provide for their comfort and security, they are unable to fulfill their emotional needs. From this perspective, only men who have been educated through schooling and exposure to television make young women truly happy, as the following testimony by a young schoolteacher suggests:

> [Men] who have money, they don't know how to treat a woman, they just give her things. A rich trader who talks to a girl, it's not the same as when I talk to her. My only ambition is to make her happy. [After bringing her a gift,] the trader says, "I have some business to attend, I'll be back next week," and leaves. Whereas the poor boy spends time singing her praise, sending her poems. He knows women like to be valorized.

Aside from hinting that finance cannot replace romance, the teacher claimed that because they had received training in the art of love, young educated men knew what women expected from their admirers.[13] By creating with words an atmosphere conducive to romance, they not only conveyed their desirability as partners but were able to offer women moments of transcendence, a chance to "escape the limits of the given" (Lindholm 2006, 17).

Language—not money—has become essential to the cultivation of emotional intimacy, this testimony suggests. It is by both speaking about love and "speaking love" that one can successfully claim the affection of another person. For young people for whom love—and the kinds of relationship it both entails and sustains—is part of the emotional apparatus of modern people, claiming to be conversant in the language of love is a way to situate themselves in opposition to the previous generation and to legitimize their gendered roles in the face of potential parental disapproval. Consider the following conversation between Ali, an unemployed high school graduate, and myself:

A.: *Feuilletons* are good.
A.M.: Why is that?
A.: They cultivate you. They develop your understanding of love. You gather ideas on love.
A.M.: What does the *feuilleton* teach you?

A.: It teaches you how to speak to a girl, how to make love to her, how to manage the relationship.

A.M.: Parents don't teach this to their children?

A.: No, we don't talk about this with them. Our religion forbids it. We feel shame.

A.M.: Did your parents have love?

A.: Well, no. It's not the same thing. Our elders did not have what we have.

A.M.: Why?

A.: In the past, if you had a girlfriend, you did not speak unless you were about to marry her. But now, our generation, we don't necessarily get married. But we speak—all the time.

For Ali and his peers, it is by verbally expressing one's attachment to a person (rather than demonstrating it by, say, buying her a cell phone or preparing his bath water) that one builds the affective bonds on which companionate marriage is predicated. In their efforts to compete with wealthier suitors who have money but no conversation, impoverished young men looking for romance have transformed love making into "an essentially narrative . . . affair" (Illouz 1997, 42), whose terms are directly inspired by the language of telenovelas.

Of Soaps and Schooling: Television as Education

Although youths acknowledge that the plots of their favorite serials may not reflect reality as they know it, they often insist that the stories are nonetheless realistic, depicting not just moments of blissful intimacy but also the heartaches that signal the end of romance. As one of them put it, "Love in *feuilletons,* it's real, it's about life and what happens in relationships." It is tempting to dismiss comments such as these on the basis that foreign teledramas tell stories of fashionably attired, jet-setting people in luxurious settings that bear little resemblance to Sahelian realities. The realism that audiences claim is part of their viewing experience must be assessed, I suggest, in light of the "mix of intimacy and distance" (Abu-Lughod 2005, 239) that characterizes viewers' responses to foreign dramas.

Though they know that the worlds presented in the serials are fictional, audiences find ways to selectively relate to them, Abu-Lughod (2005) notes of Egyptian television drama viewers. Often, meaning is derived not from a purported connection between the characters' lives and the viewers' lives, but from the familiarity the viewers come to have over time with the characters, their stories, and their struggles. Similarly, Nigerien audiences compartmentalize telenovelas as "worlds unto themselves" (Abu-Lughod 2005, 239) that are only distantly related to their own at the same time that they develop an intimate knowledge of the characters. That the dramas featured on Nigerien television are produced in Latin America complicates the process of audience identification with the fictional characters. For one thing, unlike Egyptian serials that are designed for Egyptian audiences, Latin American teledramas are not part of the technologies of nation building in Niger. The shared longings and communal fantasies that foreign teledramas inspire have little to do with what many Nigeriens would argue are the critical social issues of their time. Despite the asymmetries of power and information that separate local audiences from the makers of these serials, however, there is much in the lives of the characters that viewers can sympathize with. A young unemployed man said that he identified with Hector, Rubí's wealthy husband, because of what he knew of the man's suffering at the hands of his conniving wife: "I feel sorry for Hector. She married him for his money and then she cheated on him." Though the two belonged to different worlds, his knowledge of Hector's troubled marriage colored his perception of the architect. He saw Hector as just another victim of women who, like Rubí, put aside emotional satisfaction for the ruthless pursuit of material comforts.[14]

The instrumental value of television serials also lies in the pragmatic message that can be distilled from them. A girl explained how she drew inspiration from *Café*, a teledrama about two star-crossed lovers. "In the *feuilleton*, Carolina is rejected by the family of the man she loves, Sébastien, because they think she's a prostitute. That's exactly my situation. My boyfriend's family does not accept me." Like other youths, she saw *feuilletons* as both models *of* and *for* social realities. Far from embellishing life, *feuilletons* provided a hard-headed assessment of it.

As I previously noted, the fact that the characters they identify with are non-Muslims makes little difference. As youths see it, the issues at stake are universal enough to transcend religious sectarianism. Ultimately, the goal is to become a self-sufficient, morally engaged individual through the cultivation of affective ties—in short, a more modern person. According to one youth, teledramas function like the Qur'an by providing a set of principles aimed at leading the audience toward right action. Just as people do not follow everything the Qur'an says, so audiences must separate the wheat from the chaff before modeling their conduct after that of characters "made in Mexico." There is disagreement regarding what is and what is not acceptable. Attire is a subject of contentious debate between those who believe that dress is irrelevant to Muslim identity and those who insist that Muslims should wear modest clothing and stop trying to dress like the handsome Hector or the alluring Rubí.

Countering the perception that foreign teledramas contribute to their uprooting, youths I spoke with insisted that *feuilletons* helped solve the materialism that had infected romance instead of contributing to it. At the same time, *feuilletons* brought them hope. "I was like Alejandro," Boubacar confided. "I was poor, without a job, and I couldn't marry the woman I loved." When he was a university student, Boubacar fell in love with a young woman. At first, he brought her small gifts, but she wanted money—lots of it. Eventually, he had to give up the pretense that he could support her lifestyle. After finishing his studies, he took a teaching position in town. "Like Alejandro, I knew that with hard work, I could improve my life." Telenovelas that feature rags to riches scenarios offer Nigerien youth a way of imagining themselves out of the mediocre life poverty condemns them to. As citizens of the world's poorest nation, they are achingly aware that they are "behind" in every respect. They see foreign dramas as a tool for catching up with more industrialized countries: "*Feuilletons* show us how the world is moving. . . . They help us move forward."

Love, Poverty, and Fantasy

When you truly love someone, young people insist, it is not because of how rich that person is. Without denying that spending money can be an expression of love, many of them nonetheless condemn those who sacrifice "true" love for wealth. In our conversations about the threats that materialism poses to romantic love, they often brought up Rubí as the prototypical materialistic lover. Consider this testimony from twenty-year-old Hamissou:

> If a rich man marries a poor woman, when he loses his wealth, she will change. She will stop caring for him and eventually leave him. That's because she married for money. It's just like Rubí. Rubí is poor. Her mother advises her not to marry someone for his wealth. But Rubí loves money. So she marries a wealthy man instead of the man she loves. She thinks that once she is rich, she can marry the love of her life. Rubí is a materialist.

By defying parental authority and marrying above her station to ultimately lose everything, including her "true" love, Rubí reinforced the perception that marriages based on interest are doomed. "Wealth disparities between lovers are not good," Hamissou concluded—a veiled reference to the current debate about whether partners with different social backgrounds can enjoy fulfilling, long-lasting marriages.

Given the concern about mismatched couples, Rubí's marital history had considerable resonance among local audiences. As the central villain of the story, Rubí is the nodal point around which everything unfolds. Her wiliness is highlighted by the presence of Maribel, who is the picture of righteousness and the model young women should emulate. In a country where the ravages of polio are visible everywhere, Maribel's physical handicap spoke of a vulnerability that many found realistic:

> Girls who watch *Rubí* must follow the example of Maribel. She is patient, nice, and intelligent. But the other, she is disaster [*sic*]. She causes problems for everyone. I watch this and [I think] I would like to find a girl like Maribel. I like her style. The other, I hate her.

When I asked some young women who their favorite television character was, a few of them picked Rubí over the morally upright Maribel. I suspect that they identified with the character's predicament, her poverty, and the dilemmas that she faced, even if they did not say so explicitly. Though they disapproved of her selfish ways, Rubí's fans paradoxically admired her determination to shape her own destiny. Men, by contrast, universally condemned Rubí: She was a nagging reminder of the perils they faced in the quest for love.

What emerges from these testimonies is that the experience of poverty sharpens the tensions between emotion and materialism that remain implicit in more affluent contexts. Significantly, some youths saw *feuilletons* as educational programs that raised viewers' awareness of realities. "They inform people so that they can change their conduct accordingly," a youth said. For another,

> it is by watching televised dramas that we can begin to understand how true love manifests itself and how one demonstrates love to a person. Televised dramas provide a framework that allows people to correct the way they behave in a romantic relationship.

In the same vein, one youth compared *feuilletons* to health campaigns such as those the Nigerien government holds to promote polio or measles eradication. "*Feuilletons,*" Tahirou explained,

> function like information campaigns: People are told stories so that they can understand how to conduct themselves. Take Rubí, who married for money. She hurt many people. We all know what happened. But [to

know,] we had to watch the serials. It provided a good example of what not to do. We're not going to act like her because we don't want to end up like her.

In Tahirou's view, love was something one learned about through exposure to television. Only after having watched teledramas—and absorbed their educational message—could one measure the terrible price paid by those who, like Rubí, betrayed love and all it stood for to satisfy their lust for riches. As elsewhere in the world, the forms of intimacy and pleasure on which companionate marriage is predicated on are increasingly perceived to be expressions of modern selfhood (Wardlow and Hirsch 2006). As the primary vehicle for the dissemination of images of progressive courtship and marriage, *feuilletons* facilitate claims to modern identity.

Enabled by a savoir faire that youth claim to have acquired through the consumption of foreign cultural forms, this kind of refined love is seen as a means of both developing oneself and escaping the poverty that is associated with traditional forms of conjugality. "We are witnessing an evolution of sentiments. Love must be pure and honest. The dramas show what happens when people find true love. We must develop ourselves," a young man explained. According to another, "since watching *feuilletons*, I have become enlightened and thoroughly acquainted with the problems of love, and I know how to treat my partner right. Women are queens; they must be loved, respected, and pampered." By seeking instruction from televised serials on how to love (and be loved), youth embrace love as an emancipatory device through which they can privilege personal fulfillment over social obligation and liberate women from the grip of kinship and labor.

Within the prevailing context of poverty, romantic love and the emotional involvement it presupposes are complexly bound up with aspirations to affluent lifestyle. As is the case elsewhere (Ferguson 1999; Hansen 2005; Weiss 2002), youths are convinced that life is better just about everywhere else. Many invoke the desperate economic situation of Niger to justify their wanting to emigrate to wealthier countries. Through their engagement with Latin American teledramas such as *Rubí*, young people have begun to imagine the alternative lives they could be having outside of Niger (Appadurai 1996). In this regard, wistful comments such as wanting to "find a girl like Maribel" speak of the desire not only to build a marriage around emotional closeness, trust, and long-term commitment, but also to share the social position and lifestyle that one would presumably enjoy as Maribel's husband. Marrying for love presupposes a freedom from financial concerns such that *soyayya* will necessarily bloom into companionate mar-

FIGURE 8.1 Couple dancing at a party for young people in Dogondoutchi, Niger, 2004. Young people organize dance parties where boys pay an entrance fee and girls do not. The young woman is wearing a *tufafi serre* (tight clothing) considered fashionable among the young but strongly disapproved of by Muslim conservatives. *Photo by Adeline Masquelier.*

riage. As noted earlier, young women associate marriage with the material possessions they receive as young brides. Not unlike the young Huli women of Papua New Guinea for whom modern homes and the modern furnishings they are filled with are "necessary props for companionate marriage" (Wardlow 2006a, 57), they often see marriage as a way of moving up in the world.

Even as they decry women's acquisitive tendencies, young men too come to imagine the ideal marriage, not only in terms of particular kinds of relationship, but also in terms of a certain lifestyle—enabled by a salaried position. In the way that it summons a world of bourgeois values and practices most vividly instantiated in teledramas such as *Rubí, soyayya* has become the idiom through which to forge imaginative links to more prosperous "elsewheres" (Weiss 2002, 101). Far then from constituting escapist illusions that further marginalize them from the "real" world, fantasies of romance fed by poverty and exclusion constitute a concrete form of engagement with social realities "at the intersection of global possibility and local limitation" (Weiss 2002, 119). Fantasies, Weiss (2002, 120) notes, do not evade the reality of poverty so much as they reconfigure local places through "[their] relationship to what is recognized and treated as a more potent, forceful and *true* world." None captured better how fantasy works as a "social practice" (Appadurai 1996) than Halila when she pointed out to me that "when you watch *feuilletons*, you increase your intelligence. I would advise younger people to watch television serials in order to better build their future."

Conclusion

In my exploration of how teledramas come to inhabit the lives of their audiences, I have argued that in Dogondoutchi, notions of romantic love are informed and inflected by the language of romance supplied by foreign television. At a time when young people are debating the importance of affective bonds in their lives, teledramas provide compelling images of romance and companionship. As both a model and an anti-model of affect and intimacy, *Rubí* was an especially rich source of insights about the rewards as well as the perils of love making. It contained all the elements—passion and intrigue, love and loss, treachery and tragedy—that local audiences have come to expect of a good televised drama and offered a thoroughly enjoyable experience. More importantly, as a youth put it, it also "provided all the *données* [data] you needed to find love." If it highlighted the conflict between love and consumerism, *Rubí* also confirmed the possibility of "true" love, thereby encouraging debates about what love meant and how to love and be loved.

Despite the gap between the worlds dramatized in the telenovelas and local realities, I have suggested that it would be a mistake to discount young Nigeriens' engagement with foreign serials as mere escapism. In Dogondoutchi, *soyayya* has become the idiom through which youth engage in the practice of forging translocal solidarities. The intensity of their engagement with teledramas testifies to the vital role that imagination plays in youthful constructions of the world. In an age of widespread economic collapse when youths face unprecedented challenges in their quest for marriage and social maturity, it exemplifies an impulse to test the limits of social norms. Young Nigeriens see romantic love as the epitome of progressive individualism: It is the site through which to transcend the boundaries of a world in which most are condemned to a life of chronic poverty. As Lindholm (2006, 17) notes, young people's desire to escape the confines of the given exists "in tension with reality and with other forms of existential commitment." As a result, it is not easily fulfilled.

No matter that young men and women often manipulate and misunderstand one another in their search for affection, understanding, and material security; or that once married, they renegotiate their relationships around webs of social obligations that brings their unions more in conformity with traditional ideas of gender and conjugality. By claiming to enjoy a more privatized, romanticized experience of love than their parents, they are purposefully distancing themselves not only from the previous generation but also, and more importantly, from the hopelessness that has become the hallmark of existence in this media saturated but materially impoverished corner of the globe. If, as Halila suggested, it is only through the work of fantasy that Nigerien youth can access potential futures, we may have to rethink the notion that romance is the stuff of dreams to explore more critically how, as a means of negotiating the distance between individual agency and globally defined fields of possibility, it might also constitute the stuff of life.

NOTES

1. I draw mainly from discussions with young literate or semi-literate men and women from eighteen to thirty-five years of age, many of whom are unemployed or underemployed.
2. In Nigeria, a movie industry has recently developed around the production of low-budget videos.
3. Duma was Baba's patrilateral parallel cousin and therefore the ideal marriage partner.
4. Youths frequently defined love as a pure, refined emotion that should be distinguished from base carnal attraction. Because it could be generated only by what was inside a person, it was not to be confused with lust, even if love itself led to sexual attraction.
5. On the commoditization of sex and love, see Brennan (2004), Chernoff (2003), Cole (2004), Mark Hunter (2002) and this volume, Mills and Ssewakiryanga (2005), Rebhun (1999a), and van Wijk (2006).
6. To my knowledge, no data is available on marriage rates. It is not clear, for instance, whether delayed marriage in Niger means that some people forgo marriage altogether, as is the case in Madagascar (Jennifer Cole, personal communication), though that is certainly the perception of the older generation.
7. Cousin marriage remains part of the matrimonial picture. For parents who worry about increasing consumerism, intergenerational conflict, and permissiveness,

gidan arme, in which a man marries his cross or parallel cousin, provides a safety net.

8. I am not implying that arranged marriages are necessarily devoid of affection or that the autonomy youth enjoy when choosing marriage partners always translates into love. Rather I am alluding to the categories that youths draw on to situate themselves within modernity.

9. In Dogondoutchi, courtship is a period during which partners forge an intense personal connection through which they demonstrate their modern individuality. Postnuptially, however, this emotional bond often gives way to a more traditional pattern of conjugality: Women are expected to produce a progeny, men are expected to provide for their dependents—and this, regardless of how emotionally intimate and sexually compatible they are. The fact that husbands have extramarital affairs rarely leads to social condemnation.

10. In 2006, a young man was expelled from school for alleged theft. He had stolen money to buy gifts for his girlfriend. His parents sent him to a private school, but the thieving continued. He was eventually forced to abandon his studies.

11. In Dogondoutchi, male teachers are known to engage in affairs with female students who receive *MST,* or *moyennes sexuellement transmissibles* ("sexually transmissible passing grades"), in exchange.

12. These forms of polyandry are known among university students as *le chic, le chèque, et le choc* (Nyamnjoh 2005). *Le chic* is the well-dressed boyfriend with whom one impresses acquaintances at parties, *le chèque* is the wallet on legs or *bailleur de fonds,* and *le choc* is the man who provides emotional satisfaction.

13. Unlike other parts of the continent where Muslim-based traditions of love poetry have flourished (Abu-Lughod 1986), love is not a traditional subject of poetry in recently Islamized Dogondoutchi.

14. It has been argued that telenovelas lack realism because their sentimental, artificially plotted dramas sacrifice characterization for sensationalism. Not only are the displays of emotions exaggerated, but the narrative is filled with improbable sequences of events. Rather than seeing the sensational narratives as improbable, young Nigeriens pointed out to me that real life was similarly filled with ambushes (or conversely, triumphs) at every turn.

REFERENCES

Abdulaziz, Mohamed H. 1979. *Muyaka: 19th century Swahili popular poetry.* Nairobi: Kenya Literature Bureau.

Abu-Lughod, Lila. 1986. *Veiled sentiments: Honor and poetry in a Bedouin society.* Berkeley: University of California Press.

———. 1995. The object of soap operas: Egyptian television and the cultural politics of modernity. In *Worlds apart: Modernity through the prism of the local,* ed. Daniel Miller, 190–210. Routledge: New York.

———. 2002. Egyptian melodrama: Technology of the modern subject? In *Media worlds: Anthropology on new terrain,* ed. Faye Ginsburg, Lila Abu-Lughod, and Brian Larkin, 115–33. Berkeley: University of California Press.

———. 2005. *Dramas of nationhood: The politics of television in Egypt.* Chicago: University of Chicago Press.

Achmat, Zackie. 1993. Apostles of civilised vice: "Immoral practices" and "unnatural vice" in South African prisons and compounds, 1890–1920. *Social Dynamics* 19 (2): 92–110.

Adams, Vincanne, and Stacy L. Pigg, eds. 2005. *Sex in development: Science, sexuality and morality in global perspective.* Durham, NC: Duke University Press.

Adrian, Bonnie. 2003. *Framing the bride: Globalizing beauty and romance in Taiwan's bridal industry.* Berkeley: University of California Press.

Ahearn, Laura. 2001. *Invitations to love: Literacy, love letters and social change in Nepal.* Ann Arbor: University of Michigan Press.

Ahlberg, Beth Maina. 1994. Is there a distinct African sexuality? A critical response to Caldwell. *Africa* 64: 220–42.

Allman, Jean. 1991. Of spinsters, concubines, and wicked women: Reflections on gender and social change in colonial Asante. *Gender and History* 30: 23–41.

———. 1996. Rounding up spinsters: Gender chaos and unmarried women in colonial Asante. *Journal of African History* 37: 62–82.

Amory, Deborah P. 1997. Homosexuality in Africa: issues and debates. *Issue: A Journal of Opinion* 25: 5–10.

Amrhein, Saundra. 2007. Telling true love from immigrant Scam. *St. Petersburg Times,* July 14. http://www.sptimes.com (accessed August 16, 2007).

Anderson, Benedict. 1983. *Imagined communities: Reflections on the origin and spread of nationalism.* London: Verso.

Ang, Ien. 1985. *Watching Dallas: Soap opera and the melodramatic imagination.* London: Methuen.

———. 1991. *Desperately seeking the audience.* New York: Routledge.

Appadurai, Arjun. 1996. *Modernity at large: Cultural dimensions of globalization*. Minneapolis: University of Minnesota Press.

Argyle, John, and Eleanor Preston-Whyte. 1978. Eileen Jensen Krige: Her career and achievements, together with a bibliography. In *Social system and tradition in southern Africa: Essays in honour of Eileen Krige*, ed. J. Argyle and E. Preston-Whyte, ix–xxi. Cape Town: Oxford University Press.

Ariès, Phillipe. 1962. *Centuries of childhood: A social history of family life*. New York: Vintage.

Arnfred, Signe. 2004. "African sexuality"/sexuality in Africa: Tales and silences. In *Re-thinking sexualities in Africa*, ed. S. Arnfred, 59–76. Uppsala: The Nordic Africa Institute.

———, ed. 2004. *Re-thinking sexualities in Africa*. Uppsala: The Nordic Africa Institute, Sweden.

Ashforth, Adam. 1999. "Weighing Manhood in Soweto." *CODESRIA Bulletin* 3/4: 51–58.

Askew, Kelly Michelle. 2002. *Performing the nation: Swahili music and cultural politics in Tanzania, Chicago studies in ethnomusicology*. Chicago: University of Chicago Press.

Bailey, Beth. 1989. *From front porch to back seat: Courtship in twentieth-century America*. Baltimore: Johns Hopkins University Press.

Bailey, James. 1982. Letting the genie out of the bottle. In *The beat of Drum*, ed. Angela Caccia. Johannesburg: Ball.

Ballantine, Christopher. 1993. *Marabi nights: Early South African jazz and vaudeville*. Johannesburg: Ravan Press.

Barber, Karin. 1995. Money, self-realization and the person in Yoruba texts. In *Money matters: Instability, values and social payments in the modern history of west African communities*, ed. J. Guyer. London: Heinemann and James Currey.

———. 1997a. Audiences in Africa. Special issue, *Africa* 67 (3): 406–40.

———. 1997b. Preliminary notes on audiences in Africa. *Africa* 67 (3): 347–62.

———, ed. 1997c. *Readings in African popular culture*. Bloomington: Indiana University Press.

———. 2000. *The generation of plays: Yorùbá popular life in theater*. Bloomington: Indiana University Press.

———, ed. 2006. *Africa's hidden histories: Everyday literacy and making the self*. Bloomington: Indiana University Press.

Barnouw, Erik, and Subrahmanyam Krishnaswamy. 1963. *Indian film*. New York: Oxford University Press.

Bastian, Misty. 2001. Acadas and fertilizer girls: Young Nigerian women and the romance of modernity. In *Gendered modernities: Ethnographic perspectives*, ed. Dorothy Hodgson, 53–76. New York: Palgrave.

———. 2002. Irregular visitors: Narratives about *Ogbaanje* [spirit children] in southern Nigerian popular writing. In *Readings in African popular fiction*, ed. Stephanie Newell, 59–66. Bloomington: Indiana University Press.

Baudrillard, Jean. 1988. *The ecstasy of communication*. Brooklyn, NY: Autonomedia.

Beauvoir, Simone de. 1953 [1949]. *The second sex*. New York: Vintage.

Beecham, John. 1841. *Ashantee and the gold coast.* London: Mason.

Behrend, H. 1998. Love à la Hollywood and Bombay in Kenyan Studio Photography. *Paideuma* 44: 139–53.

Bell, Jim. 1995. Notions of love and romance among the Taita of Kenya. In *Romantic passion: A universal experience?,* ed. William R. Jankowiak, 152–65. New York: Columbia University Press.

Berlant, Lauren. 1997. *The queen of America goes to Washington city: Essays on sex and citizenship.* Durham, NC: Duke University Press.

———, ed. 2000. *Intimacy.* Chicago: University of Chicago Press.

Berlant, Lauren, and Michael Warner. 2000. Sex in public. In *Intimacy,* ed. Lauren Berlant, 311–30. Chicago: University of Chicago Press.

Berman, Bruce, and John Lonsdale. 1992. *Unhappy valley: Conflict in Kenya and Africa.* 2 vols. London: Currey.

Bernard, Guy. 1968. *Ville africaine, famille urbaine: Les enseignants de Kinshasa.* Paris: Mouton.

Bertelsen, Eve. 1998. Ads and amnesia: Black advertising in the new South Africa. In *Negotiating the past: The making of memory in South Africa,* ed. Sarah Nuttall and Carli Coetzee, 221–41. Cape Town: Oxford University Press.

Bhabha, Homi. 1994. Of mimicry and man. In *The location of culture,* 121–31. London: Routledge.

Biersteker, Ann Joyce. 1991. Language, poetry and power: A reconsideration of "*Utendi wa Mwana Kupona.*" In *Faces of Islam in African literature,* ed. K. Harrow, 59–77. Portsmouth, NH: Heinemann.

———. 1996. *Kujibizana: Questions of language and power in nineteenth- and twentieth-century poetry in Kiswahili.* African Series. East Lansing: Michigan State University Press.

Biersteker, Ann Joyce, and Shariff Ibrahim Noor. 1995. *Mashairi ya vita vya Kuduhu: War poetry in Kiswahili exchanged at the time of the Battle of Kuduhu.* MSU Press African Historical Sources. East Lansing: Michigan State University.

Birth, Kevin K., and Morris Freilich. 1995. Putting romance into systems of sexuality: Changing smart-rules in a Trinidadian village. In *Romantic passion: A universal experience?,* ed. William R. Jankoviak, 262–76. New York: Columbia University Press.

Bledsoe, Caroline H., and Barney Cohen. 1993. *Social dynamics of adolescent fertility in sub-Saharan Africa.* Washington, DC: National Academies Press.

Bledsoe, Caroline H., and Giles Pison, eds. 1994. *Nuptuality in sub-Saharan Africa: Contemporary anthropological and demographic perspectives.* Oxford: Clarendon Press.

Bloch, Maurice. 1989. The symbolism of money in Imerina. In *Money and the morality of exchange,* ed. J. Parry and M. Bloch, 165–90. Cambridge: Cambridge University Press.

Bloch, Maurice, and Jonathan Parry. 1989. Introduction: Money and the morality of exchange. In *Money and the morality of exchange,* ed. Jonathan Parry and Maurice Bloch, 1–32. Cambridge: Cambridge University Press.

Boeck, Filip de. 2002. Le "deuxième monde" et les "enfants sorciers" en République démocratique du Congo. *Mots Pluriels* 22. http://www.arts.uwa.edu.au/ MotsPluriels/MP2202fb.html (accessed August 22, 2008).

Bonner, Phil. 1990. "Desirable or undesirable Basotho women?" Liquor, prostitution and the migration of Basotho women to the Rand, 1920–1945. In *Women and gender in southern Africa to 1945,* ed. C. Walker and D. Philip, 221–50. Bloomington: University of Indiana Press.

Boserup, Ester. 1970. *Women's role in economic development.* London: Allen & Unwin.

Bozzoli, Belinda. 1991. *Women of Phokeng: Consciousness, life strategy, and migrancy in South Africa, 1900–1983.* Portsmouth, NH: Heinemann.

Breckenridge, Keith. 2000. Love letters and amanuenses: Beginning the cultural history of the working class private sphere in southern Africa, 1900–1933. *Journal of Southern African Studies* 26 (2): 337–48.

———. 2006. Reasons for writing: African working-class letter-writing in early-twentieth-century South Africa. In *Africa's hidden histories: Everyday literacy and making the self,* ed. Karin Barber, 143–54. Bloomington: Indiana University Press.

Brennan, Denise. 2004. *What's love got to do with it? Transnational desires, and sex tourism in the Dominican Republic.* Durham, NC: Duke University Press.

Brown, Barbara. 1987. Facing the "Black Peril": The politics of population control in South Africa. *Journal of Southern African Studies* 13 (3): 256–73.

Bryant, A. T. 1905. *A Zulu-English dictionary with notes on pronunciation.* Marianhill: Marianhill Mission Press.

———. 1949. *The Zulu people, as they were before the white man came.* Pietermaritzburg: Shuter and Shooter.

Bryce, Jane. 1997. Women and modern African popular fiction. In *Readings in African popular culture,* ed. Karin Barber, 118–24. Bloomington: Indiana University Press.

Buggenhagen, Beth Ann. 2004. Domestic object(ion)s: The Senegalese murid trade diaspora and the politics of marriage payments, love, and state privatization. In *Producing African futures: Ritual and reproduction in a neoliberal age,* ed. Brad Weiss, 21–53. Leiden: Brill.

Bundy, Colin. 1979. *The rise and fall of the South African peasantry.* Berkeley: University of California Press.

Burke, Timothy. 1996. *Lifebuoy men, lux women: Commodification, consumption and cleanliness in modern Zimbabwe.* Durham, NC: Duke University Press.

Burns, Catherine. 1995. Reproductive Labors: The Politics of Women's Health in South Africa, 1900 to 1960. PhD diss., Northwestern Univesity.

Burns, James McDonald. 2002. *Flickering shadows: Cinema and identity in colonial Zimbabwe.* Athens: Ohio University Press.

Butler, Judith. 1990. *Gender trouble: Feminism and subversion of identity.* New York: Routledge.

Caldwell, John, Pat Caldwell, and Pat Quiggin. 1989. The social context of AIDS in sub-Saharan Africa. *Population and Development Review* 15 (2): 185–234.

Callaway, Barbara. 1987. *Muslim Hausa women in Nigeria: Tradition and change.* New York: Syracuse University Press.

Campbell, Carol. 1983. *Nyimbo za Kiswahili:* A socio-ethnomusicological study of a Swahili poetic form. PhD diss., University of Washington.

Campbell, Colin. 1987. *The romantic ethic and the spirit of modern consumerism.* Oxford: Basil Blackwell.

Cancian, Francesca M. 1986. The feminization of love. *Signs* 11 (4): 692–709.

Carton, Benedict. 2000. *Blood from your children: The colonial origins of generational conflict in South Africa.* Charlottesville: University Press of Virginia.

Chan, Selina Ching. 2006. Love and jewelry: Patriarchal control, conjugal ties, and changing identities. In *Modern loves: The anthropology of romantic courtship and compassionate marriage,* eds. Jennifer S. Hirsch and Holly Wardlow, 35–50. Ann Arbor: University of Michigan Press.

Chanock, Martin. 1985. *Law, custom and social order: The colonial experience in Malawi and Zambia.* Cambridge: Cambridge University Press.

Chapman, Michael. 1989. *The drum decade: Stories from the 1950s.* Pietermaritzburg: University of Natal Press.

Chatterjee, Gayatri. 1992. *Awara.* New Delhi: Wiley Eastern.

Chernoff, John M. 2003. *Hustling is not stealing: Stories of an African bar girl.* Chicago: University of Chicago Press.

Cohen, David W. 1985. Doing social history from Pim's doorway. In *Reliving the past: Perspectives on social history,* ed. O. Zunz, 191–235. Chapel Hill: University of North Carolina Press.

Cole, Jennifer. 2001. *Forget colonialism? Sacrifice and the art of memory in Madagascar.* Berkeley: University of California Press.

———. 2004. Fresh contact in Tamatave, Madagascar: Sex, money and intergenerational transformation. *American Ethnologist* 31 (4): 571–86.

———. 2005. The Jaombilo of Tamatave (Madagascar), 1992–2004: Reflections on Youth and Globalization. In "Childhood and globalization," ed. P. Stearns, special issue, *Journal of Social History* 38 (4): 891–914.

———. 2008a. Fashioning distinction: Youth, consumerism and class in the context of globalization. In *Figuring the future: Children, youth and globalization,* ed. Jennifer Cole and Deborah Durham, 99–267. Santa Fe: SAR Press.

———. 2008b. *"Et plus si affinités"*: Malagasy Internet marriage, shifting post-colonial hierarchies and national honor. In "Emotional latitudes," special issue, *Historical reflections/réflections historiques* 34 (1): 26–49.

Cole, Jennifer, and Deborah Durham. 2006. Age regeneration and the intimate politics of globalization. In *Generations and globalization: Youth, age and family in the new world economy,* ed. Jennifer Cole and Deborah Durham, 1–28. Bloomington: Indiana University Press.

Cole, Jennifer, and Karen Middleton. 2001. Rethinking ancestors and colonial power in Madagascar. *Africa* 71 (1): 1–37.

Colenso, John. 1878. *Zulu-English dictionary.* Pietermaritzburg: Davis.

Collier, Jane. 1997. *From duty to desire: Remaking families in a Spanish village.* Princeton: Princeton University Press.

Collins, Marcus. 2006 [2003]. *Modern love: Personal relationships in twentieth-century Britain.* Newark: University of Delaware Press.

Comaroff, Jean, and John Comaroff. 1988. On the founding fathers, fieldwork and functionalism: A conversation with Isaac Schapera. *American Ethnologist* 15 (3): 554–65.

———. 1991. *Of revelation and revolution: Christianity, colonialism, and consciousness in South Africa.* Chicago: University of Chicago Press.

———. 1992. *Ethnography and the historical imagination.* Boulder, CO: Westview Press.

———. 2000. Millennial capitalism: First thoughts on a second coming. *Public Culture* 12 (2): 291–343.

———. 2007. The portraits of an ethnographer as a young man. In *Picturing a colonial past: The African photographs of Isaac Schapera,* ed. John L. Comaroff, Jean Comaroff, and Deborah James, 1–17. Chicago: University of Chicago Press.

Comaroff, John L., ed. 1980. *The meaning of marriage payments.* New York: Academic Press.

Comhaire-Sylvain, Suzanne. 1968. *Femmes de Kinshasa: Hier et aujourd'hui.* Paris: Mouton.

Connell, Robert W. 1995. *Masculinities.* Cambridge: Polity Press.

Constable, Nicole. 2003. *Romance on a global stage: Pen pals, virtual ethnography, and "mail order" marriages.* Berkeley: University of California Press.

———. 2005. *Cross-border marriages: Gender and mobility in transnational Asia.* Philadelphia: University of Pennsylvania Press.

Cooper, Barbara. 1997. *Marriage in Maradi: Gender and culture in a Hausa society in Niger.* Portsmouth, NH: Heinemann.

Cooper, Frederick. 1996. *Decolonization and African society: The labor question in French and British Africa.* Cambridge: Cambridge University Press.

———. 2005. *Colonialism in question: Theory, knowledge, history.* Berkeley: University of California Press.

Cooper, Frederick, and Randall Packard, eds. 1997. *International development and the social sciences: Essays on the history and politics of knowledge.* Berkeley: University of California Press.

Coplan, David. 1985. *"In township tonight!" South Africa's black city, music and theatre.* Johannesburg: Longman.

Cornwall, Andrea. 2001. Wayward women and useless men: Contest and change in gender relations in Ado-Odo, S.W. Nigeria. In *"Wicked" women and the reconfiguration of gender in Africa,* ed. D. L. Hodgson and S. A. McCurdy, 67–84. Portsmouth, NH: Heinemann.

———. 2002. Spending power: Love, money and the reconfiguration of gender relations in Ado-Obo, southwestern Nigeria. *American Ethnologist* 29 (4): 963–80.

———. 2005. Introduction. In *Readings in gender in Africa,* ed. Andrea Cornwall, 1–19. Oxford: Currey.

Couzens, Tim. 1978. A short history of "World" (and other black SA newspapers). *Inspan Journal* 1 (1): 69–92.

———. 1985. *The new African: A study of the life and work of H.I.E. Dhlomo.* Johannesburg: Ravan Press.

Crowder, Michael. 1988. *The flogging of Phinehas McIntosh: A tale of colonial folly and injustice.* New Haven: Yale University Press.

Curtin, Philip. 1964. *The image of Africa: British ideas and action, 1780–1850*. Madison: University of Wisconsin Press.

Das, Veena. 1995. On soap operas: What kind of anthropological object is it? In *Worlds apart: Modernity through the prism of the local*, ed. Daniel Miller, 169–89. Routledge: New York.

Delius, Peter, and Clive Glaser. 2002. Sexual socialisation in South Africa: A historical perspective. *African Studies* 61 (1): 27–54.

———. 2004. The myths of polygamy: A history of multi-partnership and extramarital sex in South Africa. *South African Historical Journal* 50: 84–114.

Derné, Steve. 2000. *Movies, masculinity, and modernity: An ethnography of men's film-going in India*, Contributions in Sociology, no. 129. Westport, CT: Greenwood Press.

Dickey, Sara. 1991. *Cinema and the urban poor in South India*. Cambridge: Cambridge University Press.

Dinan, Carmel. 1983. Sugar daddies and gold-diggers: The white-collar single women in Accra. In *Female and male in West Africa*, ed. C. Oppong, 344–66. London: Allen & Unwin.

Diouf, Mamadou. 2003. Engaging postcolonial cultures: African youth and public space. *African Studies Review* 46 (2): 1–12.

Dissanayake, Wimal, and Malti Sahai. 1987. *Raj Kappor's films: Harmony of discourses*. New Delhi: Stosius.

Dodson, Don. 1974. The four modes of *Drum:* Popular fiction and social control in South Africa. *African Studies Review* 15 (2): 317–45.

Douglas, Mary, ed. 1970. *Witchcraft confessions and accusations*. London: Tavistock.

Dubow, Saul. 1995. *Scientific racism in modern South Africa*. Cambridge: Cambridge University Press.

Durham, Deborah. 2002. Love and jealousy in the space of death. *Ethnos* 67 (2): 155–80.

Dworkin, Andrea. 1975. The root cause. Lecture delivered at Massachusetts Institute of Technology, Cambridge, September 26, 1975.

Dwyer, Rachel. 2000. *All you want is money, all you need is love: Sex and romance in modern India*. London: Cassell.

Dwyer, Rachel, and Christopher Pinney, eds. 2001. *Pleasure and the nation: The history, politics, and consumption of public culture in India*. SOAS Studies in South Asia: Understandings and Perspectives. New Delhi: Oxford University Press.

Dyer, Richard. 1992. Entertainment and utopia. In *Only entertainment*, ed. Richard Dyer, 17–34. London: Routledge.

Eisenberg, Andrew. 2008. The resonance of place: Vocal expression and the communal imagination in Old Town, Mombasa, Kenya, PhD. diss., Columbia University.

Ekman, Paul. 1980. Biological and cultural contributions to body and facial movement in the expression of emotions. In *Explaining emotions*, ed. A. Rorty, 73–102. Berkeley: University of California Press.

Elphick, Richard. 1987. Mission Christianity and interwar liberalism. In *Democratic liberalism in South Africa: Its history and prospect,* ed. J. Butler, R. Elphick, and D. Welsh, 64–80. Cape Town: David Philip.

Engels, Frederick. 1972 [1884]. *The origin of the family, private property, and the state.* New York: Pathfinder Press.

Epprecht, Marc. 1998. The "unsaying" of indigenous homosexualities in Zimbabwe: Mapping a blindspot in an African masculinity. *Journal of Southern African Studies* 24 (4): 631–51.

———. 2004. *Hungochani: The history of a dissident sexuality in southern Africa.* Montreal: McGill-Queen's University Press.

Etherington, Norman. 1978. *Preachers, peasants, and politics in southeast Africa, 1835–1880 African Christian communities in Natal, Pondoland, and Zululand.* London: Royal Historical Society.

Etnofoor. 2006. "Romantic love." Special issue, *Etnofoor* 19 (1).

Evans, Mary. 2003. *Love: An unromantic discussion.* Cambridge: Polity Press.

Evans-Pritchard, E. E. 1971. *The Azande: History and political institutions.* Oxford: Oxford University Press.

Fabian, Johannes. 1978. Popular culture in Africa: Findings and conjectures. *Africa* 48 (1): 315–34.

———. 1983. *Time and the other: How anthropology makes its object.* New York: Columbia University Press.

Faier, Lieba. 2007. Filipina migrants in rural Japan and their professions of love. *American Ethnologist* 34 (1): 148–62.

Fair, Laura. 1996. Identity, difference, and dance: Female initiation in Zanzibar, 1890–1930. *Frontiers: A Journal of Women Studies* 17 (3): 146–72.

———. 2001. *Pastimes and politics: Culture, community, and identity in post-abolition urban Zanzibar, 1890–1945.* Athens: Ohio University Press.

———. 2002. "It's just no fun anymore": Women's experiences of taarab before and after the 1964 Zanzibar revolution. *International Journal of African Historical Studies* 35 (1): 61–81.

———. 2004. Hollywood hegemony? Hardly: Audience preferences in Zanzibar, 1950s–1970s. *ZIFF Journal* 1 (1): 52–58.

Farrer, James. 2002. *Opening up: Youth sex culture and market reform in Shanghai.* Chicago: University of Chicago Press.

Farsy, Muhammed. 1965. *Ada za harusi katika unguja.* Dar es Salaam: East African Literature Bureau.

Feeley-Harnik, Gillian. 2003. Number One—Nambawani—Lambaoany: Clothing as an historical medium of exchange in northwestern Madagascar. In *Lova/inheritance: Past and present in Madagascar,* ed. Zoë Crossland, Genese Sodikoff, and Will Griffin. Michigan Discussions in Anthropology, 14: 63–103.

Feldman-Savelsberg, Pamela. 1999. *Plundered kitchens, empty wombs: Threatened reproduction and identity in Cameroonian grassfields.* Ann Arbor: University of Michigan Press.

Ferguson, James. 1999. *Expectations of modernity: Myths and meanings of urban life on the Zambia copperbelt.* Berkeley: University of California Press.

——. 2006. *Global shadows: Africa and the neoliberal world order.* Durham, NC: Duke University Press.

Firestone, Shulamith. 1970. *The dialectic of sex.* New York: Morrow.

Forna, Aminatta. 2002. *The devil that danced on the water: A daughter's quest.* New York: Gove Press.

Fortes, Meyer. 1978. Parenthood, marriage and fertility in West Africa. *Journal of Development Studies* 14 (4): 121-48.

Foucault, Michel. 1978. *The history of sexuality: An introduction.* New York: Pantheon.

——. 1985. *The history of sexuality: The use of pleasure.* New York: Pantheon.

Frederiksen, Bodil Folke. 1997. Gender, ethnicity and popular culture in Kenya. In *Ethnicity, gender, and subversion of nationalism,* ed. Fiona Wilson and Bodil Folke Frederiksen, 46-59. London: Routledge.

——. 2000. Popular culture, gender relations and the democratization of everyday life in Kenya. *Journal of Southern African Studies* 26: 209-22.

Friedman, Jonathan, ed. 1994. *Consumption and identity.* Chur, Switzerland: Harwood Academic.

Fuglesang, Minou. 1994. *Veils and videos: Female youth culture on the Kenyan coast.* Stockholm: Department of Social Anthropology, Stockholm University.

Fulton, Rachel. 2002. *From judgment to passion: Devotion to Christ and the Virgin Mary, 800-1200.* New York: Columbia University Press.

Furedi, Frank. 2002. The silent ascendancy of therapeutic culture in Britain. *Society* 39: 16-24.

Furlong, Patrick. 1991. *Between crown and swastika: The impact of the radical right on the Afrikaner nationalist movement in the fascist era.* Hanover, NH: University Press of New England.

Gaitskell, Deborah. 1982. Wailing for purity: Prayer unions, African mothers and adolescent daughters 1912-1940. In *Industrialisation and social change in South Africa,* ed. S. Marks and R. Rathbone, 338-57. Essex: Longman.

Garrett, Maria. 2007. My kind of woman: Making brides at the German border. Unpublished paper presented to the Alexander von Humboldt Foundation, Sacramento.

Geschiere, Peter, and Birgit Meyer. 1998. Globalization and identity: Dialectics of flow and closure. *Development and Change* 29: 601-15.

Giddens, Anthony. 1992. *The transformation of intimacy: Sexuality, love and eroticism.* Cambridge: Polity Press.

Gilette, Maris. 2000. What's in a dress? Brides in the Hui quarter of Xi'an. In *The consumer revolution in urban China,* ed. D. S. Davis, 80-106. Berkeley: University of California Press.

Gillis, John. 1988. From ritual to romance: Toward an alternative history of love. In *Emotions and social change: Towards a new psychohistory,* ed. C. Stearns and P. Stearns, 87-121. New York: Holmes and Mier.

Ginsburg, Faye D., Lila Abu-Lughod, and Brian Larkin, eds. 2002. *Media worlds: Anthropology on new terrain.* Berkeley: University of California Press.

Glassman, Jonathon. 2000. Sorting out the tribes: The creation of racial identities in colonial Zanzibar's newspaper wars. *Journal of African History* 41 (3): 395–428.

Glynn, R. R., et al. 2003. HIV risk in relation to marriage in areas with high prevalence of HIV infection. *Journal of Acquired Immune Deficiency Syndrome* 33: 526–35.

Gondola, Ch Didier. 1999. Dream and drama: The search for elegance among Congolese youth. *Africana Studies Review* 42 (1): 23–48.

Goodman, Bryna. 2006. All the feelings that are fit to print: The community of sentiment and the literary public in China, 1900–1918. *20th Century China* 27 (3): 291–327.

Goody, Jack. 1998. *Food and love: A cultural history of east and west.* London: Verso.

Gordon, Robert. 1990. Early social anthropology in South Africa. *Africa* 49 (1): 15–48.

Graeber, David. 1996. Love magic and political morality in central Madagascar, 1875–1990. *Gender and History* 8 (3): 416–39.

Grandidier, G. 1913. Le mariage à Madagascar. *Société d'Anthropologie de Paris.* 4 (6): 9–46.

Gready, Paul. 1990. Sophiatown writers of the 1950s. *Journal of South African Studies* 16 (1): 139–64.

Gregg, Jessica. 2003. *Virtually virgins: Sexual strategies and cervical cancer in Recife, Brazil.* Stanford: Stanford University Press.

———. 2006. He can be sad like that: Liberdade and the absence of romantic love in a Brazilian shantytown. In *Modern loves: The anthropology of romantic courtship and companionate marriage,* ed. Jennifer Hirsch and Holly Wardlow, 157–73. Ann Arbor: University of Michigan Press.

Gregory, Chris. 1982. *Gifts and commodities.* London: Academic Press.

Gutsche, Thelma. 1972. *The history and social significance of motion picture in South Africa, 1895–1940.* Cape Town: Timmins.

Guy, Jeff. 1979. *The destruction of the Zulu kingdom: The civil war in Zululand, 1879–1884.* London: Longman.

———. 1983. *The heretic: A study of the life of John William Colenso, 1814–1883.* Johannesburg: Ravan Press; Pietermaritzburg: University of Natal Press.

———. 1987. Analysing pre-capitalist societies in southern Africa. *Journal of Southern African Studies* 14 (1): 18–37.

Hafkin, Nancy J., and Edna G. Bay, eds. 1976. *Women in Africa: Studies in social and economic change.* Stanford: Stanford University Press.

Hammond-Tooke, David. 1997. *Imperfect interpreters: South Africa's anthropologists, 1920–1990.* Johannesburg: Witwatersrand University Press.

Hanchard, Michael. 2000. Jody. In *Intimacy,* ed. Lauren Berlant, 193–217. Chicago: University of Chicago Press.

Hanretta, Sean. 1998. Women, marginality and the Zulu state: Women's institutions and power in the early nineteenth century. *Journal of African History* 39 (3): 389–415.

Hansen, Thomas Blom. 2005. In search of the diasporic self: Bollywood in South Africa. In *Bollyworld: Popular Indian cinema through a transnational lens,* ed. by R. Kaur and A. J. Sinha, 236–90. New Delhi: Sage.

Haram, Liv. 2004. "Prostitutes" or modern women? Negotiating respectability in northern Tanzania. In *Re-thinking sexualities in Africa,* ed. S. Arnfred, 211-29. Uppsala, Sweden: Nordiska Afrikainstitutet.

Harrell-Bond, Barbara. 1975. *Modern marriage in Sierra Leone: A study of the professional group.* Paris: Mouton.

Harris, Grace Gredys. 1978. *Casting out anger: Religion among the Taita of Kenya.* Cambridge: Cambridge University Press.

Harris, Patrick. 1990. Symbols and sexuality: Culture and identity on the early Witwaterstrand gold mines. *Gender and History* 11 (3): 318-36.

Hatfield, Elaine, L. Richard Rapson, and Lise D. Martel 2007. Passionate love. In *Handbook of cultural psychology,* ed. S. Kitayama and D. Cohen, 760-79. New York: Guilford Press.

Helle-Valle, Jo. 2004. Understanding sexuality in Africa: Diversity and contextualised dividuality. In *Re-thinking sexualities in Africa,* ed. S. Arnfred, 195-207. Uppsala: Nordic Africa Institute.

Hellmann, Ellen. 1935. Native life in a Johannesburg slum yard. *Africa* 8 (1): 34-62.

———. 1937. The native in the towns. In *The Bantu-speaking tribes of South Africa,* ed. Isaac Schapera, 405-34. New York: Humanities Press.

———. 1940. *Problems of urban Bantu youth.* Johannesburg: South African Institute of Race Relations.

———. 1948. *Rooiyard: A sociological survey of an urban native slum yard.* Cape Town: Oxford University Press.

Hirsch, Jennifer. 2003. *A courtship after marriage: Sexuality and love in Mexican transnational families.* Berkeley: University of California Press.

Hirsch, Jennifer, Jennifer Higgins, Margaret E. Bentley, and Constance Nathanson. 2006. The social constructions of sexuality: Companionate marriage and STD/HIV risk in a Mexican migrant community. In *Modern loves: The anthropology of romantic courtship and companionate marriage,* ed. Jennifer Hirsch and Holly Wardlow, 95-118. Ann Arbor: University of Michigan Press.

Hirsch, Jennifer, Sergio Meneses, Brenda Thompson, Mirka Negroni, Blanca Pelcastre and Carlos del Rio. 2007. The inevitability of infidelity: Sexual reputation, social geographies, and marital HIV risk in rural Mexico. *American Journal of Public Health* 97 (6): 986-96.

Hirsch, Jennifer, and Holly Wardlow, eds. 2006. *Modern loves: The anthropology of romantic courtship and companionate marriage.* Ann Arbor: University of Michigan Press.

Hoad, Neville, Karin Martin, and Graeme Reid, eds. 2005. *Sex and politics in South Africa.* Cape Town: Double Storey.

Hodgson, Dorothy, and Sheryl A. McCurdy, eds. 2001. *"Wicked" women and the reconfiguration of gender in Africa.* Portsmouth, NH. Heinemann.

Hoernlé, Reinhold. 1934. Race-mixture and native policy in South Africa. In *Western civilization and the natives of South Africa: Studies in culture contact,* ed. Isaac Schapera, 263-81. New York: Humanities Press.

Hollos, Marida. 1997. From lineage to conjugality: The social context of fertility decisions among the Pare of northern Tanzania. *Social Science and Medicine* 45 (3): 361-72.

Honneth, Axel. 1992. Pluralization and recognition: On the self-misunderstanding of post-modern theorists. *Thesis Eleven* 31: 24–33.

Human Science Research Council. 2005. *South African national HIV prevalence, HIV incidence, behaviour and communication survey.* Cape Town: HSRC Press.

Hunt, Nancy Rose. 1999. *A colonial lexicon of birth ritual, medicalization, and mobility in the Congo.* Durham, NC: Duke University Press.

Hunter, Mark. 2002. The materiality of everyday sex: Thinking beyond "prostitution." *African Studies* 61 (1): 99–120.

———. 2005a. Building a home: Unemployment, intimacy, and AIDS in South Africa. PhD diss., University of California at Berkeley.

———. 2005b. Courting desire? Love and intimacy in late 19th century and early 20th century KwaZulu-Natal. *Passages: A Chronicle of the African Humanities,* n.s., 2. http://www.hti.umich.edu/p/passages.

———. 2005c. Cultural politics and masculinities: Multiple-partners in historical perspective in KwaZulu-Nata. *Culture, Health and Sexuality* 7 (4): 389–403.

———. 2007. The changing political economy of sex in South Africa: The significance of unemployment and inequalities to the scale of the AIDS pandemic. *Social Science and Medicine* 64 (3): 689–700.

Hunter, Monica. 1932. Results of culture contact on the Pondo and Xosa family. *South African Journal of Science* 29: 681–86.

———. 1933. The effects of contact with Europeans on the status of Pondo women. *Africa* 6 (3): 259–76.

———. 1936. *Reaction to conquest: Effects of contact with Europeans on the Pondo of South Africa.* Oxford: Oxford University Press.

Hutchinson, Sharon. 1996. *Nuer dilemmas: Coping with money, war and the state.* Berkeley: University of California Press.

Hyslop, Jonathan. 1995. White working-class women and the invention of Apartheid: "Purified" Afrikaner nationalist agitation for legislation against "mixed" marriages, 1934–39. *Journal of African History* 36: 57–81.

Illouz, Eva. 1997. *Consuming the romantic utopia: Love and the cultural contradictions of capitalism.* Berkeley: University of California Press.

Iordanova, Dina. 2006. India cinema's global reach: Historiography through testimonies. *South Asian Popular Culture* 4 (2): 113–40.

Isiugo-Abanihe, Uche. 1994. Extramarital sexual relations and perceptions of HIV/AIDS in Nigeria. *Health Transition Review* 4: 111–25.

Jahadhmy, Ali. 1977. *Anthology of Swahili poetry.* London: Heinemann.

Jahoda, Gustav. 1959. Love, marriage, and social change: Letters to the advice column of a West African newspaper. *Africa* 29 (2): 177–90.

Jankowiak, William R., ed. 1995. *Romantic passion: A universal experience?* New York: Columbia University Press.

———. 2008. *Intimacies: Love and sex across cultures.* New York: Columbia University Press.

Jeater, Diana. 1993. *Marriage, perversion, and power: The construction of moral discourse in southern Rhodesia, 1894–1930.* Oxford: Clarendon Press.

Jefferson, Thomas. 2002 [1785]. *Notes on the states of Virginia*, ed. David Waldstreicher. Boston: Bedford Books.

Jeffreys, M. 1951. Lobolo is child-price. *African Studies* 10 (4): 145–83.

Jordan, Winthrop D. 1968. *White over black: American attitudes toward the negro, 1550–1812*. Chapel Hill: University of North Carolina Press.

Junod, Henri A. 1912. *The life of a South African tribe*. 2 vols. New York: Kessinger.

Karanja, Wambui. 1987. "Outside wives" and "inside wives" in Nigeria: A study of changing perceptions. In *Transformations in African marriage*, ed. D. Parkin and D. Nyamwaya, 247–262. Manchester: International African Institute.

Kark, Sydney. 1950. The influence of urban-rural migration on Bantu health and disease. *Leech* November: 23–37.

Kaur, Raminder, and Ajay J. Sinha. 2005a. Bollyworld: An introduction to popular Indian cinema through a transnational lens. In *Bollyworld: Popular Indian cinema through a transnational lens*, ed. Raminder Kaur and Ajay J. Sinha, 302–29. New Delhi: Sage

———. 2005b. *Bollyworld: Popular Indian cinema through a transactional lens*. New Delhi: Sage.

Keane, Webb. 2007. *Christian moderns: Freedom and fetish in the mission encounter*. Berkeley: University of California Press.

Kendall, Laurel. 1996. *Getting married in Korea: Of gender, morality and modernity*. Berkeley: University of California Press.

Kenyatta, Jomo. 1938. *Facing Mount Kenya: The tribal life of the Gikuyu*. London: Secker and Warburg.

Kidula, Jean. 2000. Polishing the luster of the stars: Music professionalism made workable in Kenya. *Ethnomusicology* 4: 408–28.

King'ei, Geoffrey. 1992. Language, culture and communication: The role of Swahili taarab songs in Kenya, 1963–1990. PhD diss., Howard University.

Klausen, Susanne. 2004. *Race, maternity, and the politics of birth control in South Africa, 1910–39*. New York: Palgrave Macmillan.

Knappert, Jan. 1972. *A choice of flowers. Chaguo la maua: An anthology of Swahili love poetry*. London: Heinemann Educational.

———. 1979. *Four centuries of Swahili verse: A literary history and anthology*. London: Heinemann Educational.

———. 1983. Swahili Songs with Double-entendre. *Afrika and Ubersee* 66 (1): 67–76.

Krige, Eileen Jensen. 1936a. Changing conditions in marital relations and parental duties among urbanized natives. *Africa* 1: 1–23.

———. 1936b. *The social system of the Zulus*. Pietermaritzburg: Shuter and Shooter.

Kuper, Adam. 1982. *Wives for cattle: Bridewealth and marriage in southern Africa*. London: Routledge.

———. 1996. *Anthropology and anthropologists: The modern British school*. 3rd rev. ed. New York: Routledge.

———. 1999. *Among the anthropologists: History and context in anthropology*. London: Athlone Press.

———. 2001. Isaac Schapera—A conversation, part 1: South African beginnings. *Anthropology Today* 17 (6): 3–7.

———. 2002. Isaac Schapera—A conversation, part 2: The London years. *Anthropology Today* 18 (1): 14–19.

———. 2007. Isaac Schapera (1905–2003): His life and times. In *Picturing a colonial past: The African photographs of Isaac Schapera*, ed. John L. Comaroff, Jean Comaroff, and Deborah James, 19–41. Chicago: University of Chicago Press.

Lambek, Michael, and Jackie Solway. 2001. Just anger: Scenarios of indignation in Botswana and Madagascar. *Ethnos* 66 (1): 49–72.

Lambek, Michael, and Andrew Strathern. 1998. *Bodies and persons: Comparative perspectives from Africa and Melanesia.* Cambridge: Cambridge University Press.

Lan, David. 1989. Resistance to the present by the past: Mediums and money in Zimbabwe. In *Money and the morality of exchange*, ed. Jonathan Parry and Maurice Bloch, 191–208. Cambridge: Cambridge University Press.

Langford, Wendy. 1999. *Revolutions of the heart: Gender, power and the delusions of love.* London: Routledge.

Larkin, Brian. 1997. Indian films and Nigerian lovers: Media and the creation of parallel modernities. *Africa* 67 (3): 406–40.

———. 2005. Bandiri music, globalization and urban space in Nigeria. In *Bollyworld: Popular Indian cinema through a transnational lens*, ed. Raminder Kaur and Ajay J. Sinha. New Delhi: Sage.

Lawoyin, T. O., and Ulla Larsen. 2002. Male sexual behavior during wife's pregnancy and postpartum abstinence period in Oyo state, Nigeria. *Journal of Biosocial Science* 34 (1): 51–63.

Lears, Jackson T. J. 1983. From salvation to self-realization: Advertisement and the therapeutic roots of the consumer culture, 1880–1930. In *The Culture of consumption: Critical essays in American history, 1880–1980*, ed. Richard Wrightman Fox and Jackson T. J. Lears. New York: Pantheon Books.

Leclerc-Madlala, Suzanne. 2004. Transactional sex and the pursuit of modernity. *Social Dynamics* 29 (2): 213–33.

Lee, Haiyan. 2001. All the feelings that are fit to print: The community of sentiment and the literary public sphere in China, 1900–1918. *Modern China* 27 (3): 291–327.

———. 2007. *Revolution of the heart: A genealogy of love in China, 1900–1950.* Stanford: Stanford University Press.

Le Guennec-Coppens, Francoise. 1980. *Wedding customs in Lamu.* Nairobi: Lamu Society.

Levin, Ruth. 1947. Marriage in Langa native location. MA thesis, University of Cape Town.

Lewinson, Anne. 2006. Love in the city: Navigating multiple relationships in Dar es Salaam, Tanzania. *City and Society* 18 (1): 90–115.

Liechty, Mark. 2003. *Suitably modern: Making middle-class culture in a new consumer society.* Princeton: Princeton University Press.

Lindholm, Charles. 2006. Romantic love and anthropology. *Etnofoor* 19 (1): 5–21.

Lindsay, Lisa A. 1998. "No need . . . to think of home"? Masculinity and domestic life on the Nigerian railway, 1940–62. *Journal of African History* 39: 439–66.

———. 2003. *Working with gender: Wage labor and social change in southwestern Nigeria.* Portsmouth, NH: Heinemann.

Lindsay, Lisa A., and Stephan Miescher. 2003. *Men and masculinities in modern Africa.* Portsmouth, NH: Heinemann.

Lindsey, Ben B., and Wainwright Evans. 1925. *The revolt of modern youth.* New York: Boni and Liveright.

Lipset, David. 2004. Modernity without romance? *American Ethnologist* 31 (2): 205–24.

Little, Kenneth. 1966. Attitudes towards marriage and the family among educated young Sierra Leoneans. In *New elites of tropical Africa,* ed. P. C. Lloyd, 139–62. London: Oxford University Press for International African Institute.

———. 1973. *African women in towns: An aspect of Africa's social revolution.* New York: Cambridge University Press.

Little, Kenneth, and Anne Price. 1967. Some trends in modern marriage among west Africans. *Africa* 37 (4): 407–23.

———. 1973. Some trends in modern marriage among west Africans. In *Africa and change,* ed. C. Turnbull, 185–207. New York: Knopf.

Livingston, Julie. 2005. *Debility and the moral imagination in Botswana.* Bloomington: Indiana University Press.

Lodge, Tom. 1981. The destruction of Sophiatown. *Journal of Modern African Studies* 19 (1): 107–32.

Longmore, Laura. 1959. *The dispossessed: A study of sex-life of Bantu women in urban areas in and around Johannesburg.* London: Cape.

Luke, Nancy. 2003. Age and economic asymmetries in the sexual relationships of adolescent girls in sub-Saharan Africa. *Studies in Family Planning* 34 (2): 67–86.

———. 2005. Confronting the "sugar daddy" stereotype: Age and economic asymmetries and risky sexual behavior in urban Kenya. *International Family Planning Perspectives* 31 (1): 6–14.

Lutz, Catherine. 1988. *Unnatural emotions: Everyday sentiments on a Micronesia Atoll and their challenge to western theory.* Chicago: University of Chicago Press.

Macfarlane, Alan. 1986. *Marriage and love in England: Modes of reproduction, 1300–1840.* Oxford: Blackwell.

MacKinnon, Catherine. 1989. *Toward a feminist theory of the state.* Cambridge, MA: Harvard University Press.

Macmillan, Hugh. 1989. "Paralyzed conservatives": W. M. Macmillan, the social scientists, and "the common society," 1923–48. In *Africa and empire: W. M. Macmillan, historian and social critic,* ed. H. Macmillan and S. Marks, 72–90. London: University of London.

Mair, Lucy. 1969 [1953]. *African marriage and social change.* London: Cass.

Malinowski, Bronislaw. 1927. *Sex and repression in a savage society.* New York: Humanities Press.

———. 1929. *The sexual life of savages in north-western Melanesia.* Boston: Routledge and Kegan Paul.

———. 1938. Introductory essay: The anthropology of changing African cultures. In

Methods of study of culture contact in Africa, vii–xxxviii. London: Oxford University Press.

———. 1941. Introduction. In *Married life in an African tribe,* ed. Isaac Schapera, i–xvii. New York: Sheridan.

Mama, Amina. 1996. Women's studies and studies of women in Africa during the 1990s. CODESRIA Working Paper Series, no. 5.

Mann, Kristin. 1985. *Marrying well: Marriage, status and social change among the educated elite in colonial Lagos.* Cambridge: Cambridge University Press.

Marks, Shula. 1989. Patriotism, patriarchy and purity: Natal and the politics of Zulu ethnic consciousness. In *The creation of tribalism in southern Africa,* ed. L. Vail, 215–40. Berkeley: University of California Press.

Marris, Peter. 1962. *Family and social change in an African city.* Evanston, IL: Northwestern University Press.

Martin, Phyllis. 1995. *Leisure and society in colonial Brazzaville.* Cambridge: Cambridge University Press.

Marx, Karl. 1967 [1867] *Capital: A critique of political economy.* Vol. 1. New York: International Publishers.

Masquelier, Adeline. 2005. The scorpion's sting: Youth, marriage and the struggle for social maturity in Niger. *Journal of the Royal Anthropological Institute* 3: 59–83.

Massumi, Brian. 2002. *Parables for the virtual: Movement, affect, sensation.* Durham, NC: Duke University Press.

Matsuda, Matt K. 2005. *Empire of love: Histories of France and the Pacific.* New York: Oxford University Press.

Matthews, Z. K. 1938. The future of race relations in South Africa. *Race Relations Journal* 4 (4): 84–86.

———. 1940. Marriage customs among the Barolong. *Africa* 13 (1): 1–24.

Mauss, Marcel. 1990 [1950]. *The Gift: Forms and functions of exchange in archaic Societies.* trans. W. D. Halls. London: Routledge.

Mbembe, Achille. 1992. Provisional notes on the postcolony. *Africa* 62 (1): 3–37.

———. 2004. Aesthetics of superfluity. *Public Culture* 16: 373–405.

McClendon, Thomas V. 2002. *Genders and generations apart: Labor tenants and customary law in segregation-era South Africa, 1920s to 1940s.* Portsmouth, NH: Heinemann.

McDowell, Linda. 2003. *Redundant masculinities? Employment change and white working class youth.* Oxford: Blackwell.

McNeil, Donald G., Jr. 1995. For gay Zimbabweans. A difficult political climate. *New York Times,* September 10.

Mead, Margaret. 1928. *Coming of age in Samoa: A psychological study of primitive youth for western civilization.* New York: Modern Library.

Meillassoux, Claude. 1981. *Maidens, meal, and money: Capitalism and the domestic community.* Cambridge: Cambridge University Press.

Meyer, Birgit. 2003. Ghanaian popular cinema and the magic in and of film. In *Magic and modernity: Interfaces of revelation and concealment,* ed. Birgit Meyer and Peter Pels, 200–22. Stanford: Stanford University Press.

Mikell, Gwendolyn. 1997. Pleas for domestic relief: Akan women and family courts.

In *African Feminisms,* ed. Gwendolyn Mikell, 90–115. Philadelphia: University of Pennsylvania Press.

Miller, Daniel. *Worlds apart: Modernity through the prism of the local.* New York: Routledge.

Mills, David, and Richard Ssewakiryanga. 2005. No romance without finance: Commodities, masculinities, and relationships among Kampalan students. In *Readings in gender in Africa,* ed. Andrea Cornwall, 90–95. Bloomington: Indiana University Press.

Mishra, Vijay. 2002. *Bollywood cinema: Temples of desire.* New York: Routledge.

Mitchell, Sally. 1995. *The new girl: Girls' culture in England, 1880–1915.* New York: Columbia University Press.

Mitsunaga, T. M., A. M. Powell, N. J. Heard, and U. M Larsen. 2005. Extramarital sex among Nigerian men: Polygyny and other risk factors. *Journal of Acquired Immune Deficiency Syndrome* 39 (4): 478–88.

Mlanga, Susan. 2006. We live a different lifestyle from our parents: Young professionals from Tanzania reworking their gender norms. Pilot Study. University of Minnesota: Sociological Research Institute.

Modern Girl Around the World Research Group (Tani E. Barlow, Madeleine Yue Dong, Uta G. Poiger, Priti Ramamurthy, Lynn M. Thomas, and Alys Eve Weinbaum). 2005. Modern girl around the world: A research agenda and preliminary findings. *Gender and History* 17 (2): 245–94.

———. 2008. The modern girl as heuristic device: Collaboration, connective comparison, multidirectional citation. In *The modern girl around the world: Consumption, Modernity, and Globalization,* ed. Modern Girl Around the World Research Group. Durham, NC: Duke University Press.

Molokomme, Athaliah. 1991. Children of the fence: Maintenance of extra-marital children under law and practice in Botswana. *Research Reports,* no. 46: 32–49.

Moodie, T. Dunbar. 1994. *Going for gold: Men, mines and migration.* Berkeley: University of California Press.

Moodie, T. Dunbar, with Vivienne Ndatshe and British Sibuyi. 1988. Migrancy and male sexuality on the South African gold mines. *Journal of Southern African Studies* 14 (2): 229–45.

Morgan, Jennifer. 2004. *Laboring women: Reproduction and gender in new world slavery.* Philadelphia: University of Pennsylvania Press.

Morgan, Ruth, and Saskia Wieringa, eds. 2005. *Tommy boys, lesbian men, and ancestral wives: Female same-sex practices in Africa.* Johannesburg: Jacana Media.

Morris, Patricia. 1984. The rise and fall of "Drum." *New African* October: 53–54.

———. 1989. "The rise and fall of *Drum.*" Special issue, *Drum,* October.

Murray, Stephen O., and Will Roscoe, eds. 1998. *Boy-wives and female husbands: Studies in African homosexualities.* New York: St. Martin's Press.

Mutongi, Kenda. 1999. "Worries of the heart": Widowed mothers, daughters and masculinities in Maragoli, western Kenya, 1940–60. *Journal of African History* 40: 67–86.

———. 2000. "Dear Dolly's" advice: Representations of youth, courtship, and sexualities in Africa, 1960–1980. *International Journal of African Historical Studies* 33 (1): 1–23.

———. 2007. *Worries of the heart: Widows, family, and community in Kenya.* Chicago: University of Chicago Press.

Najmabadi, Afsaneh. 2005. *Women with mustaches and men without beards: Gender and sexual anxieties of Iranian modernity.* Berkeley: University of California Press.

Nandy, Ashis. 1998. Popular Indian cinema as a slums' eye view of politics. In *The secret politics of our desires: Innocence, culpability and Indian popular cinema,* ed. Ashis Nandy, 1–18. London: Zed Books.

Newell, Stephanie. 1997. Making up their own mind: Reader's interpretation and the difference of view in Ghanaian popular narrative. *Africa* 67 (3): 347–62.

———. 2000. *Ghanaian popular fiction: "Thrilling discoveries in conjugal life" and other tales.* Athens: Ohio University Press.

———. 2002. Introduction. In *Readings in African popular fiction,* ed. Stephanie Newell, 1–10. Bloomington: Indiana University Press.

Niehaus, Isak. 2005. Masculine domination in sexual violence: Interpreting accounts of three cases of rape in the South African Lowveld. In *Men behaving differently: South African men since 1994,* ed. G. Reid and L. Walker, 65–88. Cape Town: Double Storey Books.

Njau, Wangui. 1993. The parental role in the provision of sex education to children. Working Paper. Nairobi: Center for the Study of Adolescence.

Nolan, James L., Jr. 1998. *The therapeutic state: Justifying government at century's end.* New York: New York University Press.

Noor Shariff, Ibrahim. 1991. Islam and secularity in Swahili literature: An overview. In *Faces of Islam in African literature,* ed. Kenneth Harrow. Portsmouth, NH: Heinemann.

Ntarangwi, Mwenda. 2003. *Gender, performance and identity: Understanding Swahili cultural identity through songs.* Trenton, NJ: Africa World Press.

Nuttall, Sarah. 1994. Reading in the lives and writing of black South African women. *Journal of Southern African Studies* 20 (1): 85–98.

Nyaggah, Mouga. 2003. Gender, family, race and social change. Paper presented at the annual meeting of the Pan African Anthropology Association, Port Elizabeth, South Africa.

Nyairo, Joyce. 2005. "Modify": Jua Kali as a metaphor for Africa's urban ethnicities and cultures. Mary Kingsley Zochonis lecture, meeting of the Africa-Europe Group for Interdisciplinary Studies, London.

Nyamnjoh, Francis. 2005. Fishing in troubled waters: Disquettes and Thiofs in Dakar. *Africa* 27 (3): 295–324.

Nzioka, Charles. 1994. AIDS policies in Kenya. A critical perspective on prevention. In *AIDS: Foundations for the future,* ed. Peter Aggleton, Peter Davies, and Graham Hart, 159–75. London: Taylor and Francis.

Obbo, Christine. 1980. *African women: Their struggle for economic independence.* London: Zed Books.

Obiechina, Emmanuel, ed. 1972. *Onitsha market literature.* London: Heinemann.

———. 1973. *An African popular literature: A study of Onitsha market pamphlets.* Cambridge: Cambridge University Press.

O'Brien, Donald B. C. 1996. A lost generation? Youth identity and state decay in

West Africa. In *Postcolonial Identities in Africa,* ed. Richard Werbner and Terence Ranger, 55–74. London: Zed Books.

Odhiambo, Tom. 2003. Troubled love and marriage as work in Kenyan popular fiction. *Social Identities* 9: 423–36.

Okonjo, K. 1992. Aspects of continuity and change in mate-selection among the Igbo west of the river Niger. *Journal of Comparative Family Studies* 13 (3): 339–60.

Olaussen, Maria. 2002. About lovers in Accra: Urban intimacy in Ama Ata Aidoo's "Changes: A love story." *Research in African Literatures* 33 (2): 61–80.

Omolade, Barbara. 1983. Hearts of darkness. In *Powers of desire: The politics of sexuality,* ed. A. Snitow, C. Stansell, and S. Thompson, 350–67. New York: Monthly Review Press.

Oppong, Christine. 1974. *Marriage among a matrilineal elite.* Cambridge: Cambridge University Press.

Orubuloye, I. O., John Caldwell, and Pat Caldwell. 1991. Sexual networking in Ekiti district of Nigeria. *Studies in Family Planning* 22 (2): 61–73.

——. 1997. Perceived male sexual needs and male sexual behavior in southwest Nigeria. *Social Science and Medicine* 44 (8): 1195–1207.

Packard, Randall, and Paul Epstein. 1991. Epidemiologists, social scientists, and the structure of medical research on AIDS in Africa. *Social Science and Medicine* 33 (7): 771–94.

Padilla, M., J. Hirsch, M. Munoz-Laboy, R. Sember, and R. Parker, eds. 2007. *Love and globalization: Transformations of intimacy in the contemporary world.* Nashville: Vanderbilt University Press.

Pala, Oyunga. 2001. To be gentle or not to be gentle. *Saturday Magazine,* October 12.

Palmer, Robin, and Neil Parsons. 1977. *Roots of rural poverty in central and southern Africa.* Berkeley: University of California Press.

Parikh, Shanti. 2004. Sex, lies and love letters: Rethinking condoms and female agency in Uganda. *Agenda* 62: 12–20.

——. 2005. From auntie to disco: The bifurcation of risk and pleasure in sex education in Uganda. In *Sex in development: Science, sexuality and morality in global perspective,* ed. S. L. Pigg and V. Adams, 122–58. Durham, NC: Duke University Press.

Parker, Richard. 2001. Sexuality, culture, and power in HIV/AIDS research. *Annual Review of Anthropology* 30: 163–79.

Parkin, David, and David Nyamwaya, eds. 1987. *Transformation of African marriages.* Cambridge: Cambridge University Press.

Parry, Jonathan. 1986. The gift, the Indian gift, and the "Indian gift." *MAN (Journal of the Royal Anthropological Institute)* 21: 453–73.

Parry, Jonathan, and Maurice Bloch. 1989. *Money and the morality of exchange.* Cambridge: Cambridge University Press.

Paulme, Denise, ed. 1963 [1960]. *Women of tropical Africa.* Berkeley: University of California Press.

Pauw, Berthold A. 1963. *The second generation: A study of the family among urbanized Bantu in east London.* Published on behalf of the Institute of Social and Economic Research, Rhodes University. Cape Town: Oxford University Press.

Pendakur, Manjunath. 2003. *Indian popular cinema: Industry, ideology, and consciousness.* Cresskill, NJ: Hampton Press.

Peterson, Bhekizizwe. 2000. *Monarchs, missionaries and African intellectuals.* Johannesburg: Witwatersrand University Press.

———. 2006. The Bantu world and the world of the book: Reading, writing, and "enlightenment." In *Africa's hidden histories: Everyday literacy and making the self,* ed. Karin Barber, 236–57. Bloomington: Indiana University Press.

Piot, Charles. 1999. *Remotely global: Village modernity in West Africa.* Chicago: University of Chicago Press.

Plotnicov, Leonard. 1995. Love, lust and found in Nigeria. In *Romantic passion: A universal experience?,* ed. William R. Jankowiak, 128–40. New York: Columbia University Press.

Porter, Mary A. 1995. Talking at the margins: Kenya discourses on homosexuality. In *Beyond the lavender lexicon,* ed. W. Leap, 133–54. Amsterdam: University of Amsterdam Press.

Poulin, Michelle J. 2007. Sex, money and premarital partnerships in southern Malawi. *Social Science and Medicine* 65 (11): 2383–93.

Povinelli, Elizabeth A. 2002. Notes on gridlock: Genealogy, intimacy, sexuality. *Public Culture* 14 (1): 215–38.

———. 2006. *The empire of love: Toward a theory of intimacy, genealogy, and carnality.* Durham, NC: Duke University Press.

Powdermaker, Hortense. 1962. *Copper town: Changing Africa.* New York: Harper Colophon.

Prazak, Miroslava. 2001. Talking about sex: Contemporary construction of sexuality in rural Kenya. *Africa Today* 48: 82–98.

Pressly, Donwald. 2006. The rise and rise of South Africa's shacks. *Mail and Guardian,* January 6. http://www.mg.co.za (accessed August 16, 2007).

Projet Madio. 2001. *L'emploi, le chomage et les conditions d'activité des ménages dans les sept grandes villes de Madagascar.* Antananarivo, Madagascar: Ministère des Finances et de l'Economie, Institut National de la Statistique.

Radcliffe-Brown, Alfred R. 1923. The methods of ethnology and social anthropology. *South African Journal of Science* 20: 124–47.

———. 1950. Introduction. In *African systems of kinship and marriage,* ed. Alfred R. Radcliffe-Brown and Daryll Forde, 1–85. London: Oxford University Press.

Radway, Janice A. 1991 [1984]. *Reading the romance: Women, patriarchy, and popular literature.* Chapel Hill: University of North Carolina Press.

Rafael, Vincente L. 2000. *White love and other events in Filipino history.* Durham, NC: Duke University Press.

Ratele, Kopano. 2004. Kinky politics. In *Re-thinking sexualities in Africa,* ed. S. Arnfred, 139–54. Uppsala: Nordiska Afrikainstitutet.

Rebhun, Linda-Anne. 1999a. *The heart is unknown country: Love in the changing economy of northeast Brazil.* Stanford: Stanford University Press.

———. 1999b. For love and for money: Romance in urbanizing northeast Brazil. *City and Society* 11 (1–2): 145–64.

———. 2007. The strange marriage of love and interest: Economic change and emotional intimacy in northeast Brazil, private and public. In *Love and globalization: Transformations of intimacy in the contemporary world*, ed. Mark B. Padilla, Jennifer S. Hirsch, Miguel Munoz-Laboy, Robert E. Sember, and Richard G. Parker, 107-19. Nashville: Vanderbilt University Press.

Reddy, William. 2001. *The navigation of feeling: a framework for the history of emotions.* New York: Cambridge University Press.

———. Forthcoming. The rule of love: The history of western romantic love in comparative perspective. In *New dangerous liaisons: Discourses on Europe and love in the last century,* ed. L. Passerini. Oxford: Berghahn Books.

Richardson, Rev. J. 1885. *A new Malagasy-English dictionary.* Antananarivo: London Missionary Society.

Riesman, Paul. 1972. Defying official morality: The example of man's quest for woman among the Fulani. *Cahiers d'Etudes Africaines* 11 (44): 602-3.

———. 1973. Love Fulani style. *Society* (January/February): 27-35.

———. 1981. Love Fulani style. In *Anthropological Realities,* ed. Jeanne Guillemin, 9-25. New Brunswick, NJ: Transaction Books.

Roberts, Nomakhula. 2004. Thou shalt not moan. Know the rules of the Nyatsi game. *Sunday World,* May 2. http://www.sundayworld.co.za (accessed August 16, 2007).

Robertson, Claire C. 1997. *Trouble showed the way: Women, men, and trade in the Nairobi area, 1890-1990.* Bloomington: Indiana University Press.

Robertson, Claire, and Iris Berger, eds. 1986. *Women and class in Africa.* New York: Holmes and Meier.

Rodney, Walter. 1972. *How Europe underdeveloped Africa.* London: Bogle-L'Ouverture.

Rosaldo, Michelle. 1980. *Knowledge and passion: Ilongot notions of self and social life.* Cambridge: Cambridge University Press.

———. 1984. Toward an anthropology of self and feeling. In *Culture theory: Essays on mind, self and emotion,* eds. R. A. Shweder and R. A. LeVine, 137-57. Cambridge, MA: Harvard University Press.

Rosenwein, Barbara. 2006. *Emotional communities in the early middle ages.* Ithaca, NY: Cornell University Press.

Sachs, Wulf. 1996 [1937]. *Black hamlet.* Baltimore: Johns Hopkins University Press.

Sampson, Anthony. 1957. *"Drum": The newspaper that won the heart of Africa.* Cambridge, MA: Harvard University Press.

Schapera, Isaac. 1933a. The native as letter-writer. *The Critic* 2: 20-28.

———. 1933b. Premarital pregnancy and native opinion: A note of social change. *Africa* 6 (1): 59-89.

———. 1934. *Western civilization and the natives of South Africa: Studies in culture contact.* New York: Humanities Press.

———. 1937. Cultural changes in tribal life. In *The Bantu-speaking tribes of South Africa,* ed. Isaac Schapera, 357-87. New York: Humanities Press.

———. 1938. Contact between European and native in South Africa: In Bechuanaland. In *Methods of study of culture contact in Africa,* 25-37. London: Oxford University Press.

———. 1940. *Married life in an African tribe.* London: Faber and Faber.

———. 1990. The appointment of Radcliffe Brown to the chair of social anthropology at the University of Cape Town. *African Studies* 49 (1): 1–13.

Scheper-Hughes, Nancy. 1985. Culture, scarcity and maternal thinking. *Ethos* 13 (4): 291–317.

———. 1992. *Death without weeping: The violence of everyday life in Brazil.* Berkeley: University of California Press.

Schoenbrun, David. 1995. Gendered histories between the great lakes: Varieties and limits. *International Journal of African Historical Studies* 2: 269–90.

Schoepf, Brooke Grundfest. 1992. Women at risk: Case studies from Zaire. In *The time of AIDS: Social analysis, theory and method,* ed. G. Herdt and S. Lindenbaum, 259–86. London: Sage.

———. 1995. Culture, sex research and AIDS prevention in Africa. In *Culture and sexual risk: Anthropological perspectives on AIDS,* ed. H. Ten Brummelhuis and G. Herdt, 29–51. London: Gordon and Breach.

Schumaker, Lyn. 2001. *Africanizing anthropology: Fieldwork, networks, and the making of cultural knowledge in central Africa.* Durham, NC: Duke University Press.

Schuster, Ilsa M. G. 1979. *New women of Lusaka.* Palo Alto, CA: Mayfield.

Scott, Walter. 1808. *Marmion: A tale of Flodden field.* Edinburgh: J. Ballantyne for A. Constable.

Scorgie, Fiona. 2002. Virginity testing and the politics of sexual responsibility: Implications for AIDS interventions. *African Studies* 61 (1): 55–75.

Sedgewick, Eva Kosofsky. 1990. *Epistemology of the closet.* Berkeley: University of California Press.

Seidman, Steven. 1991. *Romantic longings: Love in America, 1830–1980.* New York: Routledge.

Selikow, Terry-Ann, Bheki Zulu, and Eugene Cedras. 2002. The Ingagara, the Regte and the cherry: HIV/AIDS and youth culture in contemporary urban townships. *Agenda* 53: 22–32.

Setel, Philip W. 1999. *A plague of paradoxes: AIDS, culture, and demography in northern Tanzania.* Chicago: University of Chicago Press.

Shadle, Brett L. 2006. *"Girl cases": Marriage and colonialism in Guisiiland, Kenya, 1890–1970.* Portsmouth, NH: Heinemann.

Shafi, Adam. 1999. *Vuta n'Kuvute.* Dar es Salaam: Mkuki na Nyota.

Shain, Milton. 1994. *The roots of antisemitism in South Africa.* Charlottesville: University Press of Virginia.

Sharpless, John. 1997. Population science, private foundations, and development aid: The transformation of demographic knowledge in the United States, 1945–1965. In *International development and the social sciences: Essays on the history and politics of knowledge,* ed. F. Cooper and R. Packard, 176–202. Berkeley: University of California Press.

Sheikh-Hashim. 1989. *Unyago: Traditional family life education among the Muslim Digo, Seguju, Bondei, Sambaa, and Sigua of Tanga region.* Dar es Salaam: Tanzania Media Women's Association.

Shepard, Gil. 1987. Rank, gender, and homosexuality: Mombasa as a key to understanding sexual options. In *The cultural construction of sexuality,* ed. Pat Caplan, 20–41. Oxford: Oxford University Press.

Shorter, Edward. 1975. *The making of the modern family.* New York: Basic Books.

Shumway, David R. 1998. The problem of modern married love for middle-class women. In *An emotional history of the United States,* ed. Peter Stearns and Jan Lewis. New York: New York University Press.

Silberschmidt, Margarethe. 2001. Disempowerment of men in rural and urban east Africa: Implications for male identity and sexual behaviour. *World Development* 29: 657–71.

Simmel, Georg. 1978 [1900]. *The philosophy of money.* T. Bottomore and D. Frisby, trans. London: Routledge and Kegan Paul.

———. 1984 [1921–22]. On love (a fragment). In *Georg Simmel: On women, sexuality, and love,* trans. Guy Oakes, 153–92. New Haven: Yale University Press.

Skillman, Teri. 1986. The Bombay Hindi film song genre: A historical survey. *Yearbook for Traditional Music* 18: 133–44.

Sklar, Robert. 1975. *Movie made America: A cultural history of American movies.* New York: Vintage.

Smith, Daniel Jordan. 2000. "These girls today *Na War-O*": Premarital sexuality and modern identity in southeastern Nigeria. *Africa Today* 47 (3–4): 98–120.

———. 2001. Romance, parenthood, and gender in a modern African society. *Ethnology* 40 (2): 129–52.

———. 2002. "Man no be wood": Gender and extramarital sex in contemporary southeastern Nigeria. *Ahfad Journal* 19 (2): 4–23.

———. 2004. Premarital sex, procreation and HIV risk in Nigeria. *Studies in Family Planning* 35 (4): 223–35.

———. 2006. Love and the risk of HIV: Courtship, marriage, and infidelity in southeastern Nigeria. In *Modern loves: The anthropology of romantic courtship and companionate marriage,* ed. Jennifer Hirsch and Holly Wardlow, 135–53. Ann Arbor: University of Michigan Press.

———. 2007a. *A culture of corruption: Everyday deception and popular discontent in Nigeria.* Princeton: Princeton University Press.

———. 2007b. Modern marriage, men's extramarital sex, and HIV risk in southeastern Nigeria. *American Journal of Public Health* 97 (6): 997–1005.

Smith, Mary F. 1954 [1981]. *Baba of Karo: A woman of the Muslim Hausa.* New Haven: Yale University Press.

Smuts, Jan. 1936. Foreword. In *Reaction to conquest: Effects of contact with Europeans on the Pondo of South Africa,* ed. Monica Hunter, vii–ix. London: Oxford University Press.

Sobo, Elisa. 1995. *Choosing unsafe sex: AIDS-risk denial among disadvantaged women.* Philadelphia: University of Pennsylvania Press.

Solomon-Godeau, Abigail. 1996. The other side of Venus: The visual economy of feminine display. In *The sex of things,* ed. Victoria de Grazia and Ellen Furlough, 112–32. Berkeley: University of California Press.

Sommer, Doris. 1991. *Foundational fictions: The national romance of Latin America.* Berkeley: University of California Press.

Southall, Aidan W., and Peter C. Gutkind. 1957. *Townsmen in the making: Kampala and its suburbs.* Kampala: East African Institute of Social Research.

Spiegel, Andrew. 1981. Changing patterns of migrant labour and rural differentiation in Lesotho. *Social Dynamics* 6 (2): 1–13.

Spitulnik, Debra. 1993. Anthropology and mass media. *Annual Review of Anthropology* 22: 293–315.

Spronk, Rachel. 2002. Looking at love: Hollywood romance and shifting notions of gender and relating in Nairobi. *Etnofoor* 15 (1): 229–39.

———. 2005a. Female sexuality in Nairobi: Flawed or favoured? *Culture, Health, and Sexuality* 7: 267–79.

———. 2005b. "There is a time to fool around and there is a time to grow up": Balancing sex, relationships and notions of masculinities in Nairobi. In *Rethinking masculinities, violence, and AIDS,* ed. Diana Gibson and Anita Hardon, 44–73. Amsterdam: Het Spinhuis.

———. 2006. *Ambiguous pleasures: Sexuality and new self-definitions in Nairobi.* Amsterdam: University of Amsterdam Press.

Standing, Hilary. 1992. AIDS: Conceptual and methodological issues in researching sexual behaviour in sub-Saharan Africa. *Social Science and Medicine* 34 (5): 475–83.

Stearns, Carol Z., and Peter N. Stearns, eds. 1988. *Emotion and social change: Toward a new psychohistory.* New York: Holmes and Meier.

Stearns, Peter N. 1994. *American cool: Constructing a twentieth-century emotional style.* New York: New York University Press.

Stearns, Peter N., and Jan Lewis, eds. 1998. *An emotional history of the United States.* New York: New York University Press.

Stewart, Kearsley. 2001. Toward a historical perspective on sexuality in Uganda: The reproductive lifeline technique for grandmothers and their daughters. *Africa Today* 47 (3–4): 122–48.

Stillwaggon, Eileen. 2006. *AIDS and the ecology of poverty.* Oxford: Oxford University Press.

Stocking, George. 1995. *After Tylor: British social anthropology, 1888–1951.* Madison: University of Wisconsin Press.

Stoler, Ann. 2002. *Carnal knowledge and imperial power: Race and the intimate in colonial rule.* Berkeley: University of California Press.

———, ed. 2006. *Haunted by empire: Geographies of intimacy in North American history.* Durham, NC: Duke University Press.

Stone, Lawrence. 1979. *The family, sex and marriage in England 1500–1800.* Harmondsworth: Penguin Books.

Stones, Christopher, and Joseph Philbrick. 1989. Attitudes toward love among Xhosa university students in South Africa. *Journal of Social Psychology* 129 (4): 573–75.

Strobel, Margaret. 1979. *Muslim women in Mombasa, 1890–1975.* New Haven: Yale University Press.

Summers, Carol. 1991. Intimate colonialism: The imperial production of reproduction in Uganda, 1907–1925. *Signs* 16 (4): 787–807.

Sweet, James. 1996. Male homosexuality and spiritism in the African dispora: The legacies of a link. *Journal of the History of Sexuality* 7 (22): 184–202.

Swidler, Ann. 2001. *Talk of love: How culture matters.* Chicago: University of Chicago Press.

Swidler, Ann, and Watkins, Susan. 2005. Ties of dependence: AIDS and transactional sex in rural Malawi. Paper prepared at the annual meeting of the American Sociological Association, Philadelphia.

Switzer, Les. 1988. "Bantu World" and the origins of a captive African commercial press in South Africa. *Journal of Southern African Studies* 14 (1): 351–70.

——. 1997. "Bantu World" and the origins of a captive African commercial press. In *South Africa's alternative press: Voices of protest and resistance, 1880s–1960s,* ed. Les Switzer, 189–212. Cambridge: Cambridge University Press.

Thomas, Lynn. 2003. *Politics of the womb: Women, reproduction and the state in Kenya.* Berkeley: University of California Press.

——. 2006. Schoolgirl pregnancies, letter-writing, and "modern" persons in late colonial East Africa. In *Africa's hidden histories: Everyday literacy and making the self,* ed. Karin Barber, 180–207. Bloomington: Indiana University Press.

Thomas, Rosie. 1989. Sanctity and scandal: The mythologization of mother India. *Quarterly Review of Film and Video* 11 (3): 11–30.

Thompson, Kristin, and David Bordwell. 2003. *Film history: An introduction.* Boston: McGraw-Hill.

Uchendu, Victor. 1965. Concubinage among the Ngwa Igbo of southern Nigeria. *Africa* 35 (2): 187–97.

Van der Vliet, Virginia. 1991. Traditional husbands, modern wives? Constructing marriages in a South African township. In *Tradition and transition in southern Africa: Festschrift for Philip and Iona Meyer,* ed. A. D. Spiegel and P. A. McAllister, 219–42. New Brunswick, NJ: Transaction Books.

Vandewiele, M., and Joseph Philbrick. 1983. Attitudes of Senegalese students toward love. *Psychological Reports* 52 (3): 915–18.

Van Onselen, Charles. 1982. *Studies in the social and economic history of the Witwatersrand, 1886–1914.* Johannesburg: Ravan Press.

van Wijk, Joan. 2006. Romance tourism on Ambergris Caye, Belize: The entanglements of love and prostitution. *Etnofoor* 19 (1): 71–89.

Vasudevan, Ravi. 1995. Addressing the spectator of a "third world" national cinema: The Bombay social film of the 1940s and 1950s. *Screen* 36 (4): 305–24.

——. 2000. Shifting codes, dissolving identities: The Hindi social film of the 1950s as popular culture. In *Making meaning in Indian cinema,* ed. Ravi Vasudevan, 99–121. New Delhi: Oxford University Press.

Vaughan, Megan. 1991. *Curing their ills: Colonial power and African illness.* Stanford: Stanford University Press.

Velten, C. 1903. *Desturi za wasuaheli.* Gottigen: Vandenhoeck and Ruprecht.

Verheijen, Janneke. 2006. Mass media and gender equality: The empowering presence of romantic love in Telenovelas. *Etnofoor* 19 (1): 23–39.

Vilakazi, Absolom. 1962. *Zulu transformations: A study of the dynamics of social change.* Second Impression. Pietermaritzburg: University of Natal Press.

Virdi, Jyotika. 2003. *The cinematic imagination: Indian popular films as social history.* New Brunswick, NJ: Rutgers University Press.

Wainaina, Binyavanga. 2005. How to write about Africa. "The View from Africa," special issue, *Granta* 92: 93-95.

Wardlow, Holly. 1996. "Bobby Teardrops": A Turkish video in Papua New Guinea. Reflections on cultural studies, feminism, and the anthropology of mass media. *Visual Anthropology Review* 12 (1): 30-46.

———. 2006a. All's fair when love is war: Romantic passion and companionate marriage among the Huli of Papua New Guinea. In *Modern loves: The anthropology of romantic courtship and companionate marriage,* ed. Jennifer S. Hirsch and Holly Wardlow, 51-77. Ann Arbor: University of Michigan Press.

———. 2006b. *Wayward women: Sexuality and agency in a New Guinea society.* Berkeley: University of California Press.

———. 2007. Men's extramarital sexuality in rural Papua New Guinea. *American Journal of Public Health* 97 (6): 1006-14.

Wardlow, Holly, and Jennifer S. Hirsch. 2006. Introduction. In *Modern loves: The anthropology of courtship and companionate marriage,* ed. Jennifer S. Hirsch and Holly Wardlow, 1-31. Ann Harbor: University of Michigan Press.

Warner, Michael. 1999. Normal and normaller: Beyond gay marriage. *GLQ: A Journal of Lesbian and Gay Studies* 5 (2): 119-71.

Watkins, Susan Cotts. 2000. Local and foreign models of reproduction in Nyanza province, Kenya, 1930-1998. *Population and Development Review* 26 (4): 725-59.

Watt, Jeffrey. 1992. *The making of modern marriage: Matrimonial control and the rise of sentiment in Neuchatel, 1550-1800.* Ithaca, NY: Cornell University Press.

Webb, Colin de B., and John B. Wright, eds. 2001. *The James Stuart archive of recorded oral evidence relating to the history of the Zulu and neighbouring peoples.* Pietermaritzburg: University of Natal Press.

Weiss, Brad. 2002. Thug realism: Inhabiting fantasy in urban Tanzania. *Cultural Anthropology* 17 (1): 93-124.

Welsh, David. 1971. *The roots of segregation: Native policy in colonial Natal, 1845-1910.* London: Oxford University Press.

White, Luise. 1990. *The comforts of home: Prostitution in colonial Nairobi.* Chicago: University of Chicago Press.

———. 1993. Cars out of place: Vampires, technology, and labor in East and Central Africa. *Representations* 43: 27-50.

Whitehead, Stephen M. 2001. *Men and masculinities: Key themes and new directions.* Chicago: University of Chicago Press.

Whitsitt, Novian. 2003. Islamic Hausa feminism meets northern Nigerian romance: The cautious rebellion of Bilkisu Funtuwa. *African Studies Review* 46: 137-53.

Willemen, Paul, and Rajadhyaksha Ashish. 1999. *Encyclopedia of the Indian cinema.* 2nd ed. London: Fitzroy Dearborn.

Wipper, Audrey, ed. 1972. "Women," special issue, *Canadian Journal of African Studies* 5 (2).

Wojcicki, Janet Maia. 2002. Commercial sex work or Ukuphanda? Sex-for-money exchange in Soweto and Hammanskraal area, South Africa. *Culture, Medicine and Psychiatry* 26: 339-70.

Wood, Katherine, and Rachel Jewkes. 2001. "Dangerous love": Reflections on violence among Xhosa township youth. In *Changing men in southern Africa*, ed. R. Morrel, 317-36. Pietermaritzburg: University of Natal Press.

Woodson, Dorothy. 1989. *"Drum": An index to Africa's leading magazine 1951-1961*. Madison: University of Wisconsin Press.

Yan, Yunxiang. 2003. *Private life under socialism: Love, intimacy and family change in a Chinese village, 1949-1999*. Stanford: Stanford University Press.

Zalduondo, Barbara. 1991. Prostitution viewed cross-culturally: Toward recontextualizing sex work in AIDS intervention research. *Journal of Sex Research* 28 (2): 223-48.

Zeff, Adam. 1999. Marriage, film, and video in TamilNadu: Narrative, image, and ideologies of love. PhD diss., University of Pennsylvania.

Zelizer, Vivianna. 2005. *The purchase of intimacy.* Princeton: Princeton University Press.

CONTRIBUTORS

JENNIFER COLE, a cultural anthropologist, is associate professor in the Department of Comparative Human Development at the University of Chicago. She is the author of *Forget Colonialism? Sacrifice and the Art of Memory*.

LAURA FAIR is an associate professor in the Department of History at Michigan State University. She is the author of *Pastimes and Politics: Culture, Community and Identity in Post-Abolition Urban Zanzibar, 1890–1945*.

MARK HUNTER, a cultural geographer, is an assistant professor in the Department of Social Sciences at the University of Toronto. He has published numerous articles on HIV/AIDS, intimacy, and gender in South Africa in journals including *Social Science and Medicine* and *African Studies*.

ADELINE MASQUELIER is an associate professor of anthropology at Tulane University. She is author of *Prayer Has Spoiled Everything: Possession, Power and Identity in an Islamic Town of Niger*.

KENDA MUTONGI is associate professor in the Department of History at Williams College. She is author of *Worries of the Heart: Widows, Family and Community in Kenya*.

DANIEL JORDAN SMITH is associate professor in the Department of Anthropology at Brown University. He has published numerous articles on HIV/AIDs, gender, and sexuality in Nigeria, in addition to his book, *A Culture of Corruption: Everyday Deception and Popular Discontent in Nigeria*.

RACHEL SPRONK, a cultural anthropologist, is a postdoctoral fellow at the Amsterdam School for Social-Science Research at the University of Amsterdam. She has published articles on sexuality, gender, and the middle class in Kenya in journals including *Culture, Health & Sexuality* and *Africa*.

LYNN M. THOMAS is associate professor in the Department of History and adjunct associate professor in the Department of Women's Studies at the University of Washington, Seattle. She is the author of *Politics of the Womb: Women, Reproduction and the State in Kenya*.

flapper. *See* modern girl

foreign men, 124–25, 126–27, 129–30, 132

Forna, Aminatta, 13–15

Foucault, Michel, 9

419 scam industry, 165

Frederiksen, Bodil, 195

Freud, Sigmund, 33, 36

Fuglesang, Minou, 60

Furedi, Frank, 184, 191

gay and lesbian relationships, 17, 34, 36, 86, 87–88, 98–102, 107n13

gender equality, 201–2

gender inequality, 25–28, 53–54, 146, 152, 158, 168, 179–80

gendering of commodities, 88–92

gender roles, 119, 130, 166, 196, 198

gender segregation, 209–10

generational difference, 15–16, 19, 65, 79–81, 141, 185, 188–89, 194, 201, 202n1

Geschiere, Peter, 187

Ghana, 11, 17, 60, 84, 86

Giddens, Anthony, 28, 30n7, 152

gifts. *See* consumption; exchange

globalization, 4–5, 162

Gora, Haji, 61

Grandidier, G., 116, 117

Gregg, Jessica, 111

Hellmann, Ellen, 32, 34, 35, 37, 38, 42, 53

Hindi films. *See* films: Hindi

Hirsch, Jennifer S., 4, 16, 21, 213

HIV/AIDS epidemic: and extramarital affairs, 158, 180; and intimacy, 4, 29; and the media, 190; and sexuality, 9–10; and transactional sex, 24, 135, 151

homosexuality. *See* gay and lesbian relationships

humor, 92–93, 95–96

Hunter, Monica. *See* Wilson (formerly Hunter), Monica

Hutchinson, Sharon, 22

identity, 20, 187–88

Igbo, 26

Illouz, Eva, 21, 183, 187, 190, 191

ilobolo. *See* bridewealth

Immorality Act, 34

independence movements. *See* nationalism

individualization, 10, 30n7, 191, 226

infertility, 138

infidelity. *See* extramarital affairs

initiation rituals, 38, 59, 68, 70, 88

International Monetary Fund, 112

Internet, 112

interracial intimacy, 34

intimacy: economies of, 21–24, 109–33; interracial, 34; same sex (*see* gay and lesbian relationships); as sex, 3–4. *See also* emotion; love

Iran, 5

Islam, 16, 210, 217–18

Jahoda, Gustav, 11, 13, 17

Jamaica, 27

jaombilo, 126–28, 129–30, 131

Jefferson, Thomas, 8, 13

Junod, Henri, 6–7, 15

Kenya, 20, 28, 60, 84, 86, 92, 142, 181–202

Khama, Tshekedi, 35

kinship. *See* family and kinship

Kipnis, Laura, 198

Krige, Eileen, 32, 34, 35, 37, 38, 53

KwaZulu-Natal, 24, 137

labor, division of, 25, 164, 166, 178

labor migrancy, 17, 38, 40, 53, 140–44, 162, 167–68, 184–85, 211. *See also* wage labor

Lan, David, 22–23